Where to Eat
In Northern Ireland

Restaurants, Coffee Shops, Pubs & Hotels - *plus* **'A Taste of Ulster'**

Northern Ireland Tourist Board

Published by the Northern Ireland Tourist Board
59 North St, Belfast BT1 1NB. ☎ (0232) 231221

Copyright © Northern Ireland Tourist Board 1994

All rights reserved. No part of this publication may be reproduced or transmitted in any form or by any means, electronic or mechanical, including photocopy, recording or any information storage and retrieval system, without permission in writing from the publisher.

ISBN 0 946871 62 0

Fourteenth edition

Printed by The Universities Press (Belfast) Ltd. 6m/11/93

Contents

	Page
Acknowledgments	5
A Taste of Ulster	6
Special mentions	22
How to use the guide	24
Belfast districts - map	28
City Centre	29
Golden Mile	39
University and Malone	43
East of the River	53
North and West of the River	59
County Antrim	65
County Armagh	99
County Down	111
County Fermanagh	153
County Londonderry	163
County Tyrone	183
Index to towns and villages	200

Acknowledgments

The editors are grateful for all the help they have received in compiling the main listings for this, the fourteenth edition of *Where to Eat in Northern Ireland*.

Information provided by organisations and individuals outside the Tourist Board has enabled us to maintain the wide coverage which makes this small book uniquely useful.

The response from local authorities was most helpful, particularly with regard to cafés and unlicensed restaurants. All twenty-six councils supplied us with information on the eating-out scene in their area. This local knowledge ensures that we continue to provide a useful service to visitors and, we hope, give some welcome publicity to small and out-of-the-way places.

Thanks are also due to the Healthy Eating Circle for keeping us up to date with details of their members.

Some places that deserve to be included in the book may not have come to our attention. In this case we would be glad to hear of them for the next edition. Please write to *Where to Eat in Northern Ireland,* Northern Ireland Tourist Board, 59 North St, Belfast BT1 1NB.

A Taste of Ulster

A Taste of Ulster's distinctive symbol is your guarantee of a menu featuring the best of Ulster produce. You will find traditional and modern dishes created from the finest local ingredients wherever you see the special hexagonal plaque on display.

Listed in this special section are restaurants, pubs and coffee shops which have attained Taste of Ulster membership (applied for under a voluntary registration scheme). These are shown in green preceded by ★ in the main listings. Many have received special mentions in well known guide books and we have indicated these in the entry. Major credit cards are accepted unless indicated otherwise.

A Taste of Ulster

Belfast

Bewleys Oriental Café (p 29)
A branch of the famous traditional Irish café company, founded over 150 years ago. Wide range of blended and roasted coffees, speciality teas and splendid home-baked pastries and savouries.

Bittles Bar (p 29)
City centre bar offering classic Belfast pub grub with fresh soups, bread and stew. Champ – a dish of creamed potatoes and scallions – served with sausage is a local favourite. Fine collection of local art. No credit cards.

Clare Connery at Malone House (p 45)
Clare Connery places a particular emphasis on fish, game and vegetables. Vegetarian dishes are a speciality. The restaurant is in a lovely Georgian mansion three miles from the city centre.

The Clarence (p 31)
Steps lead down to this attractive basement wine bar and restaurant, beside City Hall. Popular with business people. Menus change daily and home-made desserts are a speciality.

Dundonald Old Mill, Dundonald (p 54)
A splendid coffee house at one of Northern Ireland's most popular visitor attractions. The 300-year-old mill has the largest waterwheel in Ireland. Large range of local crafts on sale.

Duke of York (p 31)
In a bustling alleyway near St Anne's Cathedral, this is one of Belfast's oldest bars. Recently refurbished, the original fittings create an old style atmosphere. Food is fresh and varied and served in both bars. Live music in the evenings. No credit cards.

Dukes Hotel (p 46)
In a tree-lined avenue close to Queen's University and Botanic Gardens. Chef Gerard Manley's modern French style cooking is complemented by an extensive wine list. Snacks in the bar. Ackerman.

A Taste of Ulster

Belfast (contd)

Fillers Coffee Shop (p 54)
A bright, modern self-service restaurant featuring traditional home baking. The emphasis is on healthy eating and vegetarian alternatives are available. No credit cards.

Nick's Warehouse (p 35)
Nick Price's city centre restaurant and wine bar are on two floors of an atmospheric converted warehouse. Nick and his wife Kathy do all their own cooking and Ulster fish is their speciality. Ackerman, Bridgestone, Egon Ronay, Good Food Guide, Michelin.

Peppermill Coffee Shop (p 50)
In the university area, this welcoming coffee shop offers home-made scones, breads and pastries. Soups and salads are prepared with fresh local vegetables. No credit cards.

Roscoff (p 42)
Bright, uncluttered restaurant with a dynamic style. Paul Rankin complements classical French training with healthy Californian ideas. Creative use of organic vegetables and local seafood. Mid-way between City Hall and Queen's University. Ackerman clover, Bridgestone, Egon Ronay star, Good Food Guide, Michelin star.

Scoffs Coffee House (p 57)
Although Scoffs is in a popular shopping district, the decor is old country pine. Joanne Rodgers and Margaret Spragg prepare honey-glazed Ulster ham, seafood and vegetable bakes. No credit cards.

Skandia (p 36)
This unlicensed restaurant is ideal for family dining with special menus for children. Extensive hours allow diners to enjoy any meal from breakfast to a late supper after the theatre. Close to the Grand Opera House, central for shopping.

Stormont Hotel (p 57)
The Stormont overlooks the landscaped grounds of the former Northern Ireland parliament. In McMaster's restaurant, head chef Billy McAteer offers fine local produce. Less formal fare is served in the brasserie.

A Taste of Ulster

Belfast (contd)

White's Tavern (p 37)
This 17th-century tavern is in an old trading alley where the *Mercury* newspaper was founded in the 1850s. It enjoys an established reputation for fine home cooking with an interesting range of local dishes.

A Taste of Ulster

County Antrim

Brown Jug, Ballymoney (p 74)
Offering a good selection of home-cooked dishes, this pleasant coffee shop has convenient parking. No credit cards.

Bushmills Inn, Bushmills (p 75)
Close to the world's oldest licensed whiskey distillery, this hotel is a restored coaching inn. Specialities include salmon from the nearby Bush river with Bushmills whiskey. In summer and at weekends, the Victorian-style bar is open for simpler fare.

Grouse Inn, Ballymena (p 72)
In Ballymena's bustling town centre, the Grouse Inn is renowned for friendly service and the relaxed atmosphere of its grill bar and wood panelled Bailiff's Parlour restaurant. Chef Archie Stewart bases his menu on the best seasonal ingredients.

Hillcrest Country House, Bushmills (p 81)
A stone's throw from the Giant's Causeway, this attractive licensed restaurant has panoramic coastal views. Fine sauces accompany many dishes and local seafood is well prepared.

Londonderry Arms Hotel, Carnlough (p 76)
Charming coaching inn in a small fishing village on the Antrim coast road 14 miles north of Larne. A reputation for good food, cooked simply - wheaten bread, soups, pies, lamb and beef, and smoked Glenarm salmon.

A Taste of Ulster

Antrim *(contd)*

Magherabuoy House Hotel, Portrush (p 94)
The hotel is set in a popular seaside resort on this splendid coast. A wide range of seafood is on offer and chef Johnny McIndoer's quality dishes are served by friendly and efficient staff.

National Trust Tea Room, Giant's Causeway (p 81)
Chef/manager Adrian Fletcher offers a daily choice of home-cooked fare, including a range of delicious soups and traditional breads, scones and cakes.

Sweeney's Wine Bar, Portballintrae (p 92)
There are fine views of the north Antrim coast from the conservatory. This converted 17th-century stable block retains much of its original character. Customers come from all over for the diverse menu. No credit cards.

The Tea House, Ballymoney (p 75)
A haven for morning coffee or afternoon tea amid Victorian decor and pine furnishings. Home-baked pastries and savouries are complemented by a good selection of speciality teas. No credit cards.

Templeton Hotel, Templepatrick (p 97)
A hotel with interesting architectural features near the international airport. All tastes are catered for and local produce is used in the preparation of a wide range of dishes. One mile from M2, Templepatrick exit. Ackerman.

Wallace Restaurant, Lisburn (p 91)
This small, intimate restaurant has built up an appreciative following. The imaginative menu changes frequently and daily specials are determined by local produce in season.

A Taste of Ulster
County Armagh

Archway, Armagh (p 99)
In an old Victorian archway near the historic Mall, this pretty coffee house reflects the owner's interest in local history and crafts. The apple pies are made with local Bramleys. No credit cards.

Famous Grouse Country Inn, Loughgall (p 104)
The atmosphere of this country inn, in the heart of the orchard county, is relaxed and friendly. Careful cooking combines admirably with quality local produce. An excellent snack menu is available until 9 pm each evening.

Hearty's Folk Cottage, Crossmaglen (p 103)
Thatched country kitchen, open Sunday only, famous for its hot scones, fresh apple pie and cakes. Even the butter is home made. Irish traditional music. Antiques and crafts on sale.

Old Thatch, Markethill (p 106)
Modelled on a traditional thatched cottage, this unusual coffee shop in Alexander's busy department store has a fine range of home-made cakes and scones. Try the speciality jam!

Wheel and Lantern, Armagh (p 101)
A coffee shop in Lennox's department store. Brick, beams and oak furniture create an old-world atmosphere and freshly baked scones with Bewley's coffee is the morning speciality.

A Taste of Ulster
County Down

Adelboden Lodge, Groomsport (p 129)
The restaurant has splendid sea views and fine home cooking. The wholemeal wheaten bread is baked with a light hand by chef/owner Margaret Waterworth. Vegetarian dishes. Bridgestone.

Aylesfort House, Warrenpoint (p 151)
Easily located on the main road, the restaurant offers a buffet lunch daily, with extensive à la carte and fixed price evening menus. Head chef Peter Magill consistently emphasises local fresh produce. Adventurous bistro menu.

Back Street Café, Bangor (p 116)
Experience innovative modern cuisine in a relaxed atmosphere. Chef/proprietor Richard Gibson likes at least half his starters and entrées to be fresh fish dishes. Local produce is a main feature.

Bay Tree, Holywood (p 131)
This little coffee house is warm and welcoming. On summer days, doors open on to a pretty terrace. The soups and salads and Sue Farmer's cinnamon scones are all freshly prepared. Craft shop. A smoke-free zone!

The Barn, Saintfield (p 150)
Strangford Lough fish and local aged beef are special strengths of American chef Martin Straub's repertoire. Local artists exhibit their paintings in the lounge which has a welcoming turf fire.

The Brass Monkey, Newry (p 140)
Characterful bar with a country farmhouse atmosphere, stone floors and a spiral staircase. The fish comes from Kilkeel and meat and poultry is County Down-bred. Try the superb Ulster 'Monkey' Fry and fine steaks.

Burrendale Hotel, Newcastle (p 137)
In a magnificent setting at the foot of the Mourne mountains, Denis Orr and his team create delicate flavours, with an insistence on fresh ingredients. Families love Denis's high tea menu.

A Taste of Ulster

County Down (contd)

Carmichael's, Holywood (p 131)
An interesting and popular pub near the Belfast-Bangor railway line. The railway theme creates a unique and fun atmosphere.

Castle Espie Coffee Room, Comber (p 122)
Set in a nature reserve with views of Strangford Lough, home of Ireland's largest collection of ducks, geese and swans. A splendid backdrop for the fine food. No credit cards.

Coffee Plus, Donaghadee (p 124)
This cheerful coffee shop in a pretty fishing village is ideal for morning coffee or a light lunch. The home-baked desserts are very good. Another non-smoking coffee shop. No credit cards.

Culloden Hotel, Cultra (p 124)
Chef Paul McKnight offers a wide range of dishes in the Mitre restaurant which looks on to landscaped gardens. This characterful gothic mansion hotel is 7 miles from Belfast on the A2 Bangor road. Ackerman, Egon Ronay.

Deane's on the Square, Helen's Bay (p 129)
Mossiman-trained chef/owner Michael Deane offers modern Irish and British cooking with the emphasis on presentation and taste. Deane's was built in 1863 by the Marquis of Dufferin. The atmosphere is quite distinctive. Good Food Guide.

Dufferin Arms, Killyleagh (p 135)
A traditional Irish pub with a cellar bar/restaurant. The atmosphere is relaxed and the food delicious, with music Thursday through Saturday, Sunday brunch, the newspapers and piano.

The George, Bangor (p 117)
Chef Colin McCreedy offers an extensive menu in the refurbished 'Poacher's Arms', located in an original 1860 building. The emphasis is on healthy eating and vegetarians are particularly welcome.

A Taste of Ulster

County Down *(contd)*

Gilberry Fayre, Gilford (p 127)
This former schoolhouse has an agreeable pine interior. Even with its emphasis on healthy eating, the coffee shop has a mouth-watering array of sweets! Disabled visitors welcome. No credit cards.

Hampton's Coffee Shop, Hillsborough (p 130)
Tea and coffee is prepared from filtered water for a fuller flavour and the scones are always delicious. Another smoke-free zone. Self-service.

Heatherlea Tea Rooms, Bangor (p 117)
This pleasant coffee shop at the rear of Roulston's home bakery is popular with shoppers. Wide range of good home-baked breads. No credit cards.

Hillside, Hillsborough (p 130)
Imaginative dishes with a touch of nouvelle cuisine in this 18th-century restaurant/pub with a herb garden at the back. Off M1/A1 south of Belfast. Bridgestone, Michelin.

Ivanhoe Inn, Carryduff (p 121)
This family-run restaurant/pub is a well known landmark on the main Belfast-Newcastle road. The building dates back to the early 1900s. Specialities are Steak & Guinness pie and Ardglass prawns. The choice steaks come highly recommended.

Knott's Cake & Coffee Shop, Newtownards (p 145)
In a large Victorian building with high ceilings, this airy coffee shop offers a wide range of breads and cakes as well as hot pies, stews and casseroles. A popular lunchtime spot. No credit cards.

McLogans, Newry (p 141)
These lounge bars and restaurant are situated right beside the Buttercrane shopping centre. The daily carvery is very popular and the establishment is well known for its high quality service seven days a week.

A Taste of Ulster

County Down (contd)

No 1 Gallery, Moira (p 136)
A quaint coffee shop with stone walls and original wooden beams. The soups, salads, casseroles, and sweet and savoury pancakes are all prepared on the premises, fresh every day. Entrance through craft shop.

O'Hara's Royal Hotel, Bangor (p 118)
This family-owned hotel enjoys a reputation for good food and friendly atmosphere. Chef Alex Taylor offers French-style modern cuisine using the best county Down produce.

Old Inn, Crawfordsburn (p 123)
The hotel is one of Ireland's oldest hostelries, with records dating back to 1614. The hospitality is warm and genuine with excellent locally produced dishes from the kitchen of chef Ronnie Craythorne. Ackerman.

Old School House, Comber (p 123)
Restaurant close to Strangford Lough. Avril Brown bases her cooking on traditional methods, but experiments with new combinations of seasonal produce. A regular and happy clientèle. On A22, 3 miles south-east of Comber.

Peppercorn Court, Kilmood, Killinchy (p 134)
Stylish restaurant in a former courthouse, with gothic windows and splendid façade. The chef/patron Tolson Sherwood makes imaginative use of local products such as oysters with Guinness and sauces made from dulse (seaweed). Bridgestone.

Portaferry Hotel, Portaferry (p 147)
This country hotel, privately owned and managed, has an idyllic outlook across Strangford Lough. Chef Anne Truesdale's seafood dishes make the very best of the area's plentiful supplies of fish and shellfish. Ackerman, Bridgestone.

A Taste of Ulster

County Down *(contd)*

Primrose Bar, Ballynahinch (p 112)
A former blacksmith shop, the Primrose combines character and excellent cuisine. Discerning eaters come from a distance for Helen Gordon's open prawn sandwiches and wheaten bread.

Red Fox Coffee Shop, Hillsborough (p 130)
Just off the main street, with views of the parish church and grounds. Owner Mo Mullan offers nutritious home-made food. (Craft shop across the courtyard.) No credit cards.

Ritchies, Hillsborough (p 130)
Tradition and style combine to make eating in this pub/restaurant a pleasurable experience. The healthy-eating menu uses fresh local produce and there is a fine view of the historic parish church.

Roma's, Newtownards (p 146)
Stone walls and an art deco theme in the three bars and upstairs restaurant. Daily blackboard specials complement a full lunch menu downstairs. An à la carte menu is served in the restaurant.

Rosemary Jane Tea Room, Crossgar (p 124)
An intimate atmosphere in a fine old building. The menu includes vegetarian dishes using local organic vegetables and imaginative soups, salads and desserts. No credit cards.

The Stables, Groomsport (p 129)
Rustic brick, pitch pine and equestrian memorabilia provide the atmosphere in this pub/restaurant overlooking Belfast Lough. It won the 'Bushmills Bar of the Year' award in 1992. Snacks and grills are prepared with as much care as the extensive à la carte menu.

Wheatear Coffee Lounge, Bangor (p 119)
A bright and busy self-service coffee shop which offers a very wide range of high quality savouries and sweets. The chicken dish is a house speciality. No credit cards.

A Taste of Ulster

County Down (contd)

White Gables Hotel, Hillsborough (p 130)
Paul Cullen's inspiration comes from far and wide but he uses fresh Ulster produce – prime beef, free range poultry and organically grown vegetables. Bridgestone.

Woodlands Restaurant, Ballynahinch (p 113)
Period house, in lush countryside. Alison Sandford's accent is on local produce with seafood from Strangford and Ardglass, game from nearby estates, and home-grown vegetables. Off A24, signposted B175 to Spa. Good Food Guide, Michelin.

A Taste of Ulster

County Fermanagh

Le Bistro, Enniskillen (p 155)
Le Bistro coffee shop in the Erneside shopping centre is a friendly family-run place. The Johnstons use only the best local produce and all food is freshly prepared.

Hollander Restaurant, Irvinestown (p 159)
Interesting decor, with red brickwork, mahogany bar and souvenirs from Holland. Chef Stephen Holland produces some superb dishes – like salmon en croûte, beef Wellington and garlic chicken. On A32, 9 miles from Enniskillen. Bridgestone.

Tullyhona Guesthouse, Florencecourt (p 158)
The restaurant in this guesthouse near Florence Court stately home is open to non-residents. Rosemary Armstrong's menu features home-produced meats and vegetables and some wonderful desserts. Follow signs for Marble Arch caves. No credit cards.

A Taste of Ulster
County Londonderry

Beech Hill Country House, Londonderry (p 171)
This hotel in an 18th-century mansion retains an old-world elegance. Chef Noel McMeel's adventurous menu has more than a touch of nouvelle cuisine, and his desserts are outstanding. Bridgestone, Good Food Guide.

Brown's Restaurant, Londonderry (p 172)
Set in a refurbished railway station, Brown's presents a range of the best in local produce – meat, fowl, fish and vegetarian dishes complemented by a varied wine list.

Brown Trout Golf & Country Inn, Aghadowey (p 163)
The original hostelry here has been associated with the hospitable O'Hara family since 1725. Local pork, game and poultry are favourites and Ulster beef is a house speciality. Open fire, good 'craic' in the bar.

Cloisters Restaurant, Magherafelt (p 178)
A small family-owned restaurant. Chef Deirdre Campbell uses only the best of the county's produce, including Lough Neagh smoked eel. The restaurant offers a range of dishes from light snacks to à la carte.

Ditty's Home Bakery & Coffee Shop, Magherafelt (p 178)
This small coffee shop is in a well known home bakery. The range of breads and confectionery is excellent and there is a choice of hot dishes. No credit cards.

Everglades Hotel, Londonderry (p 173)
The hotel's restaurant facilities are varied, featuring extensive menus, with quality snacks. The Everglades chefs are committed to producing imaginative and traditional food using fresh Ulster produce, as well as a good selection for vegetarians.

Fioltas Bistro, Magherafelt (p 178)
Chef Paul Glass offers a wide range of dishes at this spacious bistro. The menu is based around the best available county Londonderry products. Lunch discounts for senior citizens.

A Taste of Ulster

County Londonderry (contd)

The Little Tea Room, Coleraine (p 166)
Decorated in a warm and cosy style, this non-smoking establishment has easy access for disabled visitors. Afternoon cream tea is a favourite and the lunch menu includes a good selection of simple well prepared family dishes.

MacDuff's, Coleraine (p 166)
The best of country house cooking, with a modern touch, in the cellar of a Georgian rectory, now a guesthouse. Game is a speciality and the seafood is caught locally. Off A29, 6 miles south of Coleraine. Ackerman, Bridgestone, Egon Ronay, Good Food Guide, Michelin.

Metro Bar, Londonderry (p 175)
Charming little pub in the shadow of the city walls. Lots of alcoves create a cosy atmosphere. Everything from soup and sandwiches to a hearty beef stew in Guinness. No credit cards.

Morelli's, Portstewart (p 181)
This bright and cheerful seafront café offers a clear view to the sea. As well as hot dishes, Morelli's is a long established and famous ice cream parlour with an amazing array of exotic ices. No credit cards.

Schooner's, Londonderry (p 176)
Overlooking Lough Foyle and the historic city of Londonderry, the restaurant/wine bar offers a high standard of cuisine. Local fish figures prominently and vegetables are treated with respect.

Waterfoot Hotel, Londonderry (p 177)
The hotel has an interesting design and offers excellent views of the River Foyle and the Donegal mountains. Chef Kevin McGowan uses fish straight from the Foyle and local vegetables.

A Taste of Ulster
County Tyrone

The Courtyard, Cookstown (p 186)
Ploughs and cartwheels create a rustic feel in this attractive coffee shop. The wholesome, home-made food echoes the theme. No credit cards.

Grange Lodge Country House, Dungannon (p 189)
An ivy-covered Georgian retreat, set in rolling countryside. Norah Brown cooks many award-winning dishes. Exit M1 at junction 15, follow A29 south for 1.5 miles, left at signpost 'Grange', right, then first house on right.

Greenmount Lodge, Omagh (p 194)
The Lodge, once part of an 18th-century estate, is renowned for its quality Ulster beef and lamb reared on its own farm, and Louie Reid is well known for her delicious desserts. Open to non-residents at weekends for dinner. No credit cards.

Greenvale Hotel, Cookstown (p 187)
Formerly a 19th-century gentleman's residence, the hotel provides a homely and cosy atmosphere in the Orchard Room, popular with families for Sunday lunch.

Hedley's Coffee House, Dungannon (p 189)
This friendly, family-run coffee shop in the town centre offers a wide range of home-cooked and baked products. The scones, wheaten bread and pavlova come highly recommended.

Inn on the Park, Dungannon (p 189)
A family hotel tucked away in wooded gardens. The extensive menu ranges from bar snacks to à la carte dining, and chefs Richard Torode and Andrew Rusk use the finest local produce.

A Taste of Ulster

County Tyrone *(contd)*

Mellon Country Inn, Omagh (p 195)
Right opposite the Ulster-American Folk Park. Rustic brick and natural wood decor. The food is traditional with perceptible French influences. Extensive menu in Mary Gray's restaurant. Paddy Brown's bar is excellent value for light snacks.

Rosamund's Coffee Shop, Augher (p 183)
In one of the old Clogher Valley Railway station houses. The cooking is simple and good and dishes feature Clogher Valley cheese. Local crafts and linen on sale. No credit cards.

Suitor Gallery, Ballygawley (p 183)
Tea room/craftshop in a converted barn at the bottom of an orchard on the Ballygawley roundabout. The vegetable soup and wheaten bread is prepared by owner/cook/artist Beryl Suitor. Wide selection of cakes and pastries.

The Woodlander, Omagh (p 195)
A modern roadhouse with several bars. Food prepared by chef John Casey is available all day and the lunch menu ranges from filled rolls in the bar to a four-course meal in the restaurant.

Special mentions

Although not members of A Taste of Ulster, these restaurants feature in the latest editions of well known guides to good eating. They too are shown in green in the main listings, preceded by ★

Belfast
Antica Roma – p 43. Good Food Guide.
Ashoka – p 43. Bridgestone.
Bananas – p 39. Bridgestone.
Belfast Castle – p 60. Ackerman, Bridgestone.
Bengal Brasserie – p 43. Egon Ronay.
Bishops – p 43. Good Food Guide.
Chez Delbart – p 45. Bridgestone.
Crown Liquor Saloon – p 40. Ackerman, Bridgestone.
French Village – p 47. Bridgestone.
Friar's Bush – p 47. Bridgestone.
La Belle Epoque – p 41. Ackerman, Bridgestone,
　　　Good Food Guide, Michelin.
La Bohème – p 41. Good Food Guide.
Long's Fish Restaurant – p 62. Bridgestone.
Mr JD's – p 55. Bridgestone.
Manor House – p 49. Bridgestone, Egon Ronay, Michelin.
Restaurant 44 – p 42. Ackerman, Bridgestone.
Saints and Scholars – p 50. Bridgestone, Michelin.
Spice of Life – p 36. Bridgestone.
Strand – p 50. Ackerman, Bridgestone, Egon Ronay,
　　　Good Food Guide, Michelin.
Truffles – p 36. Bridgestone.
Upper Crust – p 37. Bridgestone.
Welcome – p 51. Ackerman, Bridgestone, Egon Ronay.

Special mentions contd

County Antrim
Auberge de Seneirl, Bushmills – p 75. Bridgestone,
 Good Food Guide.
Dunadry Inn, Dunadry – p 80. Ackerman.
Ginger Tree, Newtownabbey – p 91. Bridgestone,
 Good Food Guide, Michelin.
Manley, Ballymena – p 72. Bridgestone, Michelin.
Ramore, Portrush – p 95. Ackerman clover, Bridgestone,
 Egon Ronay star, Good Food Guide, Michelin red M.
Sleepy Hollow, Newtownabbey – p 92. Bridgestone, Michelin.
Water Margin, Ballymena – p 74. Bridgestone, Michelin.
Windrose, Carrickfergus – p 78. Michelin.
Wysner's, Ballycastle – p 68. Bridgestone.

County Down
Gaslamp, Newtownards – p 145. Bridgestone.
Glassdrumman, Annalong – p 111. Egon Ronay, Michelin.
The Grange, Waringstown – p 151. Bridgestone, Michelin.
Iona, Holywood – p 131. Bridgestone.
Lobster Pot, Strangford – p 150. Ackerman.
Ming Court, Newtownards – p 145. Bridgestone.

County Fermanagh
Cedars, Irvinestown – p 159. Bridgestone.
Drumshane Hotel, Lisnarick – p 161. Bridgestone.
Franco's, Enniskillen – p 155. Bridgestone.
Melvin House, Enniskillen – p 157. Bridgestone.
Rafters, Newtownbutler – p 162. Bridgestone.
The Sheelin, Bellanaleck – p 153. Ackerman, Bridgestone,
 Good Food Guide.

County Londonderry
Fiorentini's, Londonderry – p 173. Bridgestone.
Kitty's of Coleraine, Coleraine – p 166. Bridgestone.

County Tyrone
Top Bar, Dungannon – p 191. Good Food Guide.

How to use the guide

This handy paperback will fit neatly into a pocket or the glove compartment of your car, The 1,800 eating places listed here range from the smallest coffee shop and fish & chip café to the smart places that get into food guides.

Everyone is familiar with that uneasy feeling when, driving through some newly discovered countryside, enjoying the sights and sounds, you are wondering all the same where to stop for a bite to eat. Might there be a tea-room in the next village? Dare you press on?

To resolve this dilemma we have listed places by town and village within each county. Some villages have only one eating place - perhaps a hotel or maybe just a pub serving hot pies and pizzas. The important thing is to know what is available in the area and this book should help you find them.

The canny traveller will plan ahead, of course, and a telephone call before setting out is sensible, particularly at weekends when many restaurants are booked and some hotels may have arranged a dinner-dance, which may not suit you.

Entries are grouped by town and village in each county. There is a map at the back of the book and an index to towns and villages. The Belfast section is divided into five areas, shown on the sketch map on page 26.

City Centre — the BT1 postcode area.
Golden Mile — includes the many restaurants along Great Victoria St (BT2).
University and Malone - area around Queen's University and Lisburn Rd (BT7 & 9).
East of the River - from the Lagan to the eastern suburbs (mostly BT4-6, 8 & 16).
North and West of the River - from the Lagan to the city limits (BT10-15 & 17).

Restaurants are divided into three price bands which are based on the average cost of a three-course meal - a starter, main course of meat or fish, plus two vegetables and a sweet. We have included 10 per cent service and VAT, but not wine or coffee.

£	£5 to £10
££	£10 to £15
£££	over £15
M	followed by £, ££, or £££ refers to average cost of lunch
E	followed by £, ££, or £££ refers to average cost of evening meal

When no symbol is used, a three-course meal or equivalent will cost less than £5. In general, midday meals cost less than evening meals. E£ means that an evening meal is £5-£10 but you can still get lunch for under £5 in the same place. Some restaurants offer special early evening menus which are good value.

If you are dissatisfied in any way, tell the waiter or ask for the manager - always more effective than writing after you get home. Your comments will help them to improve the service.

Restaurants participating in the Healthy Eating Circle are indicated by ⊖. They provide healthy food choices and set aside non-smoking areas. For further information contact the Health Promotion Agency. ☎ (0232) 311611.

You will find that hotels are good places for meals and snacks throughout the day. For many visitors afternoon tea offers a welcome break from sightseeing. Served from around three o'clock it consists of a pot of tea, sandwiches, and cakes or scones.

High tea starts at about five o'clock and is usually over by seven. Some overseas visitors are quite defeated by the notion of high tea. A typical high tea consists of sausages, or a lamb cutlet, with a plate of cakes and scones. Home-baked ham and salad may be served, and since Ulster is the country of good bread, it is not unusual to have several varieties of bread on the table.

Licensed restaurants in Northern Ireland are fortunate in that they can serve a complete range of drinks including wine, beer and all kinds of spirits. All licensed establishments are indicated by ♀ and those places which we know from experience welcome customers bringing in a bottle of wine are indicated by 🍾.

Pubs in Northern Ireland are open seven days a week. They are open all day from Monday to Saturday 1130am-11pm, with half-an-hour 'drinking up' time, so that you can savour that last pint. On Sunday most open at lunchtime and in the evening (12.30-2.30pm and 7-10pm) although some publicans continue to observe the traditional Sabbath and remain closed.

More pubs are now providing food all day and this is why we have given the full licensing hours in many cases. Even so, experience has shown that the widest choice is served around lunchtime and, in some pubs, in the early evening. Many pubs will make you a pot of tea at any time during the day.

Some telephone numbers listed here may change in the course of the year. If you cannot get through dial 100 and ask the operator for help.

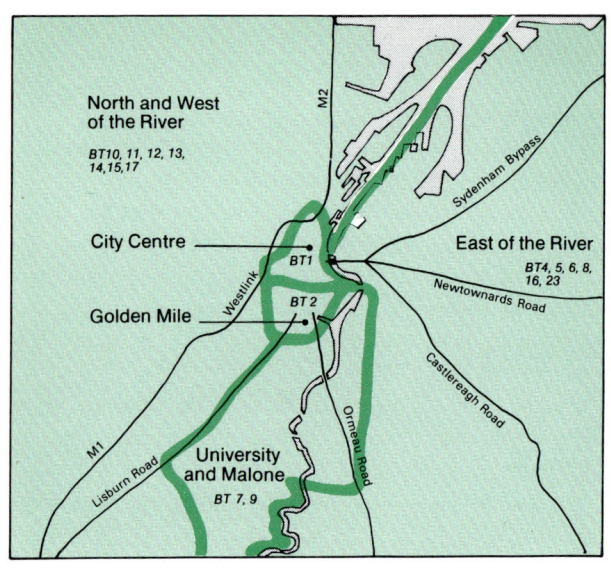

Belfast postal districts

Use this sketch map, based on postal districts, to locate restaurants in the Belfast area.

BELFAST

City Centre *(BT1)*
(STD 0232)

Alambra
114 North St, BT1. ☎ 240682.
0930-1730 Mon-Sat. Burgers,
fries, chicken.

Anderson & McAuley
1 Donegall Place, BT1.
☎ 326681. 0900-1700
Mon-Sat, 0900-2030 Thur.
Restaurant in department store.

Arizona ♀
10 Gresham St, BT1.
☎ 323590. 1130-1500
Mon-Thur, until 1700 Fri &
Sat. Pub grub.

Bambricks
58 Wellington Place, BT1.
☎ 234303. 0800-1530 Mon-
Fri, 1100-1530 Sat. Sandwich
bar & restaurant.

Bamford's Home Bakery
49A Upper Arthur St, BT1.
☎ 242284. 0800-1700
Mon-Sat. Rolls, pies,
sandwiches.

Benny's
10 Short St, BT1. ☎ 743128.
0800-1700 Mon-Fri,
0800-1300 Sat. Ulster fry,
sandwiches.

Bethel
3 Donegall Square East, BT1.
☎ 439525. 0930-1600
Mon-Sat. Chicken, salads,
pizza. Coffee shop in book
store.

★ **BEWLEY'S**
Donegall Arcade, BT1.
☎ 234955. 0830-1700
Mon-Sat, until 2030 Thur.
Breakfast, lunch, pastries,
afternoon tea, speciality
coffees. Self-service. £.

★ **BITTLES** ♀
70 Upper Church Lane, BT1.
☎ 311088. 1130-1500 Mon-
Sat. Irish stew, champ.

Blackthorn ♀
3 Skipper St, BT1. ☎ 232216.
1200-1430 Mon-Sat. Roast
beef, fish, salads.

Blinkers
1 Bridge St, BT1. ☎ 243330.
1000-2245 Mon-Sat. Grills,
burgers, set lunch.

BELFAST — City Centre

Blooms
46 Upper Arthur St, BT1.
☎ 313500. 0730-1530 Mon-Fri. Sandwiches, sausage rolls.

Bodega ♀
4 Callender St, BT1.
☎ 243177. 1130-1700 Mon-Sat, until 2000 Thur. Cajun chicken, stir fry, pub grub. E£.

Bonne Bouche
19 Fountain St, BT1.
☎ 241454. 0730-1730 Mon-Sat, until 2100 Thur. Ulster fry, set lunch.

Boots ⊙
35 Donegall Place, BT1.
☎ 242332. 0900-1730 Mon-Sat, until 2015 Thur. Coffee, cakes, baked potatoes, lasagne. Self-service restaurant in department store.

Bradan Bar ♀
83 May St, BT1. ☎ 230295. 1130-2300 Mon-Sat. Pub grub.

Brown's Fish Restaurant
30 Chichester St, BT1.
☎ 232100. 0830-1800 Mon-Wed, until 2030 Thur-Fri, 1000-1800 Sat. ££.

Burger King
Cleaver House, Donegall Place, BT1. ☎ 245314. 0800-2300 Mon-Thur, until 2400 Fri & Sat, 1000-2300 Sun. Burgers, breakfast, coffee.

C & A ⊙
46 Donegall Place, BT1.
☎ 232636. 0930-1700 Mon-Sat, until 2030 Thur. Coffee shop in department store.

Café Noir
Fountain Centre, College St.
☎ 439295. 0800-1700 Mon-Fri, 0900-1700 Sat. Breakfast, lunches, crêpes.

Café Renoir
5 Queen St, BT1. ☎ 325592. 0945-1700 Mon-Sat. Club triple sandwich, chicken & prawn open sandwiches, hot chocolate.

Campbell's
11 Donegall Square West, BT1. ☎ 322658. 0730-1700 Mon-Sat. Self-service café in cake shop.

Capstan Bar ♀
10 Ann St, BT1. ☎ 329148. 1200-1430 Mon-Sat. Hamburgers, salads, pub grub.

Carlton ♀
11 Wellington Place, BT1.
☎ 326861. 1130-1930 Mon-Sat. Steaks, haddock with mustard & banana sauce, Portavogie scampi. A la carte. E£.

City Centre — BELFAST

Casablanca
Castle Court, Royal Avenue, BT1. ☎ 235122. 1200-1600 Mon-Sat, until 2030 Thur. Moussaka, chilli, curries. £.

Castle Mews
34 Bank St, BT1. ☎ 330443. 1200-2100 Mon-Sat. Pub grub.

Chalet d'Or
48 Fountain St, BT1. ☎ 324810. 0900-1800 Mon-Sat, until 2000 Thur. Set lunch, Ulster fry, grills.

Chalet d'Or
Castle St, BT1. ☎ 249820. 0930-1700 Mon-Sat. Soup, stew, set lunch.

Chaney's
23 High St, BT1. ☎ 245688. 1000-1800 Mon-Sat, until 2100 Thur. Grills, snacks, set lunch. £.

★ **CLARENCE**
18 Donegall Square East, BT1. ☎ 238862. 1200-1430 Mon-Sat. A la carte: champagne sorbet, salmon & monkfish with ginger sauce. Bar lunch: pâté, salads, sandwiches. ££.

Crow's Nest
26 Skipper St, BT1. ☎ 325491. 1200-1500 Mon-Sat. Pub grub.

Dr B's Kitchen
5 Bridge St, BT1. ☎ 321213. 0930-1400 Mon-Fri. Baked Irish ham, pork in cider sauce, sirloin of beef in pepper sauce.

Deer's Head
5 Garfield St. ☎ 239163. 1200-1900 Mon-Sat. Soup, baked potatoes, club sandwiches, lasagne.

Delaney's
Lombard St, BT1. ☎ 231572. 0900-1700 Mon-Sat, until 2100 Thur. Breakfast, lasagne, home-baked pies, self-service. A la carte. £.

★ **DUKE OF YORK**
3 Commercial Court, BT1. ☎ 241062. 1200-1400 Mon-Fri, 1200-1700 Sat. Steaks, vegetarian lasagne, filled rolls. Live music.

Eighteen Steps
17 Ann St, BT1. ☎ 326247. 1130-1700 Mon-Wed, until 2000 Thur-Sat. Open sandwiches, home-made pies, steaks.

Fat Harry's
93 Castle St, BT1. ☎ 232226. 1200-2100 Mon-Sat. Steaks, grills, scampi. £.

Forte's
92 Castle St, BT1. ☎ 327189. 0915-1745 Mon-Sat. Soup, burgers, sandwiches.

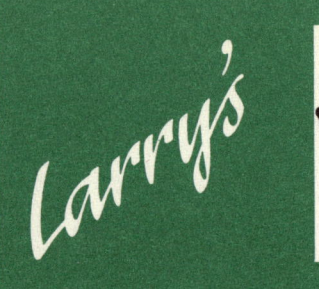

**WORLD RENOWNED PIANO BAR AND RESTAURANT
36 BEDFORD STREET, BELFAST**
(next to Ulster Hall)
Tel: 325061
Eat, drink and be entertained by our singing waitresses
and resident piano player
until 1.30 a.m.
(last orders 1.15 a.m.)

NICK'S

RESTAURANT & WINE BAR
35-39 Hill St. Belfast
Telephone: (0232) 439690

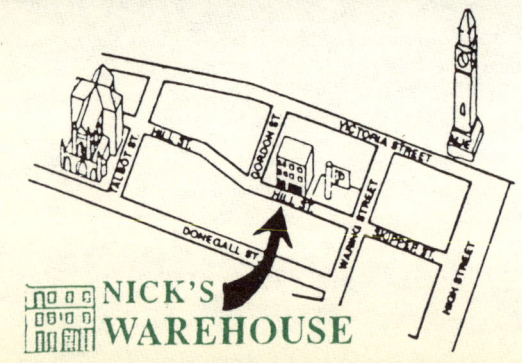

BELFAST

Fountain Tavern ♀
16 Fountain St, BT1.
☎ 242049. 1130-1900
Mon-Sat, until 2100 Thur.
Steak casserole, quiche, baked potatoes.

Frames ♀
2 Little Donegall St, BT1.
☎ 237214. 1200-1500
Mon-Fri. Moussaka, beef casserole, plaice

Frames Too ♀
2 Little Donegall St, BT1.
☎ 244855. 1200-1430
Mon-Sat, 1700-2130 Thur-Sat.
Lamb, loin of pork, mexican chicken. E£.

Front Page ♀
106 Donegall St, BT1.
☎ 324924. 1200-2130
Mon-Sat. Chilli, home-made soup, baked potatoes. Live music. £.

Garden ♀
32 Fountain Centre, BT1.
☎ 231823. 0830-1730
Mon-Sat, until 2100 Thur.
Grills, fish. A la carte. £.

Garrick ♀
29 Chichester St, BT1.
☎ 321984. 1200-1430
Mon-Sat. Home-made stew, soup, apple pie.

Globe Tavern ♀
Joy's Entry, BT1. ☎ 326711.
1130-2300 Mon-Sat. Grills, salads.

Golden Bloom
9 Wellington St, BT1.
☎ 240281. 0745-1730
Mon-Sat. Ulster fry, pies, sandwiches.

Hardy's
12 Fountain Lane, BT1.
☎ 236308. 0800-1700 Mon-Sat, until 2100 Thur. Beef & Guinness pie, home-baked scones, pancakes.

Harlequin Café
13 Union St, BT1. ☎ 236939.
0730-1500 Mon-Sat. Lasagne, chilli, stew.

Hedley's Coffee Shop ☕
103 Royal Avenue, BT1.
☎ 237077. 0930-1700
Mon-Sat. Cottage pie, casseroles.

Hercules ♀
61 Castle St, BT1. ☎ 324587.
1130-2300 Mon-Sat. Pub grub.

Just Cooking
42 Upper Arthur St, BT1.
☎ 249009. 0800-1630
Mon-Sat. Salad bar, pizzas.

Kelly's Cellars ♀
30 Bank St, BT1. ☎ 324835.
1130-1400 Mon-Sat. Pub grub, oysters, grills. Live traditional music.

BELFAST
City Centre

Kentucky Fried Chicken
7 Wellington Place, BT1.
☎ 325146. 1100-2300
Mon-Thur, until 2330 Fri &
Sat. Burgers, chips, chicken.

Kitchen Bar ♀
16 Victoria Square, BT1.
☎ 324901. 1200-1400
Mon-Sat. Ulster fry, soup,
stew, pizzas.

Krusty Korner
76 Lower North St, BT1.
☎ 232047. 0900-1700 Mon-
Sat. Set lunch, sandwiches,
coffee.

Le Café
38 Hill St, BT1. ☎ 311660.
0930-1430 Mon-Fri.
Tagliatelli, chicken curry,
vegetarian. Newspapers.

Le Petit Pain ☺
Ross's Court, William St South,
BT1. ☎ 332440. 0800-1730
Mon-Sat, until 2100 Thur.
Croissants, bagels, baguettes,
pastries.

Linen Hall Library ☺
17 Donegall Square North,
BT1. ☎ 321707. 1000-1600
Mon-Fri, until 1400 Sat. Soup,
sandwiches, scones. Café in
reading room.

Little Knife & Fork
29 North St, BT1. ☎ 439619.
0900-1800 Mon-Sat, until
2200 Thur. Fish & chips,
sausages.

Littlewoods Green Room
Ann St, BT1. ☎ 241537. 0900-
1715 Mon-Sat, until 2100
Thur. Grills, set lunch.
Restaurant in department store.

McDonald's
2 Donegall Place, BT1.
☎ 311600. 0700-2000
Mon-Sat, until 2200 Thur,
1100-1800 Sun. Breakfast,
burgers, chicken.

Mr Sandwich
20 Church Lane, BT1.
☎ 326275. 0800-1600
Mon-Fri. Irish stew,
sandwiches, snacks.

Mrs Muffins
8 Arthur St, BT1. 0800-1630
Mon-Sat. Pies, quiche,
lasagne.

Maysfield Leisure Centre
East Bridge St, BT1. ☎ 241633.
1000-2200 Mon-Fri, until
1600 Sat, 1100-1700 Sun.
Fish, chicken, lasagne.

Mermaid ♀
5 Wilson's Court, High St,
BT1. ☎ 327829. 1230-1430
Mon-Sat. Pub grub.

Miss American Pie
Ross's Court, William St South,
BT1. ☎ 311055. 0900-1730
Mon-Wed & Fri, until 2100
Thur. Chilli, club sandwiches,
doughnuts.

City Centre **BELFAST**

Monico ♀
17 Lombard St, BT1.
☎ 323211. 1200-1800
Mon-Sat. Pub grub.

Morning Star ♀
17 Pottinger's Entry, BT1.
☎ 323976. 1130-2100 Mon-Sat. Beef stroganoff, pan fried lamb fillet with ginger & garlic, carrot & stilton soup. £.

Muldoon's ♀
13 Corporation Square, BT1.
☎ 232415. 1200-1500
Mon-Sat. Burgers, salads, fish, pies.

★ **NICK'S WAREHOUSE** ♀

35 Hill St, BT1. ☎ 439690. Restaurant: 1200-1430 Mon-Fri, 1800-2100 Tues-Sat. Duck with apple, fillet of halibut with langoustine & sweet peppers. M££. Wine bar: 1200-1500 Mon-Fri, 1800-2330 Tues-Sat. Lettuce & cucumber soup, hot & sour beef with water chestnuts.

Ormeau Bakery
27 Fountain St, BT1.
☎ 328340. 0800-1630
Mon-Sat. Baked potatoes, soup, pies.

Oxford
Oxford St Bus Depot, BT1.
☎ 331289. 0830-1730
Mon-Sat. Burgers, sandwiches, coffee.

Pancake House
Haymarket, Royal Avenue, BT1. ☎ 240141. 0800-1730 Mon-Sat, until 2100 Thur. Savoury & sweet pancakes, fish, chips.

Patio Restaurant ⊙
BHS, 24 Castle Place, BT1.
☎ 243068. 0930-1700
Mon-Thur, 0900-1700 Fri & Sat. Coffee shop and restaurant in department store.

Pat's Bar ♀
19 Prince's Dock St, BT1.
☎ 744524. 1200-1430 Mon-Fri. Lasagne, pizza, set lunch. Live traditional music.

Penny Farthing ♀
94 Donegall St, BT1.
☎ 249423. 1200-1530
Mon-Sat, 1230-1430 Sun. Set meals, grills.

Poachers
Unit 10, Victoria Centre, BT1.
☎ 332162. 0900-1600
Mon-Sat. Home baking, sandwiches.

Queen's Bar ♀
4 Queen's Arcade, BT1.
☎ 321347. 1200-1800
Mon-Sat, until 2000 Thur. Club sandwich, steak pie black velvet, vegetable lasagne.

Romano's
12 Queen St, BT1. ☎ 249484.
0830-1730 Mon-Sat. Set lunch, grills.

BELFAST *City Centre*

Roost 🍷
Church Lane, BT1. ☎ 233282.
1130-2300 Mon-Sat. Irish stew, chicken in basket.

Rotterdam Bar 🍷
54 Pilot St, BT1. ☎ 746021.
1200-1400 Mon-Sat.
Sandwiches, Irish stew. Live music. Beer garden.

Rumpole's 🍷
81 Chichester St, BT1.
☎ 232840. 1200-1500 Mon-Sat, 1600-2200 Tues & Thur-Sat. Crab pâté, seafood pancake, chicken & ham pie.

Sarah's
Arthur Square, BT1.
☎ 326517. 0730-1700
Mon-Sat, until 2100 Thur.
Breakfast, sandwiches, coffee.

Shakespeare
103 Victoria St, BT1.
☎ 328788. 1130-2300
Mon-Sat. Pub grub.

Skandia 🍾 ⊘
12 Callender St, BT1.
☎ 245385. 0930-1800
Mon-Sat, until 2100 Thur.
Salads, open sandwiches, charcoal grill. £.

★ **SKANDIA** 🍾 ⊘
50 Howard St, BT1.
☎ 240239. 0930-2300
Mon-Sat. Grills, salads, open sandwiches, gateaux. E£.

Snakkers
63a Prince's Dock St, BT1.
☎ 352387. 0800-1600
Mon-Fri, until 1400 Sat.
Home-made savoury pies, casseroles, Ulster fry, roasts.

★ **SPICE OF LIFE** 🍾 ⊘
82 Donegall St, BT1.
☎ 332744. 0900-1700
Mon-Fri. Soup, lasagne, salads.
Wholefood & vegetarian.

Strikes
19 Bridge St, BT1. ☎ 320945.
0900-1800 Mon-Sat, until 2100 Thur. Set lunch, soup, grills, toasties.

Taste
Ross's Court, William St South, BT1. 0900-1730 Mon-Sat, until 2100 Thur. Chinese.

Tiffins
6 Montgomery St, BT1.
☎ 320906. 0800-1730
Mon-Fri. Coffee, scones, sandwiches.

★ **TRUFFLES** 🍷
4A Donegall Square West,
BT1. ☎ 247153. 0830-1800
Mon-Sat. Coffee shop: Ulster fry, curries. Restaurant: minute steak, stuffed pork fillet, spring chicken in barbecue sauce.

City Centre **BELFAST**

★ **UPPER CRUST**

15 Lombard St, BT1.
☎ 323132. 0930-1630 Mon-Sat. Home-made pies, chicken & broccoli bake, gateaux.

Washington ♀
15 Howard St, BT1.
☎ 241891. 1130-2300 Mon-Sat. Mexican, barbecue ribs, steaks, pancakes. Music. E££.

Whistlers I
Ross's Court, William St South, BT1. ☎ 310044. 0900-1730 Mon-Sat, until 2100 Thur. Fish & chips.

Whistlers II
Ross's Court, William St South, BT1. ☎ 310044. 0900-1730 Mon-Sat, until 2100 Thur. Burgers, salads, baked potatoes.

Whistle Stop ♀
Central Station, East Bridge St, BT1. ☎ 238637. 0800-1900 Mon-Sat. Soup, stew, fish & chips. Self-service.

★ **WHITE'S TAVERN** ♀
Winecellar Entry, High St, BT1. ☎ 243080. 1200-1430 Mon-Sat. Sandwiches, quiche, burgers, salads. Traditional music on Thur.

Windsor Dairy
4 College St, BT1. ☎ 327157. 0830-1730 Mon-Sat, until 2100 Thur. Home baking, Irish stew, coffee.

Woolworth's ⌒
11 High St, BT1. ☎ 322888. 0900-1730 Mon-Sat, until 2100 Thur. Snacks, grills, salads. Restaurant in department store.

for an
Excellent choice of beers, wines & spirits in a friendly, welcoming atmosphere

Superb food at reasonable prices
Lunch served 12 noon - 6pm
Monday to Friday
12 noon - 3pm Saturday
Try our special of the day
Private parties catered for
Portside Pubs Ltd,
Dargan Road, Belfast

ponte vecchio restaurant & pizzeria

Italian Cuisine
Large Parties catered for
Pastas/Pizzas
Fish/Meat
European Dishes

73 Gt. Victoria Street
Belfast Tel: 0232 242402

For the best Italian food right here in town

BELFAST

Golden Mile *(BT2)*
(STD 0232)

Archana ♀
53 Dublin Rd, BT2. ☎ 323713.
1200-2400 Mon-Fri, 1700-2300 Sun. Indian & European. Balti, Kashmiri bread. £££.

Arthur's ♀
7 Hope St, BT2. ☎ 333311.
1800-2300 Mon-Sat. Ginger chicken strips, lemon sole with prawns, profiteroles with peach ice cream. £££.

★ **BANANAS** ♀
4 Clarence St, BT2. ☎ 339999.
1200-1500 Mon-Fri, 1700-2300 Mon-Sat. Warm mussel & potato salad, chicken with pineapple, coconut & rum sauce, bitter chocolate truffle torte. £££.

Beaten Docket ♀
48 Great Victoria St, BT2.
242986. 1230-1500 Mon-Sat. Pub grub, champ. A la carte. ££.

Bocoose ♀
85 Dublin Rd, BT2.
☎ 238787. 1700-2130 Mon-Sat. Mexican style chilli bean soup, grilled fish, chicken & steak with spice herb butter. £££.

Boyne Bridge ♀
2 Sandy Row, BT2. ☎ 327938.
1130-1700 Mon-Sat. Ulster fry, lasagne.

Britannic ♀
Amelia St (above Crown Liquor Saloon), BT2.
☎ 249476. 1130-1430 Mon-Fri. Beef & Guinness pie, ploughman's platter, pickled beef.

Café India ♀
60 Great Victoria St, BT2.
☎ 243727. 1200-1400 & 1730-2330 Mon-Sat, 1730-2230 Sun. European & Indian. £££.

39

BELFAST

Golden Mile

Casey's
85 Dublin Rd, BT2.
☎ 238787. 1200-1500 & 1800-2300 Mon-Sat. Barbary duck with olives, monkfish medallions, lemon cabbage. £££.

China Town
60 Great Victoria St, BT2.
☎ 230115. 1200-1400 & 1700-2400 Mon-Sat, 1700-2300 Sun. Cantonese. E£.

Crescent
197 Sandy Row, BT2.
☎ 320911. 2100-0130 Mon-Sat. Pub grub.

★ **CROWN LIQUOR SALOON**
46 Great Victoria St, BT2.
☎ 249476. 1130-1430 Mon-Sat. Bar lunches, champ, oysters, stew. Victorian pub in National Trust care.

Dempsey's Terrace
45 Dublin Rd, BT2.
☎ 234000. 1200-1500 & 1700-2130 Mon-Sat. Mussels in garlic, white wine & cream sauce, duck stuffed with lime, peach & nuts. E££.

Dome & Limelight
17 Ormeau Avenue, BT2.
☎ 325942. 1900-2200 Mon-Sat. Sandwiches, grills, salads. Live music. E£.

Drury Lane
2 Amelia St, BT2. ☎ 238008.
1230-1500 & 1800-2130 Mon-Sat. Chicken, steaks. £.

Emerald City
59 Dublin Rd. ☎ 235072.
1200-1400 & 1700-2330 Mon-Thur, until 2430 Fri & Sat, 1630-2300 Sun. Chinese & European. ££.

Equinox
32 Howard St, BT2.
☎ 230089. 0930-1730 Mon-Sat. Filled croissants, tagliatelli with smoked ham & cream sauce. £.

Europa Hotel
Great Victoria St, BT2.
☎ 327000. Last orders 2330. A la carte. M£, E£££.

Explorers
89 Dublin Rd. ☎ 245550.
1700-2330 Mon-Sat, until 2300 Sun. Chicken sphinx, lamb with redcurrant & mint sauce, calypso banana.

Harvey's
95 Great Victoria St, BT2.
☎ 233433. 1700-2300 Mon-Thur & Sun, until 2400 Fri & Sat. Tacos, barbecue ribs, deep-pan pizza. E£.

Hungry Jack's
10 Bedford St, BT2.
☎ 326601. 0800-1600 Mon-Fri. Sandwiches made to order.

Golden Mile — BELFAST

Jenny's
81 Dublin Rd, BT2.
☎ 249282. 0900-1700
Mon-Sat. Lasagne, quiche, salads.

★ LA BELLE EPOQUE ♀
61 Dublin Rd. ☎ 323244.
1200-2330 Mon-Fri,
1800-2330 Sat. Fillet of beef with seed mustard cream sauce, roast breast of Barbary duck with grape sauce.

★ LA BOHÈME ♀
103 Great Victoria St, BT2.
☎ 240666. 1200-1500 &
1800-2330 Mon-Sat. Chicken pieces with prune stuffing & red wine sauce, wild salmon with fresh basil sauce.

Lacey's ♀
50 Dublin Rd, BT2.
☎ 249269. 1200-2300
Mon-Fri, 1800-2300 Sat. Cheese parcels, ribs, daily specials.

Larry's Piano Bar ♀
36 Bedford St, BT2.
☎ 325061. 1700-0130
Tues-Sat. A la carte. Pasta, steaks, fish. Live music. E£.

Morrison's ♀
21 Bedford St, BT2.
☎ 248458. 1200-1430
Mon-Sat. Oriental spiced chicken, salmon in orange sauce, salads.

No. 6
6 Great Victoria St, BT2.
☎ 244532. 0800-1700
Mon-Sat. Sandwiches, salads, pizza.

Oriental International ♀
25 Dublin Rd, BT2.
☎ 232485. 1200-1400 &
1730-2315 Mon-Thur, until 0030 Fri & Sat, 1630-2300 Sun. Peking, Cantonese & European. E£££.

Pizza Hut ♀
44 Dublin Rd, BT2.
☎ 311222. 1200-2400
Mon-Sat, 1200-2300 Sun. Pizzas, salad bar. £

Pizza Hut
Belfast Superbowl, 4 Clarence St West, BT2. ☎ 331466.
1000-0030 Mon-Sat, 1200-0030 Sun. Pizza, garlic bread.

Plaza Hotel ♀
15 Brunswick St, BT2.
☎ 333555. Last orders 2130. A la carte. Smoked salmon, steak, Belvoir pork, chocolate mousse. E£££.

Ponte Vecchio 🍷
73 Great Victoria St, BT2.
☎ 242402. 1700-2330
Mon-Sat, until 2200 Sun. Pizzas, pasta. E££.

Robinson's ♀
38 Great Victoria St, BT2.
☎ 790909. 1130-2300
Mon-Sat. Four themed bars.

BELFAST

Golden Mile

★ **RESTAURANT 44**
44 Bedford St, BT2.
☎ 244844. 1200-1500 &
1800-2300 Mon-Sat. Casserole
of shellfish, char-grilled fillet
of beef with gamba prawns &
orange butter sauce, garden
berry pudding. E£££.

Robinson's
38 Great Victoria St, BT2.
☎ 790909. 1130-2300
Mon-Sat. Five themed bars

★ **ROSCOFF**
Lesley House, Shaftesbury
Square, BT2. ☎ 331532.
1215-1415 Mon-Fri,
1830-2230 Mon-Sat. Sliced
duck breast with crispy confit,
sauté turbot & prawns,
chocolate soufflé with Black
Bush anglaise. M££. E£££.

Salvo's
117 Great Victoria St, BT2.
☎ 247891. 1700-2330
Mon-Sat. Pizza, pasta, fish,
chicken.

Speranza
16 Shaftesbury Square, BT2.
☎ 230213. 1730-2330
Mon-Sat. Italian. Pizzas,
pasta.

Spires
Church House, Fisherwick
Place, Brunswick St, BT2.
☎ 312881. 0900-1730
Mon-Sat, until 2000 Thur.
Ulster fry, chicken, scampi.

Springfellows & Joxers
12 Brunswick St, BT2.
☎ 248398. 1130-2100
Mon-Sat. A la carte. E£.

Starlite Café & Sandwich Bar
60 Great Victoria St, BT2.
1100-2400 Sun-Wed,
1100-1400 Thur-Sat. Fast
food.

Summer Palace
126 Great Victoria St, BT2.
☎ 439353. 1800-0100
Mon-Sat, until 2200 Sun.
Chinese. E££.

Tokyo Joe's Warehouse
9 Bruce St, BT2. ☎ 1800-2300
Wed-Sat. Pizzas, pasta,
desserts.

Vico's Refettorio
10 Brunswick St, BT2.
☎ 321447. 1200-2400
Mon-Sat. Italian. Pasta, veal,
salads. £.

BELFAST

University and Malone *(BT7 & 9) (STD 0232)*

Angelo's 🍷
23 Donegall Pass, BT7.
☎ 246900. 1700-2300
Tues-Sat. Italian. Garlic mussels, pasta, veal. A la carte. ££.

★ **ANTICA ROMA** 🍷
67 Botanic Avenue, BT7.
☎ 311121. 1830-2300
Mon-Sat. Salad of mussels, squid, clams & garlic, escalope of veal with cheese & ham filling. E££.

★ **ASHOKA** 🍷
363 Lisburn Rd, BT9.
☎ 660362. 1200-1400 & 1730-2330 Mon-Sat, 1730-2230 Sun. Indian & European. E££.

Attic 🍴
54 Stranmillis Rd, BT9.
☎ 661074. 1100-1500 & 1700-2230 Mon-Sat, 1100-1500 & 1630-2100 Sun. Steaks, chicken, fish.

Balmoral Inn 🍷
703 Lisburn Rd, BT9.
☎ 666109. 1200-2200
Mon-Sat. Pub grub.

Bamford's
353 Ormeau Rd, BT7.
☎ 491110. 0830-1730 Mon-Sat. Sandwiches, soup, stew.

★ **BENGAL BRASSERIE** 🍷
339 Ormeau Rd, BT7.
☎ 647516. 1200-1400 Mon-Fri, 1730-2315 Mon-Sat, until 2215 Sun. European, Indian. A la carte. E££.

★ **BISHOPS**
7 Bradbury Place, BT7.
☎ 313547. 1100-2300
Mon-Sun. Kilkeel fish, chips, Ulster fry, salads.

Bleeckers 🍷
42 Malone Rd, BT9.
☎ 663114. 1200-2400
Mon-Sat, 1200-2300 Sun. American. Burgers, pasta. E£.

NEW RESTAURANT AND BAR

Enjoy the delightful surroundings of Dempseys theme bars while sampling the delicious menu - either for lunch or evening meals.

A HOUSE OF PUBS

TASTY LUNCHES 12NOON - 3PM • SNACKS ALL DAY
EXCELLENT EVENING CUISINE FROM 5PM
CATERING FOR EVERYONE'S TASTE

45 Dublin Road • Belfast • Telephone 234000

33/35 Malone Road, Belfast BT9 6RU
Open for lunch and evening meal

FULLY LICENSED

*

The in-place in town to eat out

*

Phone NOW for reservations

*

Live entertainment Friday & Saturday Night

TELEPHONE (0232) 682929

University and Malone — BELFAST

Bluebells
50 Botanic Avenue, BT7.
☎ 322662. 0800-2200
Mon-Sat, 1000-1800 Sun.
Ice cream desserts, quiche,
cappuccino coffee.

Bob Cratchit's
Russell Court, 38 Lisburn Rd,
BT9. ☎ 332526. 1200-1900
Mon-Sat, 1230-1500 Sun.
Lasagne, club sandwich,
burgers.

Bookfinders
47 University Rd, BT7.
☎ 328269. 0930-1730
Mon-Fri, until 2100 Thur.
Soup, toasties, pasta with
courgette chicken sauce.

Botanic Inn
23 Malone Rd, BT9.
☎ 660460. 1200-1500
Mon-Sat. Pizzas, grills, pub
grub.

Café Montmartre
102 Stranmillis Rd, BT9.
☎ 668032. 1100-2300
Mon-Sat. Fish & chips, grills.

Capers
44 Bradbury Place, BT7.
☎ 247643. 1130-1430 &
1700-2330 Mon-Sat. Italian.
Pizzas, pasta, vegetarian
lasagne, curry. £.

Chelsea
346 Lisburn Rd, BT9.
☎ 665136. 1200-1800
Mon-Wed, until 2000
Thur-Sat, 1500 Sun. Pizza,
salads, open sandwiches.

★ **CHEZ DELBART**
10 Bradbury Place, BT7.
☎ 238020. 1700-2400
Mon-Sat, until 2130 Sun.
French-owned bistro. Escalope
of pork with creamy mustard
sauce, mixed kebabs, savoury
& sweet pancakes. £££.

Chicago Pizza Pie Factory
1 Bankmore Square,
Dublin Rd, BT2. ☎ 233555.
1200-2300 Mon-Thur, until
0100 Fri & Sat, 1200-2230
Sun. Pizza, burgers, salads.

Cincinnati Cooler Company
Botanic Avenue, BT7.
☎ 320570. 0800-2230
Mon-Sat, 1130-2130 Sun.
Home-made frozen yoghurts,
American apple pie.

Claire's
35 Botanic Avenue, BT7.
☎ 245321. 0900-1730
Mon-Sat. Quiche, lasagne.

★ **CLARE CONNERY AT
    MALONE HOUSE**

Barnett Demesne, BT9.
☎ 681246. 1000-1630 Mon-
Sat. Coffee, lunch, afternoon
teas. Restored 19th-century
house overlooking Lagan
Valley.

BELFAST
University and Malone

Cloisters
Queen's University,
1 Elmwood Avenue, BT9.
☎ 245133. 0900-2100
Mon-Sat. Refectory in
student's union building.
Advance booking essential.

Conversations ⌂
141 Stranmillis Rd, BT9.
☎ 664212. 0900-1700
Mon-Sat. Prawn salad, chilli,
banoffi, coffee.

Cutter's Wharf ♀
Lockview Rd, Stranmillis, BT9.
☎ 663388. Bar: 1200-1430
Mon-Sun. Irish stew, Ulster fry.
Restaurant: 1200-2230 Mon-
Fri, 1800-2230 Sat. Apple &
cheese flan, monkfish, mussels
& scampi. £££.

Dragon City ♀
82 Botanic Avenue, BT7.
☎ 439590. 1200-2400
Sun-Thur, until 0100 Fri & Sat.
Cantonese. £££.

Dragon Palace ♀
16 Botanic Avenue, BT7.
☎ 323869. 1200-1400 &
1700-2400 Mon-Thur, until
0100 Fri & Sat, 2400 Sun.
Peking & European. £££.

★ **DUKES HOTEL** ♀ ⌂
65 University St, BT7.
☎ 236666. Last orders 2130.
A la carte. £££.

Eglantine Inn ♀
32 Malone Rd, BT9.
☎ 381994. 1200-2000
Mon-Sat. Pub grub, daily
special. £.

Elms ♀
36 University Rd, BT7.
☎ 322106. 1100-1900
Mon-Sat. Champ, stew, ribs,
chilli. Live music.

Empire ♀
42 Botanic Avenue, BT7.
☎ 249276. 1200-2000
Mon-Sat. Pizza, pasta. Bar in
former variety theatre.

Errigle Inn ♀
320 Ormeau Rd, BT7.
☎ 641410. 1130-1500 &
1700-2330 Mon-Fri,
1130-2300 Sat, 1200-2200
Sun. Pub lunch, daily special.
A la carte. Roof garden. Live
music. ££.

Evergreen ♀
95 Botanic Avenue, BT7.
☎ 329303. 1200-1400 &
1700-2400 Mon-Thur,
1200-1400 & 1700-0100 Fri,
until 0100 Sat, 2300 Sun.
Chinese & European. ££.

The Fly ♀
5 Lower Crescent, BT7.
☎ 246878. 1200-1430
Mon-Sat. Soup, pub grub.

Four in Hand ♀
116 Lisburn Rd, BT9.
☎ 665440. 1200-1500
Mon-Fri. Pub grub.

University and Malone — BELFAST

★ FRENCH VILLAGE
70 Stranmillis Rd, BT9.
0915-1715 Mon-Sat.
Ploughman's lunch, gateaux.

★ FRIAR'S BUSH
159 Stranmillis Rd, BT9.
☎ 669824. 1200-1430
Tues-Fri, 1830-2300
Thur-Sat. Terrine of wild
venison, pork in cider, turbot.

Giovanni's
27 University Rd, BT1.
☎ 439300. 1700-2300
Mon-Thur, until 2400 Fri &
Sat, 1630-2100 Sun. Tagliatelli
with tomato, chilli & garlic
sauce, pizzas, steaks. £££.

Good World
627 Lisburn Rd, BT9.
☎ 666821. 1200-1400
Mon-Sat, 1700-2400
Mon-Thur & Sun, until 0100
Fri & Sat. Chinese & European.
£.

Graffiti
258 Ormeau Rd, BT7.
☎ 693300. 1000-2230
Mon-Sat, 1200-1400 Sun.
Breakfast, pasta, steak,
vegetarian.

The Greek Shop
43 University Rd, BT9.
☎ 333135. 1200-1500
Mon-Sat, 1800-2200 Tues-Sat.
Taramosalata, pikilia, sword
fish kebabs, moussaka,
baklava, Greek coffee. £££

Hatfield House
128 Ormeau Rd, BT7.
☎ 238825. 1230-1430
Mon-Sat. Pub grub.

Hong Kong
361 Ormeau Rd, BT7.
☎ 491621. 1200-1400
Mon-Sat, 1700-2400
Mon-Thur & Sun, 1700-0100
Fri. Peking, Cantonese &
European. ££.

Isibeal's
699 Lisburn Rd, BT9.
☎ 682726. 1200-2400 Mon-
Sat. Chicken, chips, sausages.

Jharna Tandoori
133 Lisburn Rd, BT9.
☎ 381299. 1200-1400 &
1730-2330 Mon-Sat, 1700-
2330 Sun. Indian. £££.

Kentucky Fried Chicken
Bradbury Place, BT7.
☎ 325129. 1000-0230 Mon &
Tues, until 0400 Wed-Sat,
0300 Sun. Hamburgers, chips,
chicken, muffins.

King's Head
Lisburn Rd, BT7. ☎ 660455.
1200-1430 Mon-Sat. Chilli,
lasagne, open sandwiches.
Opposite King's Hall. £££.

Lavery's
12 Bradbury Place, BT7.
☎ 327159. 1200-1600
Mon-Fri, until 1400 Sat. Pub
grub.

Bocoose

Licensed Restaurant

Wide variety of steak,
fish & chicken dishes
with vegetarian options
complemented by an extensive
wine list.

85 Dublin Road, Belfast.
Telephone (0232) 238787

THE BRITANNIC

AMELIA STREET, BELFAST
(upstairs in the Crown Liquor Saloon)

The White Star Liners renowned for passenger comfort

Only the very wealthy could avail themselves of the luxury which today's Britannic Lounge recreates using furnishing and superb woodwork stored when the ship was stripped in 1915. Enjoy a meal and a drink in the splendour of the Golden Age of Ship Building.

You won't sail into New York Harbour but then neither did the Britannic

University and Malone — BELFAST

Legends ♀
133 Lisburn Rd, BT9.
☎ 661652. 1730-2400
Mon-Sat, 1700-2300 Sun.
Pizza, pasta, steaks.

McDonald's
24 Bradbury Place, BT7.
☎ 332400. 1000-0200
Sun-Wed, 1000-0300
Thur-Sat. Hamburgers, french fries, milk shakes.

Mad Hatter
2 Eglantine Avenue, BT9.
☎ 681005. 0900-1715 Mon-Sat. Quiche, lasagne, gateaux.

Maharaja ♀
62 Botanic Avenue, BT7.
☎ 234200. 1200-1400
Mon-Sat, 1700-2345
Mon-Sat, until 2300 Sun.
Indian & European. E££.

Malone Lodge Hotel ♀ ⌒
60 Eglantine Avenue, BT9.
☎ 382409. 1200-1400
Mon-Sat. Lunch, coffee.

Maloney's ♀
33 Malone Rd, BT9.
☎ 682929. 1230-1430 &
1730-2300 Mon-Sat,
1730-2200 Sun. Chicken breast stuffed with tiger prawns in a lobster & Cognac sauce, seafood tagliatelli. ££.

Mandarin Palace ♀
157 Upper Lisburn Rd, BT9.
☎ 622142. 1200-1400
Mon-Sat, 1700-2400
Mon-Sun, until 0100 Fri & Sat.
Cantonese & European. E££.

The Manhattan ♀
23 Bradbury Place, BT7.
☎ 233131. 1200-2000
Mon-Sun. Clam chowder, cajun chicken. E££.

★ **MANOR HOUSE** ♀
47 Donegall Pass, BT7.
☎ 238755. 1200-2400
Mon-Sun. Exotic Chinese, Cantonese. E£££.

Mortar Board ⌒
3 Fitzwilliam St, BT9.
☎ 310313. 0900-1700
Mon-Sat, until 2300 Thur.
Salads, quiche, coffee.

New Jade Palace ♀
717 Lisburn Rd, BT9.
☎ 381116. 1200-1400 &
1700-2400 Mon-Sat,
1600-2400 Sun. Chinese, Cantonese & European. Set lunch Mon-Fri. E£££.

O'Hara's
3 Botanic Avenue, BT7.
☎ 326567. 0830-1730
Mon-Sat. Coffee shop in home bakery. Sandwiches, stew, pies.

Pavilion ♀
296 Ormeau Rd, BT9.
☎ 641545. 1200-1430 &
1700-2100 Mon-Sun. Grills, salads, set lunch. E£.

BELFAST

University and Malone

★ PEPPERMILL
112 Lisburn Rd, BT9.
☎ 666537. 0900-1700
Mon-Sat. Coffee, home-made pies, salads.

Queen's Espresso
17 Botanic Avenue, BT7.
☎ 325327. 0900-1730 Mon-Sat. Grills, salads, toasties, coffee.

Queen's University
Great Hall, University Rd, BT7. ☎ 245133. 1015-1130 & 1200-1400 Mon-Fri. Lunch, coffee, afternoon tea.

Rajput Indian Cuisine ♀
461 Lisburn Rd, BT9.
☎ 662168. 1200-1400 & 1700-2400 Mon-Sat, 1700-2300 Sun. Indian. Set meals, à la carte. £££.

Regency Hotel ♀
13 Lower Crescent, BT7.
☎ 323349. Last orders 2400. Set lunch, high tea. £££.

Renshaws Hotel ♀
75 University St. ☎ 333366. Last orders 2230. A la carte. £££.

Ruby Tuesday's ♦
629A Lisburn Rd, BT9.
☎ 661220. 0815-1915 Mon-Fri, until 1715 Sat & Sun. Breakfast, Ulster fry, chicken, pasta, salads.

★ SAINTS & SCHOLARS ♀
3 University St, BT7.
☎ 325137. 1200-2300 Mon-Sat, 1200-1430 & 1730-2130 Sun. Alsace onion flan, wok roasted monkfish, chicken bourride. £££.

Spuds ☺
37 Bradbury Place, BT7.
☎ 331541. 1000-0100 Mon-Sun. Baked potatoes, lasagne, chips with bolognese sauce & cheese, burgers.

★ STRAND ♀
12 Stranmillis Rd, BT9.
☎ 682266. 1200-2330 Mon-Sat, 1200-1500 & 1900-2200 Sun. Irish lamb noisettes, baked aubergine stuffed with minced steak, apple, nuts & raisins. ££.

The Tea House
245 Lisburn Rd, BT9.
☎ 382211. 1000-1615 Mon-Sat. Coffee, speciality teas, lasagne, open sandwiches, muffins. Café below book shop.

Terrace ♀
255 Lisburn Rd, BT9.
☎ 381655. Wine bar bistro: 1900-2130 Mon-Sat. Restaurant: 1200-1500 & 1800-2300 Mon-Sun. Smoked salmon, brill with prawns & dill butter, stuffed duck. £££.

University and Malone **BELFAST**

Three Bears
455 Ormeau Rd, BT7.
☎ 491636. 0900-1630
Mon-Sat. Shepherd's pie, quiche, open sandwiches, banoffi pie. Café above fashion shop. £.

Ulster Museum
11A Stranmillis Rd, BT9.
☎ 381251. 1000-1630
Mon-Fri, 1300-1630 Sat, 1400-1630 Sun. Lasagne, chicken tikka, pies, curries.

Villa Italia
39 University Rd, BT7.
☎ 328356. 1730-2330
Mon-Sat, 1600-2330 Sun. Italian. Pizzas, pasta, steaks. ££.

★ **WELCOME**
22 Stranmillis Rd, BT9.
☎ 381359. 1200-1400 & 1700-2330 Mon-Fri, 1730-2300 Sat & Sun. Cantonese, Hong Kong & European. £££.

Wellington Park Hotel
21 Malone Rd, BT9.
☎ 381111. Last orders 2145. Dressed crab, prawns, steaks. £££.

York Hotel
59 Botanic Avenue, BT7.
☎ 329304. Last orders 2030. A la carte. ££.

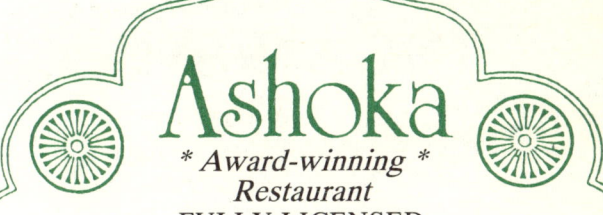

Ashoka
* Award-winning *
Restaurant
FULLY LICENSED

Special High-Tea menu
6 course meal £7.95 served every day from 5.30 - 7.00
Sunday all evening

Business Lunch £3.75 - Maharaja Lunch £6.25

à la carte menus also available • booking recommended
Opening hours: Mon-Fri 12 noon to 2 pm;
Mon-Sat 5.30 - 11.30 pm; Sun 5.30 pm - 10.30 pm

363/365 Lisburn Road, Belfast
Tel: (0232) 660362 - Fax: (0232) 660228

Situated just off Great Victoria Street and 2 minutes walk from the Opera House, this small but smart restaurant has a regular clientele who appreciate excellent cuisine and service. Fully licensed, Arthur's is a perfect place to relax and meet friends or entertain business clients.

Arthur's - Belfast's best kept secret.
Open for lunch: Mon - Fri
Evening Meals: Mon-Sat 6.00pm - 11.00pm

7 Hope Street
Belfast, Tel: 333311

Egon Ronay recommended each year 1986 - 1991
El Bar International Gastronomic Award 1987 & 1988

THE STRAND

Wine Bar and restaurant
FULLY LICENSED
12 Stranmillis Road, Belfast BT9 5AA
Reservations: Telephone 682266 Office: 663189
Opening hours: 12.00 noon - 11.00p.m. (last orders)
Full meals all day

THE ATTIC RESTAURANT

Come along anytime and enjoy the relaxed, homely atmosphere at the Attic

Open 7 days per week
LUNCHES: 11 - 3 p.m.
A la carte: 5 - 10.30 p.m.

54 Stranmillis Road, Belfast
Tel: (0232) 661074
* Private room for parties *

BELFAST

East of the River
(BT4-6, 8, 16 & 23)
(STD 0232)

Avenue One ♗
175 Newtownards Rd, BT4.
☎ 455608. 1200-1430
Mon-Thur, 1200-1430 &
1900-2300 Fri & Sat. Pub
grub.

Avoniel Leisure Centre
Avoniel Rd, BT5. ☎ 451564.
1030-2200 Mon-Fri, 1000-
1600 Sat & Sun. Chilli,
sandwiches, home baking.

Barclay ♗
Milltown Hill, Shaws Bridge,
BT8. ☎ 491203. 1200-1400 &
1730-2200 Mon-Sat,
1145-2030 Sun. A la carte,
carvery. E£.

Beechill Inn ♗
Cedarhurst Rd, BT8.
☎ 693193. 1130-2300
Mon-Sat, until 2130 Thur-Sat,
1230-1430 & 1900-2200 Sun.
A la carte, set meals. E£.

Belmont ♗
295 Upper Newtownards Rd,
BT4. ☎ 652295. 1230-1430
Mon-Sat. Pub grub.

Bethany
246 Newtownards Rd, BT4.
☎ 54498. 1130-2300 Mon-Fri,
until 2000 Sat. Fish & chips.

Castle
152 Castlereagh Rd, BT5.
☎ 731461. 1200-1400 &
1600-2245 Mon-Thur,
1200-2245 Fri & Sat. Grills.

Cedars Coffee House
334 Beersbridge Rd, BT5.
☎ 457201. 0900-1730
Mon-Sat. Quiche, lasagne,
shepherd's pie.

Chatters Coffee House
64 Bloomfield Avenue, BT5.
☎ 731654. 0930-1645
Mon-Sat. Coffee, scones,
lunch.

Coffee Corner
2 Castlereagh Rd, BT5.
☎ 732522. 0930-1600
Mon-Sat, closed Wed.
Coffee, cake, lunch.

Coffee Pot
340 Newtownards Rd, BT4.
☎ 655415. 0830-1600
Mon-Sat, until 1330 Wed,
1630 Sat. Soup, stew, desserts.

BELFAST

East of the River

Desano's
344 Newtownards Rd, BT4.
☎ 451608. 1200-2000 Tues, Thur & Fri-Sun in summer, Fri-Sun only in winter. Ice cream parlour.

Dundonald Ice Bowl
Dundonald, BT16.
☎ 482611. 1000-2215 Mon-Sun. Burgers, chips. Pins restaurant: 1500-2200 Mon-Fri, 1200-2200 Sat, until 1500 Sun. A la carte.

★ **DUNDONALD OLD MILL**

231 Belfast Rd, Dundonald, BT16. ☎ 480117.
1000-1715 Mon-Sat, 1100-1715 Sun. Home baking, quiche, lasagne, pastries. Waterwheel & craft shop.

Eda Inn ♀
41 Belmont Rd, BT4.
☎ 658810. 1700-2330 Mon-Sun. Chinese & European. E££.

Elk Inn ♀
793 Upper Newtownards Rd, Dundonald, BT16.
☎ 480004. 1130-2200 Mon-Sat. Bacon & cheese bites, pork stroganoff, banoffi. E££.

★ **FILLERS COFFEE SHOP** ⊗

233 Saintfield Rd, BT8.
☎ 701409. 1000-1730 Mon-Sat, until 1900 Thur & Fri. Lasagne, salads, apple pie, coffee.

Four Winds Inn ♀
111 Newton Park, BT8.
☎ 401957. 1200-1400 & 1900-2200 Mon-Sat, closed Xmas & Easter. Hot & cold lunch buffet, evening à la carte. Open fires. M£, E£££.

Fusco's
369 Woodstock Rd, BT6.
☎ 458736. 1030-2130 Mon-Sun. Italian. Ice cream.

The Willows Restaurant

Specials daily

Why not come and try them for yourself

273 WOODSTOCK ROAD, BELFAST

TEL: (0232) 458210

Opening hours 8.30 a.m. - 5.00 p.m.
Mon - Sat

East of the River — BELFAST

Gardener's Rest
Hillmount Nursery Centre,
Upper Braniel Rd, BT5.
☎ 448213. 0900-1645
Mon-Sat, 1400-1700 Sun.
Coffee, lunch.

Golden Bloom
47 Comber Rd, BT16.
☎ 798661. 0830-1730
Mon-Sat. Stew, curry, soup,
pies. Café in cake shop.

Holly's
74 Holywood Rd, BT4.
☎ 653345. 0830-1630
Mon-Sat, until 2200 Thur-Sat.
Chicken & ham pie, steaks,
chicken maryland.

Hong Kong ♀
9 King's Square, BT5.
☎ 792560. 1700-2400
Mon-Sun, until 0100 Fri & Sat.
Chinese & European. Set
lunch, dinner Mon-Thur. E£.

Kebab House ♀
991 Upper Newtownards Rd,
BT16. 1200-1400 & 1700-
2300 Mon-Sun. Indian &
European.

La Mon House Hotel ♀
41 Gransha Rd, BT23.
☎ 448631. Last orders 2200
Mon-Sat, 2100 Sun. Buffet
lunch, carvery Sun. A la carte.
M£, E£££.

Leaf & Berry
516 Upper Newtownards Rd,
BT4. ☎ 471774. 0930-1630
Mon-Fri, 1000-1300 Sat.
Speciality coffees, lunch.
Self-service.

★ **Mr J.D.'S**
222 Newtownards Rd, BT4.
☎ 458383. 1130-1900
Mon-Sat. Fish & chips.

Mr Pickwick's Kitchen
Connswater Shopping Centre,
BT5. ☎ 459965. 0900-1730
Mon-Sat, until 2100 Wed-Fri.
Baked potatoes, Irish stew,
doughnuts.

Melting Pot ♀
38 Mountpottinger Rd, BT5.
☎ 454080. 1200-1500
Mon-Sat. Pub grub.

Morton & Simpson ☺
Breda Shopping Centre, BT8.
☎ 491795. 0900-1630 Mon-
Sat. Sandwiches, soup, champ.

Neighbours Coffee Shop
10 Cregagh Rd, BT6.
1030-1630 Mon-Sat. Lasagne,
home-made pies, curries.

Nuts in May
24 Belmont Rd, BT4.
☎ 471109. 0930-1730
Mon-Sat. Coffee, scones,
home-made biscuits in health
food store.

Old Moat Inn ♀
993 Upper Newtownards Rd,
BT4. ☎ 480753. 1200-1500 &
1800-2130 Mon-Sat. Lasagne,
quiche, set lunch. Bistro menu.

Piggly Wiggly's Coffee Shop

**Evening Restaurant
Open for Business**

'Bring Your Own Wine'
BOOKINGS ADVISABLE
(0232) 672114

Tues.-Thurs. 6 pm - Last Orders 10 pm
Fri. & Sat. 6 pm - Last Orders 11 pm

Library Court,
Upper Newtownards Road,
Ballyhackamore, Belfast.

ANTICA ROMA
RESTAURANT

NOW OPEN FOR LUNCH

67/69 Botanic Avenue, Belfast BT7 1JL
Tel: 311121 Fax: 310787

East of the River — BELFAST

Park Avenue Hotel
Holywood Rd, BT4.
☎ 656520. Last orders 2030, Sun 1930. Closed Xmas. Smoked salmon, grilled halibut. A la carte. E££.

Peking House
374 Upper Newtownards Rd, BT4. ☎ 671033. 1200-1400 & 1700-2400 Mon-Sat, 1630-2400 Sun. Cantonese & European. E££.

Piggly Wigglys
Library Court, 3 Eastleigh Drive, Upper Newtownards Rd, BT4. ☎ 672114. 0930-1700 Mon-Sat. Feuilleté of lentils, marinated rabbit, guinea fowl with lemon grass.

Poppins Restaurant
241 Upper Newtownards Rd, BT4. ☎ 671893. 0900-1630 Mon-Sat. Pies, quiche, pizza.

Quarry Inn
Quarry Corner, Upper Newtownards Rd, BT4.
☎ 480492. 1200-1500 Mon-Sun, 1800-2130 Mon-Sat, 1230-1930 Sun. Carvery, bistro. E££.

Queen's Inn
King's Square, King's Rd, BT5.
☎ 792395. 1200-1430 Mon-Sat, 1700-1900 Fri & Sat. Set lunch, pub grub.

Rendezvous
443 Newtownards Rd, BT4.
☎ 451100. 0900-1600 Mon-Sat. Set lunch, home-baked pies, salads.

Ritchie's
142 Castlereagh Rd, BT5.
☎ 457318. 1200-1400 & 1630-1900 Mon-Sat. Fish & chips.

Rose Bowl
59 Belmont Rd, BT4.
☎ 652895. 0930-1630 Mon-Sat. Soup, sandwiches, quiche.

Rosetta
75 Rosetta Rd, BT6.
☎ 649297. 1230-1430 Mon-Sat, 1900-2100 Thur-Sat. Pub grub.

★ **SCOFFS COFFEE HOUSE**

52 Bloomfield Avenue, BT5.
☎ 450183. 0800-1730 Mon-Sat. Honey glazed Ulster ham, champ, variety of home-made scones.

Shanghai
18 Holywood Rd, BT4.
☎ 650400. 1200-1400 Mon-Sat, 1700-2400 Mon-Sun. Chinese & European. Set lunch.

Silver Leaf
15 Belmont Rd, BT4.
☎ 471164. 1200-1400 & 1600-2230 Mon-Thur, 1200-2230 Fri & Sat. Fish & chips, charcoal grills.

BELFAST

East of the River

★ STORMONT HOTEL
587 Upper Newtownards Rd, BT4. ☎ 658621. Last orders 2130. Brasserie: salads, open sandwiches. A la carte. £££££.

Stormont Inn
165 Holywood Rd, BT4. ☎ 654509. 1230-1500 Mon-Sat. Pub grub.

Trafalgar
139 Bloomfield Avenue, BT4. ☎ 451130. 1600-2300 Mon-Sat, until 1830 Wed. Pies, fish & chips.

Wellworths
1009 Upper Newtownards Rd, BT16. ☎ 481118. 0900-1700 Mon-Sat, until 2100 Wed-Fri. Daily specials, hamburgers, sausage & bacon. Restaurant in chain store.

Willows
273 Woodstock Rd, BT6. ☎ 458210. 0900-1645 Mon-Sat. Toasties, salad, chips, coffee.

Zodiac
Connswater Shopping Centre, Bloomfield Avenue, BT5. ☎ 56266. 0900-1730 Mon-Sat, 0900-2100 Wed-Fri. Grills, chicken, desserts.

North and West of the River

(BT10-15 & 17)

Alexandra 🍷
1 York Rd, BT15. ☎ 742838.
1130-2300 Mon-Sat,
1230-1430 & 1900-2200 Sun.
Pub grub.

American Bar 🍷
65 Dock St, BT15.
☎ 747494. 1130-2300
Mon-Sat, 1230-1430 Sun.
Pub grub.

Anchor
150 Sandy Row, BT12.
☎ 231415. 0830-1700
Mon-Sat. Soup, stew,
home-made ice cream.

Andersonstown Leisure Centre
Andersonstown Rd, BT11.
☎ 625211. 1100-2200
Mon-Fri, until 1600 Sat & Sun.
Chilli, sandwiches, home
baking.

Arnie's
Balmoral Fruit Market,
Boucher Rd, BT12. ☎ 663282.
0600-1500 Mon-Sat. Ulster
fry, roast beef, champ.

Balmoral Hotel 🍷
Blacks Rd, BT10. ☎ 301234.
Grill bar: 1130-2300 Mon-Sat.
Steak, chicken, fish.
Restaurant: last orders 2200.
A la carte. E£.

Bay Leaf
Park Centre, Donegall Rd,
BT12. ☎ 235773.
0900-1800 Mon, Tues & Sat,
0900-2100 Wed-Fri. Set
lunch, grills, snacks.

Beattie's Supper Saloon
220 Shankill Rd, BT13.
☎ 240273. 0930-1830
Mon-Sat. Ulster fry, fish &
chips.

Beechmount Leisure Centre
281 Falls Rd, BT11. ☎ 328631.
1200-1500 & 1800-2100
Mon-Fri, 1000-1500 Sat &
Sun. Chips, burgers.

BELFAST
North and West of the River

★ **BELFAST CASTLE** ♆
Antrim Rd, BT15. ☎ 776925.
On slopes of Cave Hill. Ben Madigan restaurant: 1215-1500 Sun. Lunch. Cellar restaurant: 1215-1430 & 1730-2130 Mon-Sat. Carrot & orange soup with croutons, grilled salmon with cajun spices & lime & sour cream dip. E££.

Belfast Zoo
Antrim Rd, BT15.
☎ 776277. Ark Restaurant: 1000-1730 Mon-Sun summer, 1000-1600 winter. Plaice, chicken nuggets, sandwiches. Mountain Tea House: 1030-1700 Mon-Sun Easter-Aug, weekends only Sept, closed winter. Sandwiches, ice cream, gateaux.

Bellybusters
50 Park Shopping Centre, BT12. ☎ 243534.
0900-1730 Mon-Sat. Burgers, fish, chips, chicken.

Big Boppers Inn
118 Antrim Rd, BT15.
☎ 752022. 1200-1430 & 1900-2130 Mon-Sat. Beef stroganoff, roast chicken, fish. E£.

Broadway Bar ♆
196 Falls Rd, BT12. ☎ 247651.
1200-1430 & 1700-2000 Mon-Sat. Scampi, chicken, lasagne.

The Burger Bar
119 Andersonstown Rd, BT11.
☎ 611465. 1200-2400 Mon-Wed & Sun, until 0100 Thur-Sat. Burgers, fish, chicken, sausages.

Chester Park ♆
466 Antrim Rd, BT15.
☎ 770811. 1200-1430 Mon-Fri, 1800-2200 Mon-Sat, 1230-1430 & 1900-2100 Sun. Set lunch, home-made soup, steaks.

Circus Bar ♆
10 Antrim Rd, BT15.
1200-1500 Mon-Sat. Salads, lasagne.

Coffee House
132 Andersonstown Rd, BT11.
☎ 617155. 0830-1730 Mon-Sat. Quiche, lasagne, pies.

Concepts ◯
100 York St, BT15.
☎ 743873. 1000-1800 Mon & Tues, until 2100 Wed-Fri, 0900-1800 Sat. Baked potatoes, quiche.

Cosy Grill
81 Upper Lisburn Rd, Finaghy, BT10. ☎ 613555. 0930-2000 Mon-Sat. Coffee, grills. E£.

Country Fayre
294 Limestone Rd, BT15.
☎ 740919. 0900-1630 Mon-Sat. Ulster fry, grills, coffee.

North and West of the River — BELFAST

Devenish Arms ♕
37 Finaghy Rd North, BT10.
☎ 301479. 1200-1500 &
1700-2200 Mon-Sat, 1230-
1500 & 1700-2100 Sun. Set
lunch, high tea. A la carte E£.

Devine's
297 Antrim Rd, BT15.
☎ 747604. 0900-1800
Mon-Sat. Sandwiches, Irish
stew.

Earl Diner
67 Duncairn Gardens, BT15.
☎ 749613. 1200-1900
Mon-Sat. Fish & chips, grills.

Ed's Bread
6 Shaw's Rd, BT11.
☎ 612077. 0900-1700
Mon-Sat. Irish stew, pasties,
sandwiches.

Fortwilliam Lodge ♕
2 Fortwilliam Park, BT15.
☎ 370537. 1030-1800
Mon-Sat. Quiche, coffee,
home-baked bread, cakes.

Gallery
333 Crumlin Rd, BT14.
☎ 745408. 0900-1500
Mon-Thur, until 1400 Fri.
Toasties, soup, burgers.

Glenowen Inn ♕
108 Glen Rd, BT11.
☎ 613224. 1130-2230
Mon-Sat, 1230-1500 &
1900-2200 Sun. Set meals.
E££.

Golden Bloom
124 Upper Lisburn Rd, BT10.
☎ 798661. 0800-1730
Mon-Sat. Pizzas, quiche, pies.

Goodman's Ice Cream Parlour
129 Andersonstown Rd, BT11.
☎ 603303. 1200-2200 Mon-
Fri, 1000-2200 Sat & Sun.
Fudge cake, ice cream, hot
scones, coffee.

Gourmet Foods
648 Antrim Rd, BT15.
☎ 778263. 0800-1900
Mon-Fri. Moussaka, roast
beef, lamb.

Hawthorne House
Fulton's Fine Furnishings,
Boucher Crescent, BT12.
☎ 382168. 0930-1730
Mon-Sat, until 2100 Thur.
Salmon, chicken & broccoli
bake, home-baked scones.

Jamaica Inn ♕
69 Jamaica St, BT14.
☎ 747112. 1900-2100
Mon-Fri, 1230-1430 Sat &
Sun. Pub grub.

Laurel Glen Road House ♕
Dairy Farm Lane,
Stewartstown Rd, BT11.
☎ 601737. 1200-1430
Mon-Sat. Pub grub, Ulster fry,
soup.

BELFAST
North and West of the River

★ **LONG'S FISH RESTAURANT**
39 Athol St, BT12.
☎ 321848. 1145-1830 Mon-Fri. Traditional fish & chips.

McErlean's
563 Antrim Rd, BT15.
☎ 370759. 0830-1730 Mon-Fri, 0900-1700 Sat. Cornish pasties, curries, Ulster fry.

Mile Cafeteria
351 Shankill Rd, BT13.
☎ 322439. 1000-2200 Mon-Fri, 1000-1800 Sat. Salads, pizzas, Ulster fry.

Moby Dick
Dargan Rd, BT3. ☎ 776208. 0800-1630 Mon-Fri. Sausage, eggs, daily special.

Mount Inn ♀
156 North Queen St, BT15.
☎ 741769. 1230-1430 Mon-Sat. Set lunch.

Muldoon's ♀
13 Corporation Square.
☎ 232415. 1200-1500 Mon-Sat. Burgers, salads, fish, pies.

NG's
Ballysillan Leisure Centre, 71 Ballysillan Rd, BT14.
☎ 391040. 1000-2200 Mon-Fri, until 1600 Sat, 1100-1700 Sun. Pies, stew, sandwiches.

Olympia Leisure Centre
Boucher Rd, BT12.
☎ 233369. 1000-1400 & 1600-2200 Mon-Fri, 1000-1600 Sat. 1200-1800 Sun. Ulster fry, coffee.

Opels Recreation Centre
41 Suffolk Rd, BT11.
☎ 601386. 0900-2100 Mon-Fri. Pizza, soup, desserts.

Orpheus ♀
59 York St, BT15. ☎ 238967. 1200-1430 & 1600-1800 Mon-Sat. Pub grub.

Patio
Kennedy Centre, 564 Falls Rd, BT12. ☎ 628118. 0900-2000 Mon-Fri, 0900-1730 Sat, 1100-1730 Sun. Home-made pies, lasagne, burgers.

Piper
17 York Rd, BT15.
☎ 749545. 0830-2230 Mon-Fri, until 1900 Sat. Bacon rolls, egg soda, spicy pork, fish & chips.

Portside Inn ♀
Dargan Rd, BT3. ☎ 370746. 1200-1700 Mon-Sat. Grills, salads.

Red Barn Barbeque
127 Andersonstown Rd, BT11.
☎ 625558. 1200-0030 Mon-Sun. Fish & chips, pasties.

North and West of the River — BELFAST

Rocktown Bar ♆
120 Great Georges St, BT15.
☎ 242414. 1200-2100
Mon-Fri. Pub grub.

Rosebank Tavern ♆
Rosebank Enterprise Park,
Flax St, BT14. ☎ 753329.
1900-2130 Fri & Sat,
1230-1430 & 1900-2200 Sun.
Soup, Irish stew, toasties,
grills.

Saltshaker Centre
174 Antrim Rd, BT15.
☎ 747114. 1000-1700
Mon-Sat. Grills, burgers, chilli.

Sandwich Choice
Unit 9A, Hillview Trade
Centre, Crumlin Rd, BT14.
☎ 740759. 0900-1630
Mon-Fri. Salads, filled rolls,
bacon sodas.

Shaftesbury Inn ♆
739 Antrim Rd, BT15.
☎ 370015. 1200-1430 &
1800-2130 Mon-Sat,
1900-2030 Sun. Beef
stroganoff, carvery, salads. E£.

Shankill Leisure Centre
Shankill Rd, BT13.
☎ 241434. 1000-2200
Mon-Fri, 1000-1600 Sat &
Sun. Burgers, salads, stew.

Somerton Inn ♆
1 Somerton Rd, BT15.
☎ 778016. 1200-1500
Mon-Sat. Chicken, scampi.

Sports Tavern ♆
91 Falls Rd, BT12.
☎ 331523. 1230-1430
Mon-Sat. Grills.

Strathmore Inn ♆
192 Cavehill Rd, BT15.
☎ 391071. 1200-1500
Mon-Sat, 1900-2200
Mon-Sun. Set lunch, salads,
steaks, grills. A la carte. E£.

Swiss Lodge ♆
77 Ballyutoag Rd, BT14.
☎ 825686. 1230-1430 &
1900-2200 Mon-Sun. A la
carte. E£.

Three Kegs Inn ♆
Boucher Rd, BT12. ☎ 664018.
1130-1430 Mon-Sat. Pizzas,
grills.

Taversa
151 Upper Lisburn Rd,
Finaghy, BT10. ☎ 603322.
1200-1400 & 1700-0100
Mon-Thur, until 0200 Fri,
1700-0200 Sat, until 0100
Sun. Pizzas, burgers, pasta.

Trinity Lodge ♆
2 Monagh Grove, BT11.
1200-1400 Mon-Fri. Pub grub.

Tudor Coffee House
123 Falls Rd, BT12. ☎ 231035.
0800-1700 Mon-Sat.
Home-made vegetable soup,
Ulster fry, gammon, shepherd's
pie, Danish pastries.

BELFAST *North and West of the River*

Tudor Lodge ⚲
778 Shore Rd, BT15.
☎ 777017. 1200-1500
Mon-Sat, 1900-2130 Thur-Sat.
Chicken kiev, scampi, home-made pies.

Whitefort Inn ⚲
67 Andersonstown Rd, BT11.
☎ 613427. 1200-1700
Mon-Wed, 1200-1900
Thur-Sat. Pub grub.

Whiterock Leisure Centre
195 Whiterock Rd, BT12.
☎ 233239. 1000-2100 Mon-Fri, 1000-1700 Sat & Sun.
Soup, sandwiches, pies.

Stage Coach Inn

𝕰njoy the 𝕺lde 𝖂orlde experience in our 𝕱ully 𝕷icensed 𝕽estaurant and 𝕭ars.

Come along and sample the fine cuisine of our à la carte and table d'hote menus.

Private parties and business meetings catered for.

52 Queensway, Derriaghy, Dunmurry.
Tel: (0232) 625141

COUNTY ANTRIM

AHOGHILL
(STD 0266)

Diamond Bar ♗
17 The Diamond.
☎ 871251. 1200-1500
Mon-Sat. Pub grub.

Fair Hill Tavern ♗
29 Church St. ☎ 871223.
1200-1500 Mon-Fri, until 1700
Sat, 1230-1430 Sun. Pub grub.

ALDERGROVE

Food Court ♗
Belfast International Airport.
☎ (084 94) 53630.
0630-2200 Mon-Sun.
Hot & cold buffet, burger
bar, salad bar, snacks,
pastries. Self-service.

Le Grill ♗
Novotel, Belfast International
Airport. ☎ (084 94) 22033.
1800-2400 Mon-Sun. French.
E££.

White Horse Inn ♗
20 Dungonnell Rd.
☎ (084 94) 28341.
1930-2230 Fri & Sat,
1230-1430 Sun. Steaks,
chicken, duck. E£.

ANTRIM
(STD 0849)

Bailiwick Inn ♗
Market Square. ☎ 428807.
1200-1800 Mon-Wed, until
2000 Thur-Sat. Pub grub.

Carriage Room
Shane's Castle. ☎ 462216.
1230-1830 Tues-Thur, Sat &
Sun July-Aug & bank hols.
Sandwiches, burgers.

Deerpark Hotel ♗
71 Dublin Rd. ☎ 462480.
Last orders 2100 Mon-Sat,
2015 Sun. Sunday high tea.
A la carte. E£££.

Furama ♗
68 Church St. ☎ 465585.
1200-1400 & 1700-2330
Mon-Wed, until 0100 Fri &
Sat, 1300-2400 Sun. European
& Cantonese. E££.

Galley
Antrim Arcade, High St.
0900-1730 Mon-Wed & Sat.
Fish, chicken.

Griddle
Castle Shopping Centre.
☎ 461193. 0900-1730
Mon-Wed & Sat, until 2130
Thur & Fri. Grills, pastries.

Co. ANTRIM — Antrim

Hong Kong ♀
69 Church St. ☎ 428513.
1200-1400 & 1700-0030
Mon-Thur, 1200-0130
Fri & Sat, 1300-2400 Sun.
Chinese & European. £££.

Lough Shore Café
Lough Shore, Sixmilewater.
1200-sunset Mon-Sun.
Grills, snacks, coffee.

Mrs Mac's
Castle Shopping Centre.
☎ 468151. 0930-1700
Mon-Wed & Sat, 0900-2030
Thur & Fri. Set lunch, curries,
chicken.

Madden's ♀
51 High St. ☎ 462177.
1130-1600 Mon-Wed,
1130-1800 Thur-Sat.
A la carte. Pub grub.

Market Bar ♀
19 Market St. ☎ 467447.
1230-1430 Mon-Sat. Grills.

Morwood's ☻
47 High St. ☎ 463575. 0900-
1700 Mon-Sat. Sandwiches,
home-baked bread, pastries.

Mullin's
30b Fountain St.
☎ 461478. 1400-2200
Mon-Sun. Ice cream,
sandwiches, coffee.

Old Rogue Bar ♀
19 Market Square. ☎ 466966.
1200-1430 Mon-Sat. Pub grub.

Old School House ♀
106 Ballyrobin Rd,
Muckamore. ☎ (0849)
428209. 1200-1500 & 1800-
2200 Mon-Sun. Set meals.
Consommé, supreme of
chicken, cheesecake. £££.

Pepper Pot
Castle Shopping Centre.
☎ 460955. 0900-1730
Mon-Wed & Sat, 0900-2100
Thur & Fri. Set lunch, lasagne,
quiche, beef stroganoff.

Railway Bar ♀
24 Railway St. ☎ 428261.
1230-1430 Mon-Sat.
Toasties, stew.

Ramble Inn ♀
236 Lisnavenagh Rd.
☎ 428888. 1200-2115 Mon-
Sat, 1230-1430 & 1900-2045
Sun. Sunday lunches, grills.
A la carte. ££.

Riverbank Café
Antrim Forum, Lough Rd.
☎ 464131. 1000-2200 Mon-
Fri, until 1800 Sat, 1400-1800
Sun. Burgers, plaice, chicken
chasseur, gateaux. £.

Shalimar ♀
4 Bridge St. ☎ 468684. 1700-
2400 Mon-Sat, 1700-2230
Sun. Indian. ££.

Shanogue House ♀
51 Sevenmile Straight.
☎ 428510. 1230-1430
Mon-Sat. Lunches, grills.

Skeffington
88 Church St. ☎ 428098.
1230-1500 Mon-Sat. Grills.

Steeple Inn ♀
11 High St. ☎ 428527.
1200-1500 Mon-Sat. Burgers,
fish & chips, daily specials.

Top Of The Town ♀
77 Fountain St. ☎ 428146.
1200-1500 Mon-Sat. Fish,
chicken, salads.

Upper Deck ♀
18 High St. ☎ 460744.
1130-1500 Mon-Sat,
2000-2200 Thur-Sat.
Grills, set lunch.

BALLINTOY

Carrick-a-Rede ♀
21 Main St. ☎ (026 57) 62241.
1200-2100 Mon-Sat,
1230-1430 & 1900-2200 Sun
in summer. Weekends in
winter. Grills, carvery.

Roark's Kitchen
Ballintoy Harbour.
☎ (026 57) 62225.
1100-1900 Mon-Sun
June-Aug, Sat & Sun only
May & Sept. Snacks.

BALLYCASTLE
(STD 026 57)

Antrim Arms Hotel ♀
Castle St. ☎ 62284.
Last orders 2030. Closed 2nd
& 3rd weeks in Oct. A la carte.
E££.

Beach House
Bayview Rd. ☎ 62262.
0900-2200 Mon-Sun
Mar-Oct. Lasagne, pizza,
home-made pies.

Checkers Bistro
43 Castle St. 1130-2400
Mon-Thur, until 0200 Fri &
Sat, 1430-2400 Sun. Burgers.

Donnelly's Coffee Shop
28 Ann St. ☎ 63236.
0900-1800 Mon-Sat,
until 1700 Sun. Soup,
pizza, quiche, pies.

Drumawillan House
1 Whitepark Rd. ☎ 62539.
Evening meals. Booking
essential.

Gawn Inn ♀
Silvercliffs, Clare Rd.
☎ 62550. 1200-1500 Mon-Sat,
1230-1430 Sun. Pub grub.

Hillsea
28 Quay Hill. ☎ 62385.
1700-1930 Mon-Sun
June-Aug. Home cooking.
Booking essential.

Co. ANTRIM — Ballycastle-Ballyclare

Lakeside Tea Room
Watertop Farm. ☎ 62576.
1030-1730 Mon-Sun July
& Aug. Coffee, salads, pastries.

Lammas Café
21 Clare Rd. ☎ 62550.
Easter-Sept 1000-1800 Sat &
Sun, July & Aug 1000-2000
Mon-Sun. Pizza, burgers,
salads.

McCarroll's ♀
7 Ann St. ☎ 62123.
1130-2300 Mon-Sat,
1200-1400 & 1900-2200 Sun.
Lasagne, sandwiches, curries.

Marine Hotel ♀
1 North St. ☎ 62222.
Last orders 2045. A la carte.
££.

Open Door
74 Castle St. ☎ 62251.
0900-1730 Mon-Sat, until
1430 Wed, 0900-1900
Mon-Sat July & Aug. Quiche,
curry, teas.

The Strand ♀
9 North St. ☎ 62349.
1000-2130 Mon-Sun.
Pub grub.

★ **WYSNER'S** ♀
16 Ann St. ☎ 62372.
0800-1730 Mon-Thur, until
2200 Fri & Sat. 0800-2200
Mon-Sat in summer. Steak,
gammon, Ulster fry. A la carte.
££££.

BALLYCLARE
(STD 0960)

The Ballyboe ♀
2 North End. ☎ 352997.
1130-1430 Mon-Sat.
Breakfast. Pub grub.

Chez Nous
3 Rashee Rd. ☎ 323173.
0900-1700 Mon-Sat.
Set lunch, scones.

Chimes
4a The Square. ☎ 352166.
0900-1700 Mon-Sat.
Pizza, salads, curries.

Gathering Inn ♀
42 The Square. ☎ 352636.
1700-2400 Sun-Thur, until
0100 Fri & Sat. Chinese &
European. E££.

Golden Dragon ♀
15 Rashee Rd. ☎ 340013.
1200-1400 & 1700-2400
Tues-Sat, 1730-2330 Sun.
Chinese & European. E£.

The Grange ♀
22 The Square. ☎ 323393.
1200-1430 & 1730-2130
Mon-Sat. Set lunch, rolls,
salads.

Market Bar ♀
The Square. ☎ 322239.
1130-2300 Mon-Sat.
Pub grub.

Ballyclare-Ballymena — Co. ANTRIM

Red Hand Bar
20 The Square. ☎ 323724.
1130-2300 Mon-Sat.
Sandwiches, soup.

Square Bar
16 Main St. ☎ 323789.
1130-2300 Mon-Sat,
1230-1430 & 1900-2200
Sun. Soup, hamburgers, pies.

BALLYGALLEY
(STD 0574)

Ballygally Castle Hotel
274 Coast Rd. ☎ 583212.
Last orders 2130. Set lunch.
A la carte. £££.

Halfway House Hotel
Coast Rd. ☎ 583265
Last orders 2130, 2000 Sun.
Bar lunch, set lunch weekend.
A la carte. £££.

Lough's Restaurant
260 Coast Rd. ☎ 583294.
1100-1900 Tues-Sun winter.
1100-2100 Mon-Sun summer.
Fish, salads. ££.

Lynden Heights
97 Drumnagreagh Rd.
☎ 583560. 1700-2100
Wed-Sat, 1230-2000 Sun.
Baked trout. Salmon, scampi.
££.

Meeting House
120 Brustonbrae Rd.
☎ 583252. 1130-2300
Mon-Sat, 1230-1430 Sun.
Pub grub.

BALLYMENA
(STD 0266)

Adair Arms Hotel
Ballymoney Rd. ☎ 653674.
Last orders 2130, Sun 1945.
Grill bar, set lunch. A la carte.
£££.

Camerons
Broughshane St. ☎ 48821.
0900-1700 Mon-Sat. Soup,
sandwiches, desserts.

Caspers
19 Mill St. ☎ 49303.
0900-1800 Mon-Thur & Sat,
until 2100 Fri. Grills, set
lunch, desserts.

Central Bar
36 Linenhall St. ☎ 49282.
1230-1400 Mon-Sat. Pub
grub.

Confucius
45 Springwell St. ☎ 651638.
1200-1400 Mon-Sat,
1700-2400 Mon-Sun. Chinese
& European. £££.

Countryman Inn
Grove Rd. ☎ 44814.
1230-1430 & 1730-2130
Mon-Sat. A la carte. Wine
bar, buffet.

Crusty Kitchen
Fairhill Shopping Centre,
Thomas St. ☎ 651436. 0900-
1730 Mon-Wed, until 2100
Thur & Fri, until 1800 Sat.
Sandwiches, baked potatoes,
pies.

Tullymore House

2 Carnlough Road, Broughshane, Ballymena
Telephone: (0266) 861233   Fax: (0266) 862238

Situated in 16 acres of gardens in the heart of the Braid Valley below Slemish mountain

Pheasantry Carvery open 7 Days lunch & dinner
Draymans Rest - Enjoy a quiet relaxing drink
Chez Maud Bistro open Wed - Sun 5.00pm - 10.00pm
Slemish Suite - ideal for weddings, dinners, conferences
10 ensuite bedrooms - all facilities
Tel: (0266) 861233

Table D'Hote at Lynden Heights

£10.95 - 4 Course
*Wednesday, Thursday, Friday Evenings
from 7 o' Clock*

Experience the *height* of good taste

Good food, relaxed surroundings, and one of the most spectacular views in the country
Sunday Lunch 12.30 - 3.00p.m.
High Tea:
Wednesday, Thursday, Friday 5.00p.m. - 7.00p.m.
Saturday 5.00p.m. - 6.30p.m. Sunday 4.00p.m. - 8.00p.m.
A la carte
from 7 o'clock Wednesday, Thursday, Friday, Saturday
Weddings, Private Parties Up to 40 catered for
97 Drumnagreagh Road, Ballygalley.
Tel: (0574) 583560

Ballymena · Co. ANTRIM

Daisy May Café
25 William St. ☎ 41543.
1000-1730 Mon, Tues &
Thur-Sat, 1100-1500 Wed.
Fish & chips, sandwiches.

Desperate Dan's
12 Ballymoney St. ☎ 49677.
0900-1700 Mon-Sat.
Sandwiches, snacks.

Dunvale Arms ⚍
Dunclug Shopping Centre.
☎ 45159. 1130-2300
Mon-Sat, 1230-1430 &
1900-2200 Sun. Pub grub.

Fern Room
80 Church St. ☎ 656169.
0900-1700 Mon-Sat. Home-
made soup, salads, vegetarian.
Self-service in department
store.

Food Web
Fairhill Shopping Centre,
Thomas St. ☎ 655838. 0900-
1730 Mon-Wed, until 2100
Thur & Fri, 1800 Sat. Soup,
sandwiches.

Fort Royal ⚍
4 Loughmagarry Rd, Crankill.
☎ 685588. 1200-2200
Mon-Sat, 1230-1430 & 1900-
2200 Sun. A la carte, grills.
E££.

Galgorm Manor ⚍
☎ 881001. 1230-1430 &
1900-2130 Mon-Sat, 1800-
2030 Sun. Dundrum oysters
with smoked halibut, Donegal
salmon with granary mustard,
steamed chocolate pudding.
E£££.

Gateway Café
52 Henry St. ☎ 47794.
0900-1700 Mon, Tues, Thur &
Fri, until 1600 Wed & Sat.
1000-1300 Wed. Pizzas,
sandwiches, desserts.

George Buttery ⚍
56 Mill St. ☎ 656170.
1130-1430 Mon-Sat,
1730-2100 Wed-Sat.
Grills, salads.

Go Sun ⚍
43 Bridge St. ☎ 656774.
1200-1400 Mon-Sat,
1700-2300 Mon-Thur,
until 2330 Sun, 1700-2430
Fri & Sat. Chinese & European.
££.

Greenhills ⚍
166 Glenravel Rd.
☎ (026 673) 743.
1700-2100 Mon-Sat,
1230-1430 Sun. A la carte,
steak, gammon.

Griddle Room
Morton & Simpson, Tower
Centre. ☎ 48106.
0900-1730 Mon-Wed & Sat,
0900-2130 Thur & Fri.
Soup, bacon rolls, open
sandwiches, Ulster fry.

Co. ANTRIM

Ballymena

★ **GROUSE INN**
2 Springwell St. ☎ 45234.
1100-2130 Mon-Thur, until 2200 Fri & Sat. Grill bar. A la carte 1800-2130 Wed-Sat, until 2200 Fri & Sat. £££.

The Inn
36 William St. ☎ 652319.
1200-1530 Mon-Sat. Pub grub.

Jane's Kitchen
4 Pats Brae. ☎ 656481.
0930-1630 Mon-Wed, until 2130 Thur-Sat. Soup, sandwiches, stew.

Jaunty's
9 Larne St. ☎ 45978.
1200-2400 Tues-Sat, 1700-2330 Sun.
Fish & chips, chicken.

Kentucky Fried Chicken
27 Queens St. ☎ 46355.
1100-2400 Sun-Wed, 1300-0200 Thur-Sat. Chicken, barbecued ribs, coleslaw, apple pie.

Knockeden Lodge
15 Crebilly Rd. ☎ 43334.
1130-1500 Mon-Fri, 1800-2000 Thur, 1730-2030 Fri & Sat, 1230-1430 Sun. Pub grub.

Leighinmohr House Hotel
Leighinmohr Avenue.
☎ 652313. Last orders 2130 Mon-Sat, 2100 Sun. M£, £££. Trout in white wine, flambé steaks. A la carte. Oyster bar and grill. ££. Buffet lunch Sun.

Lug o' th' Tub
133 Ballycregagh Rd, Clough.
☎ 685423. 1230-1430 & 1800-2100 Mon-Sat. Pies, hamburgers.

McKendry's Bar
19 Broughshane St. ☎ 47849.
1200-1500 Mon-Sat. Grills, Ulster fry.

Maine Restaurant
113 Church St. ☎ 47981.
0900-1700 Mon-Tues & Thur-Sat. Lunches, snacks, sweets.

★ **MANLEY**
State Cinema Arcade, 70a Ballymoney Rd. ☎ 48967.
1200-1400 & 1730-2400 Mon-Thur, until 0030 Fri & Sat, 1730-2400 Sun.
Cantonese, Peking & European. £££.

Mr Pickwick's Baked Potato
Tower Shopping Centre.
☎ 42801. 0900-1730 Mon-Sat, 0900-2100 Thur & Fri. Baked potatoes with various fillings.

No. 77
77 Church St. ☎ 653699.
0900-1730 Mon-Sat. Set lunch, soup, salads, desserts.

Old Oak
26 Broughshane St.
☎ 49029. 0900-1730 Mon-Sat. Set lunch.

Ballymena — Co. ANTRIM

Pizza Hut
Fairhill Shopping Centre.
☎ 658989. 1200-2400
Mon-Sat, 1200-2300 Sun.
Pizzas, pasta, salad,
vegetarian.

Pizza Parlour
Springwell St. ☎ 49245.
1700-2300 Mon, Tues & Sun,
1200-1400 & 1700-2300 Wed
& Thur, 1200-2400 Fri & Sat.
Pizzas, pasta.

Pound Bar
18 Corkey Rd. ☎ (026 564)
41287. 1300-2300 Mon-Sat,
1230-1430 & 1900-2200 Sun.
Pub grub.

Raglan Bar
20 Queen St. ☎ 652203.
1130-2300 Mon-Sat.
Pub grub.

Red Peaches
88 Lower Mill St. ☎ 651170.
1200-1400 & 1700-2400
Mon-Sat, until 2300 Sun.
Cantonese & European. E££.

Rendezvous
48 Ballymoney St. ☎ 44092.
0900-1730 Mon-Sat.
Grills, toasties, curries.

Skandia
Tower Shopping Centre.
☎ 46781. 0930-1730
Mon-Wed, until 2100
Thur & Fri, 1900 Sat.
A la carte. £.

Solomon Grundy's
64 Wellington St. ☎ 659602.
0900-1730 Mon-Wed,
0900-2230 Thur-Sat.
Pizza, chilli, vegetarian.

Sugar 'n' Spice
7 Church St. ☎ 46010.
0900-1730 Mon-Sat.
Soup, salads, pies.

Terry's Burger Bar
Tower Shopping Centre.
☎ 40940. 1000-1730
Mon-Sat, until 2130 Thur &
Fri. Burgers.

Towers Tavern
Unit 9, Ballee Centre.
☎ 48969. 1200-1500 Mon-Sat.
Pub grub.

Tubz
State Cinema Complex.
☎ 45177. 1000-2230 Sun-Sat.
Quiche, lasagne, ice cream.

Tullyglass House Hotel
178 Galgorm Rd. ☎ 652639.
Last orders 2145, Sun 2045.
A la carte. E££.

Village Restaurant
7 Fenaghy Rd, Galgorm.
☎ 491515. 0900-2200 Mon &
Tues, until 2300 Wed-Sat.
Chicken, fish, Ulster fry.

Vintage Bar
9 Galgorm St. ☎ 651255.
1200-1430 Mon-Sat.
Grills, steaks, salads.

Co. ANTRIM — Ballymena-Ballymoney

★ **WATER MARGIN** ♎
8 Cullybackey Rd. ☎ 48868.
1200-1400 Mon-Sat,
1700-2400 Mon-Thur & Sun,
until 0030 Fri & Sat.
Cantonese & European. E£££.

YMCA Café
44 Church St. ☎ 49335.
0830-1500 Mon-Thur, until
1230 Fri. Stew, lasagne, pizza.

Young Sing ♎
83 Broughshane St. ☎ 45101.
1200-1400 & 1700-2400
Mon-Sat, until 2300 Sun.
Chinese & European. E££.

BALLYMONEY
(STD 026 56)

Angler's Rest ♎
139 Vow Rd. ☎ Kilrea
(026 65) 40280. 1230-1430
Mon-Sun, 1930-2100
Mon-Sat, 1900-2200 Sun.
A la carte. Sunday carvery.
££.

Anne's Hot Bread Shop
Main St. ☎ 62979.
0830-1800 Mon-Sat.
Snacks, soup.

Arches
29 Church St. ☎ 66088.
0900-1730 Mon-Sat.
Lasagne, steak, à la carte. £.

Blinkers
9 Charles St. ☎ 66514.
1130-2300 Mon-Sat.
Set lunch, grills.

★ **BROWN JUG**
23 Main St. ☎ 62351.
0830-1730 Tues-Sat, until
1700 Mon. Salads, quiche,
vegetarian, home baking.

Bush Tavern ♎
15 Market St. ☎ 63167.
1200-1500 Mon-Sat.
Lasagne, scampi.

Century Arms ♎
9 Church St. ☎ 63924.
1230-1800 Mon-Sat.
Pub grub.

Grandma Smyth's
7 High St. ☎ 65990.
0900-1715 Mon-Sat.
Grills, snacks.

Hoi Yun ♎
Charles St. ☎ 63419.
1200-1400 Mon-Sat,
1700-2400 Mon-Fri,
1200-0030 Sat, 1700-2330
Sun. Chinese & European. E£.

Hot Food Bar
53 Main St. ☎ 63475.
0930-1730 Mon-Sat.
Fish & chips, burgers.

Leslie Hill Farm
Leslie Hill. ☎ 63109.
1400-1800 Wed-Sun Easter &
summer. Teas, scones, cakes.

Manor Hotel ♎
69 Main St. ☎ 63208.
Last orders 2030 Mon-Fri,
2230 Sat. A la carte. Set lunch.
E£.

Ballymoney-Bushmills — Co. ANTRIM

Parklight Restaurant ♀
57 Main St. ☎ 67111.
1200-1430 Mon-Sun, 1700-2130 Wed-Sat, until 2000 Sun. Fish, chicken, steaks, salads, à la carte. £££.

Raymond's ♀
2 Market St. ☎ 65834.
0900-1830 Mon-Sat,
1000-1830 Sun.
Set lunch, grills.

Riada Centre Cafeteria
33 Garryduff Rd. ☎ 65792.
1145-1400 & 1715-2045 Mon-Fri winter, 1145-2045 Mon-Fri summer. 1145-1715 Sat all year. Fish, chicken, burgers.

★ TEA HOUSE ⊙
24 Church St. ☎ 67000.
0900-1700 Mon-Sat. Soup, baked potatoes, sandwiches, home baking. £.

BROUGHSHANE
(STD 0266)

Thatch Inn ♀
57 Main St. ☎ 861223.
1200-1430 Mon-Fri.
Steaks, salads, grills.

Tullymore House ♀
2 Carnlough Rd. ☎ 861233.
1200-1500 Mon-Sun. Carvery. 1700-2130 Wed-Sun. Bistro. £££.

BUSHMILLS
(STD 026 57)

★ AUBERGE DE SENEIRL ♀
28 Ballyclough Rd. ☎ 41536.
1930-2200 Mon, Wed, Fri & Sat. Open bank hols. French. £££.

★ BUSHMILLS INN ♀
25 Main St. ☎ 32339.
Last orders 2130. Restaurant: salmon, strips of beef fillet in cream & Bushmills whiskey. ££££. Brasserie: Ballyblue brie & beef tomatoes. Weekends & summer only. £.

Coffee Shop
65 Main St, The Diamond.
☎ 31706. 0900-1730
Mon-Sat, until 1900 in summer. Sandwiches, grills, cakes.

Dunluce Tea Room
Dunluce Rd. ☎ 31145.
1100-1830 Mon-Sun
Easter-Sept. Home baking, tea, coffee.

Olde Mill ♀
45 Main St. ☎ 32067.
1130-2000 Mon-Sat.
Pub grub.

Riverdale Lodge ♀
7 Dunluce Rd. ☎ 32104.
1200-1430 & 1645-2100
Mon-Sun Easter-Sept, variable hours in winter. Causeway crab, steaks, vegetarian.

Co. ANTRIM
Bushmills-Carrickfergus

Sportsman 🍷
150 Main St. ☎ 32334.
1130-2300 Mon-Sat,
1230-1400 & 1900-2200
Sun. Pub grub.

CARNLOUGH
(STD 0574)

Black's Bar 🍷
Harbour Rd. ☎ 885226.
1130-2300 Mon-Wed,
1130-0100 Sun. Sandwiches, hamburgers.

Bridge Inn 🍷
2 Bridge St. ☎ 885669.
1200-2000 Mon-Sun.
Set lunch.

Glencloy Inn 🍷
2 Harbour Rd. ☎ 885226.
1400-1800 Mon-Sat winter,
1200-1900 Mon-Sat summer.
Pub grub.

★ **LONDONDERRY ARMS** 🍷

20 Harbour Rd. ☎ 885255.
1200-1400 Mon-Sat, 1200-1500 Sun. Last orders 2100
Mon-Thur, 2130 Fri & Sat,
2000 Sun. Fresh lobster,
scallops, home-made wheaten
bread. M£, E£££.

Marine Café
9 Marine Rd. ☎ 885509.
1100-2030 Mon-Sun.
Fish & chips.

Waterfall Bar 🍷
1 High St. ☎ 885606.
1230-1730 Mon-Sat summer,
until 1500 winter, 1230-1430
Sun. Pub grub.

CARRICKFERGUS
(STD 0960)

Bamboo
Market Place. ☎ 3364314.
0830-1630 Mon-Sat.
Coffee bar in cake shop.

Brown Cow 🍷
9 Woodburn Rd. ☎ 364815.
1130-2300 Mon-Sat,
1230-1430 & 1900-2200.
Sun. Pies, hamburgers.

Café No 10
10 West St. ☎ 360306.
0900-1600 Mon-Sat.
Snacks, grills.

Castle Fast Food
10 Castle St. ☎ 368859.
1030-2400 Mon-Wed,
1030-0100 Thur, 1030-0200
Fri & Sat, 1400-2330 Sun.
Fish & chips, chicken,
hamburgers.

Central Bar 🍷
15 High St. ☎ 362282.
1130-2300 Mon-Sat.
Pub grub.

Coast Road Hotel 🍷
28 Scotch Quarter. ☎ 351021.
Last orders 2045. Closed
25-26 December. Steak,
scampi, chicken. E£££.

Carrickfergus   **Co. ANTRIM**

Courtyard Coffee House
Scotch Quarter. ☎ 351881.
1000-1630 Mon-Sat.
Pies, lasagne, salads.

Dobbins Inn Hotel ♀
6 High St. ☎ 351905.
Last orders 2115. Closed
25-26 December. Flambé
steak, sweets. Set lunch, bar
meals. A la carte. £££.

Fergus Inn ♀
75 Belfast Rd. ☎ 364556.
1230-1430 & 1730-2200
Mon-Sat, 1230-1430 & 1730-
2030 Sun. Pub grub, à la carte.
£££.

Galley Café
Knight Ride Heritage Plaza,
Antrim St. ☎ 365853. 0900-
1700 Mon-Fri, 1000-1700 Sat,
1200-1700 Sun. Chicken, fish,
Ulster fry.

Gate & Northgate ♀
59 North St. ☎ 364136.
1200-1445 Mon-Sun,
1700-2200 Mon-Sat.
Steaks, chicken. A la carte.
£££.

Leisure Centre
Prince William Way.
☎ 351711. 1030-2200 Mon-
Fri, 1030-1530 Sat. Snacks.

Margaret's
10 West St. ☎ 360306. 0900-
1600 Mon-Sat. Snacks, grills.

Mermaid ♀
2 Governor's Place.
☎ 364257. 1130-2300
Mon-Sat. Soup, hamburgers.

New Four Seas ♀
9 Governor's Place.
☎ 351226. 1200-1400 &
1700-2400 Mon-Thur,
1700-0100 Fri & Sat,
1700-2400 Sun. Chinese &
European. A la carte. ££.

Old Tech Griddle
20 High St. ☎ 351904.
0900-1730 Mon-Sat. Stew,
curries, home-baked bread.
Bakery & restaurant.

Park Coffee Shop
Kilroot Industrial Estate.
☎ 369941. 0930-1630
Mon-Sat. Set lunch.

Pheasant Inn ♀
Woodburn Rd. ☎ 361094.
1130-2300 Mon-Sat,
1230-1430 & 1900-2200
Sun. Grills, chicken, salads,
snacks.

Prospect House ♀
Woodburn Rd. ☎ 365577.
1730-2115 Mon-Sat,
1230-1430 & 1700-2030
Sun. Set lunch, high tea.
A la carte. £££.

The Sandwich Centre
6 North St. ☎ 367369. 1000-
1630 Mon-Sat. Sandwiches,
scones, tray bakes.

Co. ANTRIM — Carrickfergus-Crumlin

Smugglers' Restaurant
Albert Edward Pier, The Harbour. ☎ 366538. 1830-2130 Mon-Thur & Sun, until 2200 Fri & Sat. Skewered prawns, swordfish, steak Hornblower. Bistro Sun-Thur. E££.

Tourist Inn
149 Larne Rd. ☎ 351708. 1130-2300 Mon-Sat, 1230-1430 Sun. Irish stew, filled rolls.

★ **WINDROSE**
Rodgers Quay. ☎ 364192. 1200-1400 Mon-Sat, 1900-2130 Tues-Sat, 1230-1430 Sun. A la carte. E£££.

YMCA
Lancastrian St. ☎ 363223. 1030-1400 Mon-Wed & Fri, 0800-1400 Thur. Soup, stew, hamburgers.

CLOUGHMILLS
(STD 026 563)

Roadside Restaurant
Logan's Fashion Store, 232 Frosses Rd. ☎ 656. 1000-1800 Mon, Tues & Sat, 1000-2100 Wed-Fri. Stuffed chicken, haddock, curries, pastries. Set lunch May-Sept.

CRUMLIN
(STD 0849)

Airport Road Café
11 Tully Rd, Nutts Corner. 0730-1730 Mon-Fri, 0730-1400 Sat. Grills, set meals.

Breadbasket
78 Main St. ☎ 423073. 0900-1730 Mon-Sat. Home baking, toasties, pies, stew.

Bushe
47 Main St. ☎ 452411. 1230-1430 Mon-Sat. Pub grub.

Caldhame Lodge
102 Moira Rd. ☎ 423099. Dinners, home cooking. Booking essential.

Camlin
67 Main St. ☎ 453624. 1230-1430 & 1900-2200 Mon-Sun. A la carte.

Chestnut Inn
126 Lurgan Rd. ☎ 453165. 1130-2300 Mon-Sat, 1230-1430 & 1900-2200 Sun. Pub grub.

Fiddlers Inn
36 Main St. ☎ 452221. 1200-1430 Mon-Sat, 1800-2230 Mon-Thur. Grills, salads.

CULLYBACKEY
(STD 0266)

Village Inn
Main St. ☎ 871251.
1230-1500 Mon-Thur,
1700-2030 Fri & Sat.
Set lunch, grills.

Wylie's
93 Main St. ☎ 880200.
1130-2300 Mon-Thur,
until 0100 Fri. Pub grub.

CUSHENDALL
(STD 026 67)

Central Bar
7 Bridge St. ☎ 71730.
1130-2300 Mon-Sat,
1230-1430 & 1900-2200
Sun. Roast beef, plaice,
chicken, lamb. £.

Gillan's
6 Mill St. ☎ 71404.
0900-1800 Mon-Sat,
1300-1800 Sun in summer.
Salads, sandwiches, hot dogs.

Half Door Restaurant
6 Bridge St. ☎ 71300.
1100-2100 Mon-Sun summer.
More limited hours in winter.
French ££.

Lurig Inn
Bridge St. ☎ 71527.
1130-2300 Mon-Sat,
1230-1430 & 1900-2200
Sun. Chicken, curries, steak.

Thornlea Hotel
6 Coast Rd. ☎ 71223.
Last orders 2115. Set lunch,
high tea, carvery. A la carte.
M£, E££.

CUSHENDUN
(STD 026 674)

Bay Hotel
20 Strandview Park. ☎ 267.
Last orders 2045. Garlic
mushrooms, steak in whiskey
sauce. A la carte. E£.

National Trust Tea Room
☎ 506. 1100-1900 Mon-Sat,
until 2000 Sun summer,
weekends only rest
of year. Soup, quiche, salads,
home baking. Teas in garden
at rear.

Villa
185 Torr Rd. ☎ 252.
1300-1930 Mon-Sun. Booking
essential. Salmon in season,
home baking.

DERVOCK
(STD 026 57)

North Irish Horse
15 Carncullagh Rd. ☎ 41205.
1130-2200 Mon-Sat. Own
smoked trout & eel, dressed
crab & lobster, porterhouse
steaks. A la carte. E££.

Co. ANTRIM — *Dervock-Dunmurry*

Safari Wonderland
☎ 41474. 1030-1830 Mon-Sun Easter & June-Aug, Sat & Sun in May, Sun only Sept. Fish, snacks, salads. In wildlife park.

DOAGH

McConnell's
4 Main St. ☎ (096 03) 52352. 1200-1400 Mon-Sat. Scampi, soups, burgers.

DUNADRY

★ **DUNADRY INN**
2 Islandreagh Drive.
☎ (084 94) 32474.
Last orders 2145, Sun 2045. Closed 24-25 Dec. Smoked eel, veal, partridge, salmon. E£££.

DUNMURRY

Beechlawn Hotel
4 Dunmurry Lane. ☎ (0232) 612974. Last orders 2130 Mon-Sat. Seafood, steaks. A la carte. E££.

Cobblestone Coffee Shop
236 Kingsway. ☎ (0232) 612324. 0900-1700 Mon-Sat. Coffee, quiche, lasagne, apple pie.

Colin Mill Lodge
Good Shepherd Rd, Poleglass.
☎ (0232) 601238.
1800-2300 Mon & Thur-Sat. Chicken, curry, steak.

Derby Bar
Stewartstown Rd. ☎ (0232) 611157. 1200-1500 & 1900-2230 Mon-Sat, 1230-1430 Sun. Pub grub.

Dunmurry Inn
195 Kingsway. ☎ (0232) 611653. 1130-2330 Mon-Sat. Sandwiches, stew, salads.

Farmer's Inn
91 Colinglen Rd. ☎ 600135. 1200-1430 & 1700-1900 Mon-Sun. A la carte.

Jeffer's
174 Kingsway. ☎ (0232) 617938. 0830-1700 Mon-Sat. Coffee shop in home bakery.

Kentucky Fried Chicken
181 Kingsway. 1100-0100 Sun-Thur, 1100-0200 Fri & Sat. Chicken, barbecued ribs, apple pie.

Little Mermaid
Kingsway Shopping Centre.
☎ (0232) 612268. 0930-1730 Mon-Wed, until 2100 Thur & Fri, until 1900 Sat. Omelettes, baked potatoes, chilli.

Dunmurry-Glenariff — Co. ANTRIM

Pizza Bellezza
232 Kingsway. ☎ (0232) 600202. 1600-2400 Sun-Thur, 1100-0100 Fri & Sat, 1300-2400 Sun. Pizzas.

The Pyramids
180 Kingsway. ☎ 624972. 1200-1400 Mon-Sat, 1700-2300 Mon-Thur, until 2400 Fri & Sat. Kebabs, pizza, lasagne.

Sportsman Inn ♀
101 Queensway. ☎ (0846) 663994. 1230-1430 Mon-Sat, 1730-2100 Fri & Sat, 1730-2100 Sun. Steaks, chicken, scampi. ££.

Stagecoach Inn ♀
52 Queensway, Derriaghy. ☎ (0232) 301018. 1200-1430 & 1730-2130 Mon-Sat, 1200-1430 & 1730-2030 Sun. Carvery, set lunch. A la carte. ££.

Swillybrin Inn ♀
Suffolk Rd. ☎ (0232) 614754. 1130-1430 Mon-Sat. Pub grub.

GIANT'S CAUSEWAY

Causeway Hotel ♀
40 Causeway Rd. ☎ (026 57) 31226. Last orders 2130. A la carte, carvery. £££.

★ **HILLCREST COUNTRY HOUSE** ♀
306 Whitepark Rd. ☎ (026 57) 31577. 1930-2130 weekends in winter, 1200-1400 & 1700-1930 Mon-Sun in summer. A la carte, high tea. ££.

★ **NATIONAL TRUST TEA ROOM**
Giant's Causeway Centre. ☎ (026 57) 31582. 1045-1715 Mon-Sun Mar-June & Sept, until 1845 July & Aug. Soup, snacks, home baking.

GLARRYFORD
(STD 0266)

Crankhill Stores Café
133 Crankhill Rd. ☎ 85507. 0800-1930 Mon-Sat. Hot dogs, sandwiches, pastries.

GLENARIFF

Glenariffe Inn
16 Main St. ☎ (026 67) 71339. Breakfast, lunch, high tea.

Glen Tea House
99a Glen Rd. ☎ (026 67) 71402. 1400-1800 Mon-Sun in summer, Sat & Sun only rest of year. Home baking, pastries, biscuits.

Harvey's Bar ♀
4 Main St. ☎ 71383. 1200-1730 Mon-Sat, 1230-1430 Sun. Baked potatoes, salads.

WYSNER'S

LICENSED RESTAURANT
16 ANN STREET BALLYCASTLE 02657 62372

WYSNER'S
A TRADITION OF EXCELLENCE

RECOMMENDED BY -
BRIDGESTONE GOOD FOOD GUIDE
AND THE HEALTHY EATING CIRCLE

NEED WE SAY MORE

The George Buttery

54 MILL STREET,
BALLYMENA
Tel: (0266) 656170

Lunches served daily from
11.30 a.m. - 2.30 p.m.
Monday - Saturday

NOW OPEN

THE GEORGE BISTRO

Serving evening meals
Thursday - Friday
Monday - Saturday
5.00 p.m. - 9.00 p.m.

Cantonese Restaurant

NO.1 FOR CANTONESE CUISINE
Why not treat yourself to a delicious meal
in our luxury restaurant
Our proprietor Mr Chan selects our food
daily to ensure maximum freshness

DISHES MADE TO ORDER
Sit-in or take-away service available
ENJOY SUNDAY LUNCH
THREE-COURSE MEAL £4.00
FROM 1 p.m. - 3 p.m.

Opening hours: Mon. - Thurs. 12 noon - 2 p.m.
and 5 p.m. - 12 midnight
Friday & Saturday 12 noon - 2 p.m.
& 5 p.m. - 1 a.m., Sunday 1 p.m. - midnight

68-70 CHURCH STREET,
ANTRIM
Tel: (0849) 465585

 **MADDENS BAR** and restaurant

Meals served daily
11.30 a.m. - 3.30 p.m.

Entertainment & late bars
Wednesday - Comedy Store

Thursday - Disco

Friday - Live Band

Saturday - Disco

51 High Street,
Antrim, Co. Antrim

Glenariff-Glengormley — **Co. ANTRIM**

Manor Lodge ♀
Glenariff Glen.
☎ (026 673) 221. 1100-2330
Mon-Sat, 1200-2130 Sun.
Grills, high tea.

Mariners Bar ♀
7 Main St. ☎ (026 67) 71330.
1200-1500 Mon-Sun. Salads,
burgers.

Waterfall Restaurant
Glenariff Forest Park.
☎ (026 67) 58769. 1100-2000
Mon-Sun Mar-Oct. Set meals,
quiche, salads, high tea.

GLENARM
(STD 0574)

Coast Road Inn ♀
3 Toberwine St. ☎ 841207.
1200-1500 Fri-Mon winter,
1200-1500 Mon-Sat, 1230-
1430 Sun summer. Pub grub.

Drumnagreagh Hotel ♀
Coast Rd. ☎ 841651.
Last orders 2230. A la carte.
E££.

Heather Dew Tavern ♀
1 New Row. ☎ 841221.
1200-1500 & 1700-2000
Mon-Sat, 2100-2300 Fri
& Sat, 1230-1430 & 1900-
2100 Sun. Grills, salads.

Rock-View
32 Drumcrow Rd. ☎ 841225.
1700-2130 Mon-Sun. High
tea.

GLENGORMLEY
(STD 0232)

Beck's
329 Antrim Rd. ☎ 833854.
0900-1700 Mon-Sat. Coffee,
snacks.

Bellevue Arms ♀
129 Antrim Rd. ☎ (0232)
773041. 1230-2200 Mon-Sat,
1230-1430 & 1900-2200
Sun. Pub grub. Set meals.
A la carte. E££.

Cavalier
8 Portland Avenue. ☎ 836759.
1000-2300 Mon-Thur, until
0100 Fri & Sat. Grills, fish &
chips, coffee.

Chimney Corner Hotel ♀
630 Antrim Rd. ☎ 844925.
Last orders 2130. A la carte.
E££.

Coffee Corner
14 Farmley Shopping Centre.
☎ 833031. 0900-1630
Mon-Sat, closed Wed. Coffee,
cakes, snacks.

Huckleberry's ♀
Unit 8, Farmley Shopping
Centre. ☎ 838282. 1200-1430
& 1700-2200 Mon-Fri, 1200-
2300 Sat, 1400-2130 Sun.
Modern American. ££.

Co. ANTRIM
Glengormley-Larne

Jasmin House ♀
17a Ballyclare Rd. ☎ 841705.
1200-1400 & 1700-2400
Mon-Thur, until 0100 Fri &
Sat, 1300-2400 Sun. Chinese
& English.

Kentucky Fried Chicken
376 Antrim Rd. ☎ 843040.
1100-0100 Sun-Wed, until
0200 Thur, 0230 Fri & Sat.
Chicken, barbecued ribs,
coleslaw, apple pie.

Peking Inn ♀
377 Antrim Rd. ☎ 848189.
1200-1400 & 1700-2400
Mon-Thur, until 0100
Fri & Sat, 1230-2400 Sun.
Peking & Cantonese. £££.

Swiss Chalet ♀
81 Ballyclare Rd. ☎ 848630.
1230-1430 Mon-Sat.
A la carte. £.

Village Inn ♀
350 Antrim Rd. ☎ 836077.
1215-1445 Mon-Sat.
A la carte.

GREENISLAND

Knockagh Lodge ♀
236 Upper Greenisland Rd.
☎ (0232) 861444.
1130-2300 Mon-Sat, 1230-
1430 & 1900-2200 Sun. Pub
grub, set lunch, grills, Sunday
high tea. £££.

KELLS
(STD 0266)

Country House Hotel ♀
20 Doagh Rd. ☎ 891663.
Last orders 2115. Buffet lunch,
Sunday high tea, à la carte.
Lobster, zabaglione. ££££.
(From Ballymena A36 (Larne
road) 2m, B59 to Doagh,
3.5m).

LARNE
(STD 0574)

Ann's Pantry
64 Main St. ☎ 260474.
0900-1730 Mon-Sat. Quiche,
baked potatoes.

Apsley's Scullery
11 Main St. ☎ 260510.
0930-2100 Mon-Sun. Stew,
sandwiches, pastries.

Ardella
3 Upper Cross St. ☎ 270908.
0930-1730 Mon-Thur & Sat,
0900-1900 Fri. Chicken, fish,
grills, desserts.

The Bailie
111 Main St. ☎ 273947.
1200-1500 & 1700-2100
Mon-Sat, 1230-1430 &
1900-2100 Sun. Evening à la
carte. ££.

Bric-a-brac
4 Riverdale. ☎ 275657.
0930-1700 Mon-Sat, until
1400 Tues. Home-made broth,
coffee. In antique shop.

Larne — **Co. ANTRIM**

Butter Churn
61 Main St. ☎ 260575.
0900-1630 Mon-Sat, until 1400 Tues. Quiche, baked potatoes.

The Cabin
6 Upper Main St. ☎ 270070.
0900-1730 Mon-Sat. Quiche, pies, lasagne, pavlova.

Captain's Kitchen
Harbour Terminal. ☎ 270284.
0600-2230 Mon-Sun. Burgers, pies, fish, salads.

Carnfunnock Country Park
☎ 270541. 1200-1800 Mon-Sun in summer, 1400-1700 weekends Easter-June. Coffee, biscuits.

Carriages ♀
105 Main St. ☎ 275132.
1700-2300 Mon-Sat, 1700-2200 Sun. Grills, pizza. E£.

Central Bakery & Cottage Restaurant
21 Lower Cross St. ☎ 260293.
0900-1730 Mon-Sat. Grills, snacks.

Chekkers Wine Bar ♀
33 Lower Cross St. ☎ 275305.
1200-1430 Mon-Sun, 1730-2130 Mon-Sat, 1200-1430 & 1900-2130 Sun. Steaks, lasagne.

Connor's Kitchen
38 Main St. ☎ 274701.
0930-1730 Mon-Wed & Sat, until 2100 Thur & Fri. Set lunch, baked potatoes.

Country Kitchen
Murrayfield Shopping Centre.
☎ 278306. 0900-1730 Mon & Wed-Sat, 0900-1400 Tues. Soups, stews, burgers.

Country Kitchen
968 Main St. ☎ 275811. 0815-1730 Mon-Sat. Stew, home-made broth, sandwiches.

Curran Court Hotel ♀
84 Curran Rd. ☎ 275505.
Last orders 2115, Sun 2015. Set lunch, Sunday high tea. A la carte. E££.

Dan Campbell's ♀
2 Bridge St. ☎ 277222. 1700-1900 Mon-Sat, 1230-1400 Sun. High tea. A la carte. £££.

Die Windmolen
68 Main St. ☎ 275370.
0900-1800 Mon-Thur & Sat, until 2000 Fri. Chicken Kiev, lasagne, stew.

Eagle Bar ♀
1 Station Rd. ☎ 273817.
1130-2300 Mon-Sat. Pub grub.

Food For Thought
83 Main St. ☎ 279666.
0900-1730 Mon-Sat. Lasagne, sandwiches, coffee.

Co. ANTRIM — Larne-Lisburn

Harbour Diner
25 Olderfleet Rd. ☎ 272386.
0700-2300 Mon-Sun. Stews,
grills.

Highways Hotel ⚜
Ballyloran. ☎ 272272.
Last orders 2110, Sun 2000.
Roast ham, mixed grill.
A la carte. £££.

Kiln ⚜
Old Glenarm Rd. ☎ 260924.
1200-1430 & 1700-2200
Mon-Sat, 1230-1430 &
1900-2130 Sun. Home-made
chicken & ham pie, steak &
kidney pie, rainbow trout.
A la carte. £££.

Kilwaughter House Hotel ⚜
61 Shanes Hill Rd. ☎ 272591.
Last orders 2130, Sun 2030.
Grills, scampi, steaks. ££.

Loafers ◠
8 Penny Lane, Point St.
☎ 273322. 0900-1700
Mon-Sat. Sandwiches, salads,
lasagne, pastries.

Lotus Flower
117 Main St. ☎ 272102.
1200-1400 Mon-Sat,
1700-0030 Mon-Thur,
1600-0200 Sat, 1700-2400
Sun. Chinese & European.

Magheramorne House Hotel ⚜
59 Shore Rd. ☎ 279444. Last
orders 2130. A la carte. £££.

Rafters ⚜
13 Point St. ☎ 274368.
1130-1430 Mon-Fri. Pub grub.
Home-made soup, Irish stew.

Silver Lounge
124 Main St. ☎ 260040.
0930-1800 Mon-Sat, until
1430 Tues in winter. Fish &
chips. Set lunch.

LISBURN
(STD 0846)

Admiral Benbow ⚜
15 Market Square.
☎ 671788. 1130-2300
Mon-Sat. Lasagne, stews,
grills.

Aldo Raffo
25 Market St. ☎ 662960.
1000-1800 Mon-Sat. Baked
potatoes, salads, fish.

Al Pacino's
4 Smithfield Square.
☎ 661177. 1000-2400 Mon,
Wed & Thur, until 0100 Fri,
0900-2400 Tues, 0930-0200
Sat, 1430-2330 Sun. Ulster fry,
kebabs, fish.

Andrews
23a Market Square.
☎ 673189. 0900-1830
Mon-Sat. Ulster fry, silverside
of beef, coffee.

Lisburn — **Co. ANTRIM**

Bow Street Brasserie ☺
Bow Street Mall. ☎ 661650.
0900-1700 Mon & Tues, until
2100 Wed-Fri, 1730 Sat.
Devon teas, grills, salads,
pastries.

Burger King
1 Bow St. ☎ 660663.
1000-1900 Mon-Wed, until
2200 Thur-Sun. Burgers, chips,
coffee.

Chico's
158 Longstone St. ☎ 662182.
0900-2130 Mon-Sat, 1200-
2130 Sun. Ice cream, baked
potatoes, burgers.

Cooke Pot
134 Longstone St.
☎ 671204. 0900-1630
Mon-Sat. Irish stew, broth,
chicken pie, shepherd's pie.
Set lunch Tues & Fri.

Down Royal ♀
62 Ballinderry Rd. ☎ 602870.
1200-2130 Mon-Sat. Buffet
lunch, à la carte 1900-2130
Wed-Sat. Chilli, open
sandwiches, baked potatoes.
E££.

Eats
25 Market Square.
☎ 662960. 1000-1800
Mon-Sat. Hamburgers, fries.

Fonzie's
158 Longstone St. ☎ 662182.
0900-2130 Mon-Sun. Home-
made ice cream, coffees,
salads, baked potatoes.

Gaffe Cutter ♀
25 Market Place. ☎ 666950.
1200-1430 Mon-Fri, 1500-
2000 Thur, 1700-2100 Fri,
1200-2100 Sat. Burgers, open
sandwiches. A la carte Sat. E£.

Golden Garden ♀
140 Longstone St.
☎ 671311. 1200-1400 &
1700-2400 Mon-Thur, until
0100 Fri & Sat, 1700-2400
Sun. Chinese & European. E£.

Golden Pheasant ♀
Aughnaleck, Baillies Mills.
☎ 638056. 1200-2200
Mon-Sat, 1230-1430 &
1900-2200 Sun. Lunch, high
tea. A la carte. E£.

Green Hall ♀
4 Airport Rd. ☎ 651617.
1230-1430 & 1730-2130
Mon-Sat, until 2015 Sun.
A la carte, high tea, set lunch.
18th-century manor house.
E££.

Grooms ♀
Down Royal Park,
6 Dunygarton Rd, Maze.
☎ 621668. 1230-1430 &
1800-2200 Tues-Sat. Steaks,
chicken, salads. A la carte.
E££.

Co. ANTRIM — Lisburn

Hagues Bar 🍷 ⊙
32 Chapel Hill. ☎ 663224.
1230-1430 Mon-Sat. Chicken, plaice, home-made bread, teas.

Hedley's ⊙
43 Bow St. ☎ 681337.
0900-1700 Mon-Sat. Home baking, savoury pies, curries.

Holmstead Inn 🍷
314 Hillhall Rd. ☎ (0232) 826763. 1200-1500 Mon-Thur, until 1900 Fri & Sat, 1230-1430 Sun. Steak, chicken, fish. £.

Horseshoe Inn 🍷
24 Crumlin Rd, Upper Ballinderry. ☎ 651087.
1130-2300 Mon-Sat, 1230-1430 & 1900-2200 Sun. Soup, hamburgers, grills, steak, basket meals. E£.

Inglenook ⊙
17 Market St. ☎ 665401.
0930-1700 Mon-Wed, until 2145 Thur-Sat. Lemon chicken, casseroles, chocolate cake. E££.

Jeffers ⊙
20 Market Square.
☎ 663210. 0845-1700 Mon-Sat. Salads, sandwiches, desserts.

La Piazza
13a Market Square.
☎ 673158. 1100-1430 & 1730-2200 Mon-Sat. Chicken, prawns, seafood, steak. E££.

Laurel House 🍷
99 Carryduff Rd. ☎ 638422.
1730-2130 Mon-Sat,
1230-1430 & 1730-2130 Sun.
Set menu. A la carte. ££.

Lisnoe Nursery
Duneight. ☎ 663565.
1400-1800 Sat & Sun in summer except July.
Scones, coffee, cakes.

Lotus House 🍷
58 Bow St. ☎ 678669.
1200-1415 Mon-Sat,
1700-2400 Mon-Thur & Sun,
1700-0100 Fri & Sat. Chinese & European. E££.

Manor Inn 🍷
29 Longstone St. ☎ 662386.
1200-1445 Mon-Sat. Scampi, roasts.

Maze Station 🍷
228 Moira Rd, Maze.
☎ 621538. 1130-2300 Mon-Sat, 1230-1430 & 1900-2200 Sun. Scampi, chicken, salads.

Montgomery's
28 Castle St. ☎ 662656.
1000-1600 Mon-Fri, until 1800 Sat. Fish & chips, hot dogs, ice cream.

Lisburn   **Co. ANTRIM**

Morton & Simpson
Bow Street Mall. ☎ 661330. 0900-1730 Mon, Tues & Sat, until 2100 Wed-Fri. Ulster fry, stew, lasagne.

Old Castle
50 Bridge St. ☎ 672181. 1200-1500 & 1900-2100 Mon-Sun. Set lunch. Salads, quiche.

Peking Palace
58 Chapel Hill. ☎ 670445. 1200-1400 & 1700-2400 Mon-Thur, until 0030 Fri & Sat, 1700-2400 Sun. Chinese & European. E£.

Penny Farthing
5 Antrim St. ☎ 663392. 0900-1700 Mon-Sat. Home baking.

Pizzarelly's
10 Bachelor's Walk.
☎ 671980. 1000-2200 Mon-Sat. Pizzas, soup, pasta, grills.

Racecourse Inn
60 Gravel Hill Rd. ☎ (0846) 621685. 1230-1430 & 1730-2130 Mon-Sat. High tea, à la carte, Sunday carvery.

Restbite
Lisburn Leisure Centre.
☎ 679564. 1030-2130 Mon-Fri, until 1700 Sat. Fish & chips, salads.

Roadside Café & Restaurant
1 Glenavy Rd. ☎ 651379. 0900-1700 Mon-Sat. Toasties, burgers, pastries.

Robin's Nest
41 Railway St. ☎ 678065. 1130-2300 Mon-Sat. Pub grub, pies, scampi.

Rumbles
42 Longstone St. ☎ 676292. 1100-0100 Mon-Sun. Burgers, fish, chicken.

Sprucefield Shopping Centre
Mount Charles Catering.
☎ 661244. 1000-2000 Mon & Tues, 0930-2100 Wed-Fri, until 1900 Sat. Lasagne, beef stroganoff, chicken à la king.

Super Fry
19 Antrim St. ☎ 675857. 1100-1800 Mon-Sat, closed Wed. Fish & chips, grills.

Tidy Doffer
133 Ravarnet Rd. ☎ 689188. 1200-2200 Mon-Sat, 1230-1430 & 1700-2100 Sun. Garlic prawns, ribs, steaks, fish. E£. Themed linen restaurant and bar, spinning equipment, photographs.

Toffs
6 Railway St. ☎ 671369. 0930-1630 Mon-Sat. Curry, lasagne, quiche.

BELLEVUE ARMS

129 Antrim Road, Newtownabbey
Tel: (0232) 777138 Restaurant - (0232) 773041 Bar

Restaurant & Grill Bar
Open all day Mon-Sat 12 noon-10.00 p.m.
Menu ranging from bar snacks to a la carte.
Sunday opening hours -
12.30 p.m. - 2.30 p.m. 7.00p.m. - 9.00 p.m.

Try our traditional Sunday lunch

*Choice of several main courses
Evening meals:- Choice of a la carte menu
pleasant staff and comfortable surroundings*

North Irish Horse Inn
Dervock

Nestling in the Bush
Valley in the Blue
Antrim Hills

Restaurant
Open 12.00 noon - 9.30 pm
Mon - Sun
A la Carte menu all day

Function Suite
Private functions
with late extensions

Croopers Lounge
Available for small
private parties

Public Bar
Bar meals, pool and various
other games

*Tel: Dervock
(026 57) 41205/41209*

Knockagh Lodge

(formerly The Coaches)

The newly refurbished
restaurant, bar
and conservatory
commands outstanding
views over Belfast Lough

Morning coffee, lunches,
bar snacks and
evening meals.
Weddings and functions
catered for.

**236 Upper Road,
Greenisland, Co. Antrim.**

Tel: (0232) 861444/852930

Lisburn-Newtownabbey — Co. ANTRIM

Tormore
Temple Shopping Centre,
Carryduff Rd. ☎ 638633.
1000-1800 Mon-Wed,
0930-1900 Thur-Sat. Ulster
fry, steak pie, pastries, coffee.

★ THE WALLACE ♷
12 Bachelor's Walk.
☎ 665000. 1200-1500
Tues-Fri & Sun, 1800-2230
Tues-Sat. A la carte. Duck,
turbot, fish, steaks.

MALLUSK

Good Evening Roughfort ♷
230 Mallusk Rd. ☎ (084 94)
32963. 1700-2300 Mon-Thur,
1130-2300 Fri & Sat, 1900-
2200 Sun. Grills, snacks.

NEWTOWNABBEY

Bumper's
1 Abbey Centre,
Longwood Rd. 0900-1730
Mon, Tues & Sat, 0900-2100
Wed-Fri. Fish & chips, apple
pie, doughnuts.

Cloughfern Arms ♷
214 Doagh Rd. ☎ (0232)
862387. 1200-1430 Mon-Sat.
Pub grub.

Corr's Corner ♷
Ballyhenry. ☎ (0232) 849221.
1130-2230 Mon-Sat. Set
lunch. A la carte, carvery. £££.

Cottonmount Arms ♷
128 Mallusk Rd. ☎ (0232)
832006. 1130-1430 &
1700-1900 Mon-Sat,
1230-1430 & 1900-2200
Sun. Toasties, grills.

Fern Lodge ♷
76 Doagh Rd.
☎ (0232) 867394.
1200-1430 Mon-Sat,
2130-2330 Fri & Sat.
Ploughman's lunch, scampi.

The Gallery ♷
28 Mallusk Rd. ☎ 838457.
1130-2200 Mon-Sat, 1230-
1430 Sun. A la carte.

★ GINGER TREE ♷
29 Ballyrobert Rd.
☎ (0232) 848176.
1200-1430 Mon-Fri,
1900-2200 Mon-Sat.
Japanese. £££age.

Glenavna House Hotel ♷
588 Shore Rd. ☎ (0232)
864461. Last orders 2200,
Sun 1930. Masquerades:
kebabs, stir fry ravioli,
carpetbagger steak. ££.

Ivy Inn ♷
Jordanstown Rd. ☎ (0232)
862429. 1200-1500 Fri & Sat,
1900-2200 Thur-Sat,
1230-1430 Sun. Grills, salads.

Co. ANTRIM — Newtownabbey-Portballintrae

Lady Love
158 Antrim Rd. ☎ (0232) 771383. 1200-1400 Mon-Fri, 1700-0030 Mon-Thur, until 0130 Fri, 1600-0130 Sat, 1300-2400 Sun. Chinese & European. E££.

Maggie's Kitchen
14 Abbotts Cross. ☎ (0232) 863045. 0900-1730 Mon-Sat. Breakfast, coffee.

Mulvenna's
607 Shore Rd, Jordanstown. 1200-1430 Mon-Sat. Pub grub.

Skandia
Abbey Centre. ☎ (0232) 365960. 0900-1730 Mon & Tues, 0900-2130 Wed-Fri, 0900-1800 Sat. Salads, desserts. A la carte.

★ **SLEEPY HOLLOW**
15 Kiln Rd. ☎ (0232) 342042. 1900-2130 Wed-Sat. Set menu. Pigeon breasts in red wine, lamb with raisin & rum sauce. Art gallery. E£££.

Texas Pantry
Texas Homecare, Longwood Rd. ☎ (0232) 868886. 0900-1730 Mon-Sat, until 2100 Wed-Fri. Restaurant in DIY store.

Valley Leisure Centre
Church Rd. ☎ (0232) 861211. 1100-2200 Mon-Sat, until 1730 Sun. Grills, sandwiches.

Whittley's
401 Ballyclare Rd. ☎ (0232) 832438. 1200-1400 & 1700-2130 Mon-Fri, 1200-2130 Sat, 1900-2130 Sun. Steaks, vegetarian dishes, garlic prawns. E£££.

PORTBALLINTRAE

Bayview Hotel
Seafront. ☎ (026 57) 31453. Last orders 2200. Set meals. A la carte. E££.

Beach House Hotel
Seafront. ☎ (026 57) 31214. Last orders 2100. Set meals. A la carte. ££.

Sallie's Craft 'n' Coffee Shop
47 Beach Rd. ☎ (026 57) 31328. 1100-1800 Fri-Sun Easter-end June; 1100-1800 Tues-Sun July & Aug. Pizzas, baked potatoes, pastries.

★ **SWEENEY'S WINE BAR**
6b Seaport Avenue.
☎ (026 57) 31279.
1230-1430 & 1730-2030 Mon-Sat, 1900-2030 Sun. Char grill steaks, ribs, vegetarian dishes.

PORTGLENONE
(STD 0266)

Bann Restaurant
30 Main St. ☎ 821267.
0900-1800 Mon-Wed,
until 2000 Thur-Sat. Burgers,
pizza.

Coffee Garden
36 Main St. ☎ 822362.
0900-1730 Mon-Sat. Burgers,
pizza.

Golden Hill ♀
11 Clady Rd. ☎ 822168.
1700-2400 Mon-Sun. Chinese
& European. E£.

Hawthorne Inn ♀
54 Kilrea Rd. ☎ 821523.
1930-2145 Thur-Sat. Pub
grub.

Pat's Bar ♀
71 Main St. ☎ 821231.
1130-2300 Mon-Sat, 1230-
1430 & 1900-2200 Sun. Steak,
chicken, trout.

Teague's Bar ♀
Clady. ☎ 821288. 1800-2200
Thur-Sun. Grills.

Wild Duck ♀
93 Main St. ☎ 821232.
1200-1400 & 1700-2145
Tues-Sat, 1200-1400 &
1700-2130 Sun. Set lunch,
à la carte, pub grub. E£.

PORTRUSH
(STD 0265)

Alpha Bar ♀
63 Eglinton St. ☎ 823889.
1130-2300 Mon-Sat,
1230-1430 & 1900-2200
Sun. Pub grub.

Bethel
7 Lansdowne Crescent.
☎ 822354. Lunch, dinner.
Booking essential.

Black Swan House
61 Coleraine Rd. ☎ 822205.
0830-2030 Mon-Sat. Ulster
fry, grills, salads.

Café-de-Lux
4 Main St. 1100-1900
Mon-Sun June-Sept. Fish &
chips, ice cream, cakes.

Carousel
6 Main St. ☎ 824411.
0900-2200 Mon-Sun in
summer, until 2100 winter.
Set lunches, chicken, grills.

Causeway Coast Hotel ♀
36 Ballyreagh Rd. ☎ 822435.
Last orders 2200. A la
carte. ££.

China House ♀
55 Eglinton St. ☎ 822889.
1700-2330 Mon-Sun.
Cantonese & European, set
lunch. E£.

Co. ANTRIM

Portrush

Coffee Pot
Dunluce St. ☎ 823554.
0930-2300 Mon-Sun summer,
until 1700 winter. Savoury
pies, Irish stew.

Dionysus ⌘
53 Eglinton St. ☎ 823855.
1700-2230 Mon-Sat,
until 2130 Sun. Greek &
English. Souvlaki, mezze. £££.

Eglinton Hotel ⌘
49 Eglinton St. ☎ 822371.
Last orders 2130. Fresh
haddock, Ulster fry, black
pudding. A la carte. ££.

Graham's
48 Main St. ☎ 822427.
0930-2300 Mon-Sun summer.
1100-1730 Mon & Tues,
1300-1800 Thur-Sat winter.
A la carte in Tudor Room.

Harbour Inn ⌘
5 Harbour Rd. ☎ 825047.
1200-2200 Mon-Sun
April-Dec, 1230-1500 &
1700-2100 Jan-April. Fresh
seafood. ££.

Kentucky Fried Chicken
54 Main St. ☎ 824689.
1100-0230 Mon-Sun
July & Aug, until 2400
Mon-Wed, 0200 Thur-Sun rest
of year. Chicken, barbecued
ribs, coleslaw, apple pie.

Langholm Hotel ⌘
15 Eglinton St. ☎ 822293.
Last orders 2130. A la carte. £.

★ **MAGHERABUOY HOUSE HOTEL** ⌘ ⊙
41 Magheraboy Rd.
☎ 823507. Last orders 2130.
Fresh baked salmon, grills.
£££.

Ma-ring
17 Kerr St. ☎ 822765.
Lunches, dinner. Booking
essential.

Morelli's
7 Eglinton St. ☎ 824848.
1100-2200 Mon-Sun. Pizza,
lasagne, toasties, home-made
ice cream.

Mount Royal
2 Mount Royal. ☎ 823342.
1200-2100. A la carte. £.

Nibblers
50 Main St. ☎ 824017.
1100-0300 Mon-Sun
July & Aug, earlier closing rest
of year. Burgers, hot dogs.

Nobody's Inn ⌘
50 Ballyreagh Rd.
☎ 823509. 1130-2300
Mon-Sat, 1230-1430 &
1900-2200 Sun. Pub grub.

Rathlin House
2 Ramore Avenue. ☎ 824834.
1500-1930 Mon-Sun. Booking
advisable.

Portrush **Co. ANTRIM**

★ RAMORE
The Harbour. ☎ 824313. Wine bar 1200-1400 & 1730-2100 Mon-Sat. Restaurant 1830-2230 Tues-Sat. Tempura prawns, Thai chicken, hot fresh fruit & Grand Marnier souffle. £££.

Rascals
31 Main St. ☎ 822069. 1200-1430 Mon-Sat. Lasagne, quiche, burgers.

Rogues Wine Bar
54 Kerr St. ☎ 822076. 1200-1430 & 1700-2200 Mon-Sat, 1900-2130 Sun. Spinach flan, moussaka.

Rowland's
92 Main St. ☎ 822063. 1700-2230 Mon-Sun June-Sept; 1900-2200 Tues-Sun Oct-May. Lasagne, tagliatelli, pizza. A la carte. £££.

Royal Court Hotel
White Rocks. ☎ 822236. Last orders 2130, Sun 2100. Grill bar. Steak, open sandwiches, vegetarian. ££. A la carte. £££.

Shirley's Diner
26 Causeway St. ☎ 823581. 1100-2200 Mon-Sun in summer, more limited opening in winter. Scampi, lasagne, steaks.

Silver Sands
27 Eglinton St. ☎ 824113. 0900-2300 Mon-Sun summer, until 1900 winter. Fish & chips, Ulster fry.

Some Plaice Else
21 Ballyreagh Rd. ☎ 824945. 1700-2130 Mon-Sat, 1230-1430 & 1700-2130 Sun. Seafood. £££.

Spinnaker
25 Main St. ☎ 822348. 1000-2100 Mon-Sun Easter-Sept, more limited hours in winter. Set lunch, home-baked cakes. A la carte. £.

Station Bar
16c Eglinton St. ☎ 822112. 2000-2200 Mon-Sat. Coffee, sandwiches. In nightclub.

Uncle Sams
35 Eglinton St. ☎ 824796. 0900-2100 Mon-Sun. Chicken, steaks, salads.

The Victoriana
Dunluce Centre. ☎ 824400. May-Aug 1000-2200 Mon-Sun; Sept 1100-1800 Mon-Thur, 1100-2200 Fri-Sun; Oct-April 1400-2100 Fri-Sun. Ulster fry, chicken, fish. ££.

Waterworld
The Harbour. ☎ 822001. 1000-2200 Mon-Sat, 1400-2200 Sun in summer. Lunch, coffee.

Co. ANTRIM — Portrush-Stoneyford

West Bay View
48 Mark St. ☎ 823375. 1230-1330 & 1730-1830 Mon-Sun. Booking essential.

West Strand Guest House
18 Kerr St. ☎ 822270. 1200-1800 Mon-Sun. Lunch, high tea. Vegetarian, fresh fish, home baking.

The Village
18 New St. ☎ 479740. 0900-1800 Mon-Sat. Gammon & pineapple, Irish stew, cheesecake.

Waves
56 Main St. ☎ 472680. 1030-2400 Mon-Thur, 1030-0100 Fri & Sat. Fish & chips, curry.

RANDALSTOWN
(STD 0849)

Cranfield Inn ♀
34 Cranfield Rd. ☎ 472342. 1900-2300 Mon-Fri, 1500-2300 Sat, 1230-1430 & 1900-2200 Sun. Fish, eel suppers, sausages.

Granagh House ♀
9 New St. ☎ 472758. 1100-2200 Mon-Sat, 1230-1430 & 1900-2200 Sun. Lunch, grills. A la carte.

Marrion's ♀
10 Main St. ☎ 472487. 1130-2300 Mon-Sat, 1230-1430 & 1900-2200 Sun. Pies.

O'Kane's ♀
22 Main St. ☎ 473101. 1230-1430 & 1930-2200 Mon-Sat, 1200-1430 & 1900-2100 Sun. Ulster fry, plaice, hokey in breadcrumbs, toasties. 'Bushmills Bar of the Year 1991'.

RATHLIN ISLAND
(STD 026 57)

Rathlin Guesthouse 🍾
The Quay. ☎ 63917. Open Mon-Sun. Snacks, sandwiches, soup. High tea, dinner. Booking essential. E£.

Rathlin Restaurant 🍾
The Harbour. ☎ 63939. 1100-1800 Mon-Sun June-Sept, weekends Easter-June. Speciality seafood.

STONEYFORD
(STD 084 664)

Ballymac ♀
7a Rock Rd. ☎ 313. 1130-2300 Mon-Sat, 1230-1430 & 1930-2200 Sun. Restaurant: 1230-1430 & 1830-2130 Mon-Sun. E££. A la carte.

Stoneyford-Whitehead — Co. ANTRIM

Stoneyford Inn ♀
68 Stoneyford Rd. ☎ 288. 1500-2330 Mon-Sat, 1230-1430 & 1900-2200 Sun. Hamburgers, chicken, pies.

TEMPLEPATRICK
(STD 0849)

Airport Inn ♀
745 Antrim Rd. ☎ 432775. 1200-2100 Mon-Sat, 1230-1430 & 1900-2130 Sun. Carvery, à la carte. ££.

Happy Inn ♀
Unit 8, Twelfth Milestone. ☎ 433717. 1200-1400 & 1700-2330 Mon-Wed, until 0030 Thur & Fri, 1600-0030 Sat, 1300-1500 & 1700-2400 Sun. ££.

Lyle Hill Tavern ♀
96 Lylehill Rd. ☎ 432451. 1230-1430 Mon-Sun. Ulster fry, stew, pies.

★ TEMPLETON HOTEL ♀
882 Antrim Rd. ☎ 432984. 1230-1345 Mon-Sun, Last orders 2145. A la carte. ££££.

Wayside Inn ♀
25 New Mill Rd, Ballywee. ☎ (0960) 324276. 1200-2300 Mon-Sat. Chicken, chips, salad, grills.

TOOMEBRIDGE
(STD 0648)

Drumderg Café
177 Moneynick Rd. ☎ (0648) 50306. 0800-1900 Mon-Sat. Grills, coffee.

Elk Bar & Restaurant ♀
38 Hillhead Rd. ☎ 50155. 1130-1700 Mon-Fri, until 2100 Sat, 1700-2100 Sun. Toasties, grills, pub grub. On A6.

Elver Inn ♀
100 Moneynick Rd. ☎ (0648) 50362. 1230-1430 Mon-Sat. Pub grub.

O'Neill Arms Hotel ♀
Main St. ☎ 50202. Last orders 2200. £.

T-Junction Café
62 Hillhead Rd. ☎ 50095. 0930-1900 Mon-Sat. Grills. On A6.

WHITEHEAD
(STD 096 03)

Coffee & Cream
10 King's Rd. ☎ 78757. 0900-1900 Mon-Sat. Chicken, fish, salads, coffee, snacks.

Pizza Plaice 'n' Chips
Marine Avenue. ☎ 53276. 1145-1400 Mon-Sat, 1700-2200 Tues-Thur, until 2400 Fri & Sat, 2000 Sun. Pizzas, ribs, burgers.

Calvert's Tavern and The Kerry Lynn Restaurant

* Lunches: 12 noon till 2.30 pm
* A La Carte nightly 6pm till 10pm
* Private Parties Catered for

★ Live Entertainment ★
Tuesday, Thursday, Friday, Saturday and Sunday

3 SCOTCH STREET, ARMAGH
Tel. (0861) 524186

THE OLD SCHOOLHOUSE INN

DINE IN INTIMATE SURROUNDINGS & ENJOY FIRST CLASS FRENCH CUISINE IN OUR CHARMING CENTURY-OLD SCHOOLHOUSE WITH THE ATMOSPHERE ENHANCED BY A TRADITIONAL OPEN TURF FIRE

106 BALLYROBIN ROAD, TEMPLEPATRICK, CO. ANTRIM BT41 4TF
(NEAR AIRPORT)

**ANTRIM
(0849) 428209**

Carnwood Lodge Hotel

121 Castleblaney Road, Keady, Co. Armagh

Full à la Carte menu available

Booking Essential

Last orders 21.30

Tel: (0861) 538935

COUNTY ARMAGH

AGHALEE

Greenhall ⌁
4 Airport Rd. ☎ (0846) 651997.
1200-1430 & 1730-2130 Mon-Sat, 1230-1430 & 1730-2100 Sun. A la carte, high teas. £.

ARMAGH
(STD 0861)

★ ARCHWAY
5 Hartford Place, The Mall.
☎ 522532. 1000-1700
Tues-Sat. Danish pastries, apple pie. Set lunch.

Armagh Fine Foods
24 Scotch St. ☎ 522805.
0900-1730 Mon-Sat. Morning coffee, sandwiches, salads. In delicatessen.

Armstrong's Bar ⌁
21 Linenhall St. ☎ 524345.
1230-1430 Mon-Sat,
1700-2130 Sun. Pub grub.

Barnaby's Restaurant at Harry Hoots ⌁
143 Railway St. ☎ 522103.
1230-1430 Mon-Sat, 1900-2200 Wed-Sat, 1230-1430 & 1800-2130 Sun. Meatballs in Guinness sauce, smoked salmon & cream cheese pancake. £££.

Bramley Family Kitchen
Orchard Centre, Folly Lane.
☎ 522892. 1000-2200
Mon-Fri, until 1730 Sat,
1400-1730 Sun.
Burgers, chips, rolls.

Calvert's Tavern ⌁
3 Scotch St. ☎ 524186.
1200-2200 Mon-Sun.
A la carte, seafood. ££.

Cellar Lounge ⌁
55 Thomas St. ☎ 525147.
1230-1430 Mon-Sat.
Pub grub.

Charlemont Arms Hotel ⌁
63 English St. ☎ 522028.
Last orders 2130. Seafood, duckling. Set lunch. A la carte. £££.

Cottage Restaurant
Gazette Arcade, Scotch St.
☎ 528582. 0830-1730 Mon-Sat, until 1400 Wed. Morning coffee, lunch, home baking.

Diamond Bar ⌁
21 Lower English St.
☎ 522645. 1200-1430
Mon-Sat. Soup, Irish stew, lunches.

Downtown Café
13 Dobbin St. ☎ 523538.
0900-1800 Mon-Sat, until
1400 Wed. Burgers, grills, fish.

Drumsill House Hotel 🍷
35 Moy Rd. ☎ 522009. Last orders 2130. Salmon, lobster. Lunchtime carvery. E££.

Fat Sam's
7 Lower English St. ☎ 525555. 0845-1800 Mon-Fri, 0915-1700 Sat. Sandwiches, lasagne, salads.

Four Trees Lounge 🍷
Nursery Rd. ☎ 525393. 1300-1600 Mon-Sat. Pub grub.

Glencoe 🍷
72 Scotch St. ☎ 522994. 1130-2300 Mon-Sat. Pub grub.

Hester's Place
12 English St. ☎ 522374. 0900-1730 Mon-Sat, closed Wed. Ulster fry, stew, grills.

Jodie's 🍷
37 Scotch St. ☎ 527577. 1200-1500 Mon-Sat, 1800-2200 Wed-Sun. Steaks, à la carte.

Johnston's Coffee Lounge
9 Scotch St. ☎ 522995. 0900-1730 Mon-Sat, closed Wed. Stew, lasagne.

Ken's
16 Barrack St. ☎ 525692. 0900-2100 Mon-Sat. Grills, snacks, pies.

Lantern
40 Scotch St. ☎ 524395. 0930-1700 Mon-Sat, closed Wed. Fish, chicken, salads.

Loudan's Cellars 🍷
49 English St. ☎ 522015. 2000-2130 Thur-Sat. Pub grub.

McAnerney's
Irish St. ☎ 522468. 0900-1730 Mon-Sat. Coffee, salads, rolls.

Mandarin House 🍷
30 Scotch St. ☎ 522228. 1200-1400 & 1700-2400 Mon-Thur & Sun, until 0100 Fri & Sat. Chinese & European. ££.

Northern Bar 🍷
100 Railway St. ☎ 527316. 1130-1500 Mon-Sat. Salads, scampi.

Orr's Corner 🍷
36 Barrack St. ☎ 522052. 1230-1400 Mon-Sat. Pub grub.

Palace Stables
Palace Demesne. ☎ 522722. 1000-1900 Mon-Sat, 1300-1900 Sun, April-Sept; 1000-1700 Mon-Sat, 1400-1700 Sun, Oct-Mar. Morning coffee, filled rolls, lasagne, steaks. In heritage centre.

Co. ARMAGH

Armagh–Blackwatertown

Pub With No Beer
30 Thomas St. ☎ 523586.
0900-2230 Mon-Sat. Chips, burgers, lasagne. Non-alcoholic drinks.

Rainbow
13 Upper English St.
☎ 525391. 0830-1730
Mon-Sat. Coffee, grills.

Restaurant No. 12
14 English St. ☎ 522374.
0900-1730 Mon-Sat, closed Wed. Soup, salads.

Shambles Bar ♀
9 Lower English St. ☎ 524107.
1230-1430 Mon-Sat. Soup, sandwiches.

Station Bar ♀
3 Lower English St. ☎ 523731.
1230-1430 & 1600-2000
Mon-Sat. Pub grub.

Strawberry Bar ♀
23 Lower English St.
☎ 523865. 1230-1430
Mon-Fri. Lasagne, chicken, plaice.

Tino's
11 Thomas St. ☎ 523187.
0900-1800 Mon-Sat.
Pasta, chicken, fish.

★ **WHEEL & LANTERN**
Market St. ☎ 522288.
1000-1700 Mon-Sat, closed Wed. Quiche, pies, pastries. Coffee lounge in department store.

BELLEEKS

Glenside Bar & Lounge ♀
15 Main St. ☎ (0693) 878280.
1900-2330 Mon-Thur, 1600-2330 Fri, 1130-0100 Sat.
Soup, steak, chips, salads, sweets.

Mountain House ♀
Drumilly. ☎ (0693) 838766.
1900-2200 Thur-Sun.
A la carte.

BESSBROOK
(STD 0693)

Country Folk Inn ♀
Drumnahuncheon, 114
Tullyah Rd, Whitecross.
☎ 830230. 1130-2300
Mon-Sat. Hamburgers, pies.

Millvale ♀
Millvale. ☎ 830306.
1130-2300 Mon-Sat,
1230-1430 & 1900-2200
Sun. Pub grub.

BLACKWATERTOWN

Portmor House ♀
44 Main St. ☎ (0861) 548053.
1230-1430 Wed-Sun, 1900-2130 Fri-Sun. Hamburgers, pies. A la carte. ££.

CAMLOUGH

Doyle's 🍷
22 Main St. ☎ (0693) 830269.
1130-2300 Mon-Sat, 1230-1430 & 1900-2200 Sun.
Stew, pies, pub grub.

Finnegan's 🍷
25 Main St. ☎ (0693) 830044.
1200-1500 Mon-Sat. Pub grub.

Village Inn 🍷
21 Main St. ☎ (0693) 838537.
1200-1430 & 1700-2100 Mon-Sat. Pub grub. A la carte.

CRAIGAVON
(STD 0762)

Brownlow Centre
Brownlow Rd. ☎ 341333.
1200-1400 & 1700-2130 Mon-Fri, 1000-1700 Sat. Fish & chips, curries, hamburgers.
Café in recreation centre.

Captain's Table
Craigavon Lakes. ☎ 342669.
1000-2100 Mon-Fri, 1000-1700 Sat & Sun, June-Sept & Easter. Ice cream, coffee.

Cove Inn 🍷
Craigavon Shopping Centre.
☎ 341044. 1130-2300 Mon-Sat, 1900-2200 Sun.
Pub grub.

Drumgor Tavern 🍷
Drumgor. ☎ 342187.
1130-2300 Mon-Sat, 1230-1430 & 1900-2300 Sun. Pub grub.

Irwin's
Craigavon Shopping Centre.
☎ 342629. 0900-1730 Mon-Sat, until 2100 Thur & Fri. Self-service, snacks.

Laganview 🍷
Donacloney. ☎ (0762) 881232.
1130-2300 Mon-Sat.
Sandwiches, coffee.

Loughside Café
Lough Neagh Discovery Centre, Oxford Island.
☎ 322205. 1000-1430 Mon-Sun. Soup, pies, lasagne.

Mr Pickwick's Kitchen
Craigavon Shopping Centre, 15 Market Lane. ☎ 341025.
0900-1730 Mon-Wed & Sat, until 2100 Thur & Fri. Baked potatoes (20 fillings), pizzas.

Pinebank Centre
Tullygully Rd. ☎ 341033.
0830-1700 & 1930-2300 Mon-Sat. Coffee, snacks.

Tannaghmore Gardens
Tannaghmore. ☎ 341199.
1400-1730 Mon-Sun July-Aug. Self-service, snacks.

CROSSMAGLEN
(STD 0693)

Ashfield Golf Club
Freeduff, Cullyhanna.
☎ 861315. 1000-1700
Mon-Sun. Grills, salads.

Cartwheel
20 The Square. ☎ 861285.
1800-2300 Mon-Sat.
Pub grub. E£.

Chums
46 The Square. ☎ 868413.
1230-1430 Mon-Sat.
Steaks, grills.

Conalig House
124 Concession Rd.
1200-1430 Mon-Sat. Pub grub.

★ HEARTY'S FOLK COTTAGE

Glassdrummond. ☎ 861916.
1400-1900 Sun. Coffee,
home-baked scones. Live
music. Antiques/crafts sales.

Keenan's Bar
42 The Square. ☎ 868071.
1200-1430 Mon-Sat.
Daily specials.

Kerryman
36 The Square. ☎ 861589.
1900-2200 Mon-Sun.
A la carte.

Lima Country House
16 Drumalt Rd. ☎ 861944.
1800-2200 Mon-Sat.
American. Booking essential.

Lite & Easy
Tullynavall Rd. ☎ 868262.
1830-2230 Mon-Sat,
1230-1430 Sun. Pub grub.

McConville's Place
12 The Square. ☎ 861212.
1200-1500 Mon-Sat.
Pub grub.

Murtaghs Bar
15 North St. ☎ 861378.
1230-1500 Mon-Sat. Pub grub.

FORKHILL
(STD 0693)

The Forge
100 Carrickasticken Rd.
☎ 888175. 1130-2300
Mon-Sat, 1230-1430 &
1900-2200 Sun. Pub grub.

Welcome Inn
35 Main St. ☎ 888273.
1130-2300 Mon-Sat,
1230-1430 & 1900-2200
Sun. Soup, sandwiches.

HAMILTONSBAWN

Bawn Inn
25 Main St. ☎ (0762) 871239.
1130-2330 Mon-Sat. Bar snacks.

Corner Bar
Main St. ☎ (0762) 871070.
1130-2300 Mon-Sat.
Hamburgers, stew, pies.

Co. ARMAGH — Keady-Lurgan

KEADY
(STD 0861)

Callan River Inn ♟
2 The Square. ☎ 539679.
1230-1500 Mon-Sat.
Chicken, scampi, plaice.

Carnwood Lodge Hotel ♟
121 Castleblaney Rd.
☎ 538935. Last orders 2130. ££.

Rock Bar ♟
Granemore. ☎ 531992.
2000-2200 Mon-Sat.
Pub grub.

The Trap ♟
37 Kinelowen St. ☎ 538556.
1800-2130 Wed-Sun.
Pub grub. A la carte.

KILLYLEA

Digby's & Red Grouse ♟
53 Main St. ☎ (0861) 568330.
1230-1430 Mon-Sun, 1830-2400 Fri-Sun. Steaks, kebabs.
A la carte. ££.

LOUGHGALL
(STD 0762)

★ THE FAMOUS GROUSE ♟
6 Ballyhegan Rd. ☎ 891778.
1130-2100 Mon-Sat,
1230-1430 & 1900-2200 Sun.
A la carte 1900-2200 Wed-Sun. Poached Irish salmon, steaks, duckling. Bar lunches.
£££.

LURGAN
(STD 0762)

Alpine Lodge
Ski Centre, Turmoyra Lane, Silverwood. ☎ 326606.
1100-1900 Mon-Fri,
0900-1800 Sat & Sun.
Chicken, salads, vegetarian.

Andrea's Coffee House
64 Belfast Rd. ☎ 324950.
1000-1630 Mon-Sat. Scones, pastries, salads, lunch.

Ashburn Hotel ♟
81 William St. ☎ 325711. Last orders 2045, Fri & Sat 2145.
A la carte. £.

Brindle Beam Tea Rooms
20 Windsor Avenue.
☎ 321721. 1000-1700
Mon-Sat. Chicken & broccoli crunch, home-made savoury pies, salads. M£.

Byrne's ♟
Main St, Magheralin.
☎ (0846) 611506.
1130-2300 Mon-Sat.
Sandwiches, grills.

Cafolla
51 Church Place. ☎ 324022.
1000-1800 Mon-Sat, until
1430 Wed. Fish & chips, chicken, grills.

Cafolla
2 Carnegie St. ☎ 323331.
1000-1730 Mon-Sat. Snacks, grills, fish & chips, ice cream.

Lurgan — Co. ARMAGH

Castle Park Inn
Robert St. ☎ 322726.
1200-1430 Mon-Thur,
1700-1930 Fri & Sat.
Pub grub.

Cellar Lounge
50 Church Place. ☎ 327994.
1230-1430 Mon-Sat.
Pub grub.

Centrepoint Leisure
Portadown Rd. ☎ 321997.
1230-1430 Mon-Sun, later
opening weekends. Kebabs,
garlic bread, pancakes &
maple syrup. Cinema &
bowling alley. E£.

Corner House
93 Silverwood Rd,
Derrymacash. ☎ 341817.
1200-1500 & 1830-2400
Mon-Sat, 1230-1430 Sun.
Soup, baked ham, pork chops,
gateaux. A la carte. E£.

Gemini
2 Church Place. ☎ 327323.
0900-1730 Mon-Wed, until
1900 Thur, 2000 Fri & Sat.
Set lunch. A la carte.

Long Hall
22a High St. ☎ 328974.
0930-1700 Mon-Sat, closed
Wed. Grills, afternoon tea.

The Mall
Waves Complex, Robert St.
☎ 322906. 1000-2130 Mon-
Sat. Closed Thur. Home-made
pies, Irish stew, salads.

Peking Chinese
86 William St. ☎ 342290.
1700-2330 Tues-Sun.
Chinese & European. E££.

Pizza Pasta Hut
42 Church Place. ☎ 326444.
1700-2300 Mon-Sat, until
2200 Sun. Pizza, pasta.
A la carte.

Rumpoles
High St. ☎ 321747.
0900-1730 Mon-Sat, until
1400 Wed. Burgers, fish.

Sesame
41 High St. ☎ 327412.
1000-1700 Mon & Tues,
1000-2130 Wed-Sat, 1200-
1430 & 1730-2000 Sun. Set
menu. High tea. A la carte
E££.

Silverwood Hotel
Kiln Lane. ☎ 327722. Last
orders 2130, Sun 2030. Beef
stroganoff, steaks. Set lunch,
à la carte. E£.

Spades
Grattans Centre. ☎ 343558.
0900-1730 Mon-Wed & Sat,
until 2100 Thur & Fri.
Quiche, lasagne, pie.

Stables
Old Portadown Rd.
☎ 323974. 1200-1430 Mon
& Thur-Sat. Pub grub.
Grills, salads.

Co. ARMAGH — *Lurgan-Middletown*

Vintage ♀
31 Church Place. ☎ 328757.
1230-1430 & 1900-2100 Sat.
Pies, pub grub.

Wellworths
Market St. ☎ 325842.
0900-1730 Mon, Wed & Sat,
until 2100 Thur & Fri.
Breakfast, grills, salads.

White Wren
45 Market St. ☎ 325418.
0900-1800 Mon-Sat. Grills.

Wilton Cross ♀
38 Church Place. ☎ 322076.
1230-1500 Mon-Sat,
1830-2130 Wed-Sun.
Daily special. A la carte. £.

Woodville Arms ♀
111 Lake St. ☎ 324005.
1230-1430 Fri & Sat.
Pub grub.

MARKETHILL
(STD 0861)

Buttery ♀
103 Main St. ☎ 551237.
1130-2300 Mon-Sat,
1230-1600 Tues-Fri.
A la carte. E£.

Corner Bar ♀
110 Main St. ☎ 551887.
1230-1500 Tues-Fri,
1900-2200 Fri & Sat.
A la carte. Pub grub.

Gosford House Hotel ♀
Main St. ☎ 551676. Last orders
2200. Lemon sole, beef
stroganoff. A la carte. ££.

Old Barn
5 Mowhan Rd. ☎ 551082.
0900-2300 Mon-Sat. Coffee
shop & restaurant. A la carte.
£.

★ OLD THATCH

3 Keady St. ☎ 551261.
0900-1300 & 1400-1700
Mon-Fri, 0900-1700 Sun.
Home-made jam, chocolate
fudge cake, carrot cake.
Coffee shop in Alexander's
department store.

MIDDLETOWN

Commercial Bar ♀
Main St. ☎ (0861) 568407.
1230-1430 Mon-Sat.
Pub grub.

Fedara's
4 Main St. ☎ (0861) 568189.
1030-2230 Mon-Sat, until
2100 Sun. Steaks, salmon,
grills, stroganoff, sandwiches.
A la carte.

Longnancy's Bar ♀
Tamlaght, Madden.
☎ (0861) 568437. 1130-2300
Mon-Sat, 1230-1430 &
1900-2200 Sun. Pub grub.

MOUNTNORRIS

Port Bar 🍷
Main St. ☎ (086 157) 204.
1130-2200 Mon-Sat.
Pub grub.

NEWTOWNHAMILTON
(STD 0693)

Canteen
The Commons. ☎ 878250.
1000-1500 Thur, 1000-2000 alternate Sats (market days). Irish stew, sandwiches, Ulster fry, pastries.

Slane's
Dundalk St. ☎ 878249.
1230-1400 Mon-Sat.
Snacks, grills.

South Side 🍷
47 Dundalk St. ☎ 878620.
1130-2300 Mon-Sat,
1230-1430 & 1900-2200
Sun. Pub grub.

PORTADOWN
(STD 0762)

Abra-Kebabra
Magowan Buildings, Borough Place. ☎ 335075. 1100-2400 Mon-Sat, 1600-2400 Sun. Indian & European.

Bennett's Bar 🍷
46 Mandeville St. ☎ 350778.
1200-1530 Mon-Sat. Soups, salads, roasts.

Brambles
2 Borough Place, Magowan Buildings. ☎ 351000. 0900-1700 Mon-Sat. Lasagne, shepherd's pie, quiche.

Carn Restaurant
21 Craigavon Enterprise.
☎ 338801. 0900-1600 Mon-Fri. Set lunch, afternoon tea.

Carngrove Hotel 🍷
2 Charlestown Rd.
☎ 339222. Last orders 2130, Sun 2100. Duckling, paella. A la carte. E££.

Carol's
15 Mandeville St. ☎ 337814.
0900-1700 Mon-Sat,
0900-2200 Sat. Grills, set lunch, coffee.

Cascades
Swimming Pool, Thomas St.
☎ 332802. 1500-2030 Mon-Fri, 0930-1730 Sat. Café in swimming pool complex.

Chalet 🍷
111 Armagh Rd. ☎ 336980.
1230-1430 Mon-Sat. Set lunch, steak & kidney pie, roasts.

Cosy Corner 🍷
Teagy Rd. ☎ 852211.
1230-1430 & 1830-2130 Thur-Sat. Salads, grills.

Co. ARMAGH — Portadown

Dragon Inn ♆
34 Carleton St. ☎ 350761.
1700-2400 Mon-Sat,
1200-1500 & 1700-2400
Sun. Chinese & European. E£.

Ells
42 Dobbin Rd. ☎ 336326.
0900-2300 Mon-Sat.
Breakfast, grills. Set lunch.
A la carte E£.

Ferguson's Bar ♆
91 Markethill Rd.
☎ 840230. 1130-2300
Mon-Sat. Hamburgers, pies.

Gallery Tea Shop
16 Church St. ☎ 331796.
0900-1730 Tues-Sat, until
2000 Thur. Cream teas,
dietary meals.

Golden Bridge ♆
71 Bridge St. ☎ 333028.
1200-1400 & 1700-2400
Mon-Thur, 1200-0100 Fri &
Sat, 1300-2400 Sun. Chinese
& European. E£.

Hanging Sign ♆
8 Birches Rd. ☎ 851988.
1130-2130 Mon-Sat. Grills,
scampi, steak.

JR's Restaurant
16 Loughgall Rd. ☎ 330332.
1200-1400 & 1700-2100
Tues-Fri, until 2300 Sat,
2200 Sun. A la carte. E£.

Killycomain Inn ♆
Killycomain Rd. ☎ 337304.
1130-2300 Mon-Fri.
Set lunch. A la carte.

Lunch Box
1 Carleton St. ☎ 337663.
0945-1700 Mon-Fri. Toasties,
baked potatoes, burgers.

McCann's
250 Obin St. ☎ 332668.
0900-2400 Mon-Sat,
until 2100 Sun.
Fish & chips, chicken.

Meeting Place
20 Woodhouse St. ☎ 332735.
1230-1430 Mon-Sat.
Grills, salads.

Minella
22 Market St. ☎ 355911.
0900-1700 Mon-Sat,
until 1400 Thur.
Grills, sandwiches.

New Mandarin House ♆
34 West St. ☎ 351034.
1200-1400 & 1700-2330
Mon-Sat, 1730-2300 Sun.
Cantonese & European. E££.

No. 7
7 High St. ☎ 350808.
0900-1730 Mon-Sat. Lasagne,
curries, home-baked pastries.

Parkside Inn ♆
Garvaghy Rd. ☎ 330260.
1200-1430 Mon-Sat.
Pub grub.

Portadown-Tandragee — Co. ARMAGH

Pie Man
74 Woodhouse St.
☎ 330743. 0930-1645
Mon-Sat. Savoury & sweet
pies (28 varieties), pizza,
vegetarian, afternoon tea.

Queen's ♀
1 Thomas St. ☎ 334644.
1230-1400 Mon-Thur, until
1700 Fri & Sat. Pies,
hamburgers, grills.

Railway Arms ♀
28 Woodhouse St.
☎ 332054. 1200-1500
Mon-Sat. Pub grub, set lunch.

Seagoe Hotel ♀
Upper Church Lane.
☎ 333076. Last orders 2200.
Irish brotchan, planter's beef,
seafood, local vegetables.
Carvery. A la carte. E££.

Shalamar ♀
121 Bridge St. ☎ 350922.
1200-1400 Tues-Sat,
1700-2200 Mon, until 2330
Tues-Sun. Indian & European.

Spades
Portadown Shopping Centre.
☎ 339420. 0900-1730
Mon-Sat, until 2100 Fri.
Breakfast, Irish stew, sweets.

Upper Crust
16 West St. ☎ 332114.
0900-1730 Mon-Sat.
Snacks, grills, sweets.

Welcome ♀
16 Bridge St. ☎ 332325.
1200-1400 & 1700-2400
Mon-Wed, 1200-2400
Thur-Sat, 1300-2330 Sun.
Chinese & European.

Whistles Coffee Lounge
43 High St. 0900-1700
Mon-Sat. Lunch, coffee.

RICHHILL
(STD 0762)

Ballynahinch House ♣
47 Ballygroobany Rd.
☎ 870081. 1900-2200
Mon-Sat. Buffets, party
functions. Booking essential.

Normandy Inn ♀
6 Main St. ☎ 871386.
1230-1430 Mon-Sat,
1800-2100 Fri & Sat. Open
sandwiches, grills, burgers.

Ye Olde House Bar ♀
9 Irish St. ☎ 871616.
2000-2200 Thur-Sat. Pub
grub, scampi. E£.

TANDRAGEE
(STD 0762)

Cullen's ♀
114 Market St. ☎ 840327.
1130-2300 Mon-Sat,
1230-1430 & 1900-2200
Sun. Hamburgers, pies.

Farmer's Inn 🍷
2 Mill St. ☎ 840928.
1130-2300 Mon-Sat,
1230-1400 & 1900-2200
Sun. Toasties, hamburgers.

Huntsman 🍷
65 Market St. ☎ 841115.
1230-1430 Mon-Fri,
1800-2230 Mon-Sun. Pork in barbecue sauce, prawns, steaks. A la carte. E£.

WHITECROSS

Country Folk Inn 🍷
114 Tullyah Rd. ☎ (0693) 830230. 1800-2300
Fri & Sat. Pub grub.

Whitecross Bar 🍷
☎ (086 157) 642.
1700-2200 Thur-Sat. Steaks, roast beef, chicken.

COUNTY DOWN

ANNALONG
(STD 039 67)

★ GLASSDRUMMAN HOUSE ♀
224 Glassdrumman Rd.
☎ 68585. 1200-2130 Mon-Sat.
Kitchen Garden: steak, fish. ££.
Memories restaurant: French, set meals. £££.

Half Way House ♀
138 Glassdrumman Rd.
☎ 68224. 1200-1800 Mon-Sun, 1700-2200 Fri-Sun. Scampi, plaice.

Harbour Inn ♀
6 Harbour Drive. ☎ 68678.
1230-1430 Mon-Thur, 1830-2100 Fri & Sat. Fish, steaks, stuffed turkey, desserts. £.

Marlino's
224 Glassdrumman Rd.
☎ 67080. 1030-2230 Mon-Sun Apr-Sept, 1100-1800 Mon-Sun Oct-Mar. Soup, sandwiches, toasties, ice cream.

Mill Coffee Shop
Marine Park. ☎ 68736.
1000-2000 Mon-Sun in summer, 1000-1700 Sat & Sun in winter. Snacks.

Shirley's
21 Main St. ☎ 68468.
1000-2200 Mon-Sat in summer, 1200-1400 & 1700-2200 Mon-Sat in winter. Irish stew, salads.

ARDGLASS
(STD 0396)

Aldo's ♀
7 Castle Place. ☎ 841315.
1700-2200 Wed-Sun, 1230-1430 Sun in summer, 1800-2200 Thur-Sun in winter. A la carte. Steak chasseur, chicken kiev, seafood. £££.

Angus Cochrane's
The Harbour. ☎ 841551.
0800-2200 Mon-Sun. Sandwiches, prawns, potted herrings, cockles, mussels.

Harbour Restaurant
4 Quay St. ☎ 842200.
0930-2400, Mon-Sun. Steak, chicken, scampi.

Roadside Tavern ♀
83 Strangford Rd, Chapeltown.
☎ 841341. 1830-2230 Mon-Fri, 1130-2300 Sat. Pub grub.

Co. DOWN — Ballynahinch

BALLYNAHINCH
(STD 0238)

Coffee Nook
17 Main St. ☎ 563152. 0945-1630 Tues-Fri, 0930-1700 Sat. Sandwiches, pastries.

The Connoisseur
51 High St. ☎ 561797. 0900-1700 Tues-Sat. Shepherd's pie, minced beef pie, salads, coffee.

Corner Restaurant
1 Main St. ☎ 562264. 0900-1400 Mon, until 1800 Tues-Thur, 2300 Fri & Sat. Grills, self-service.

Foo Kwai
25 Dromore St. ☎ 563214. 1700-2400 Mon-Fri, until 0100 Sat & Sun. Cantonese.

Fortune ♀
25 High St. ☎ 561030. 1200-1400 Thur-Sat, 1700-2400 Mon-Fri & Sun, until 0100 Sat. Chinese & European. E££.

Ginesi
34 Main St. ☎ 562653. 1130-2330 Mon-Sat, 1400-2330 Sun, closed Tues. Steak, scampi, fish & chips.

Graham's
37 Dromore St. ☎ 563868. 2000-2400 Mon, until 2300 Tues-Thur, 1700-2430 Fri & Sat, 1800-2300 Sun. Grills, fish.

Hideaway
19 Main St. ☎ 565450. 0945-1630 Tues-Fri, 0930-1700 Sat. Coffee, scones, quiche.

Millbrook Lodge Hotel ♀
5 Drumaness Rd. ☎ 562828. Last orders 2115. A la carte. M£, E££.

The Pharaoh
10 Main St. ☎ 565252. 1200-1400 & 1630-2300 Mon-Sat, 1630-2030 Sun. Pizzas, pasta, fish, chicken, kebabs.

★ PRIMROSE ♀
30 Main St. ☎ 563177. 1200-2200 Mon-Sat. Casseroles, shellfish, trout, salmon, home-made bread. E£.

Primrose Pop In
30a Main St. ☎ 563872. 0900-1730 Mon-Sat. Afternoon tea, quiche, pies.

Ramery Inn ♀
45 Windmill St. ☎ 562171. 1130-0100 Thur-Sat, 1230-1430 & 1930-2330 Sun. Daily specials.

White Horse Hotel ♀
17 High St. ☎ 562225. Last orders 2115. A la carte. E££.

Windmill
5 Windmill St. ☎ 561111. 1200-1430 Mon-Sun, 1730-2130 Mon-Sat. Roasts, beef, pork, gammon.

★ WOODLANDS 🍷
29 Spa Rd. ☎ 562650.
1915-2330 Thur-Sat. Game in season, Strangford scallops, hazelnut & apricot meringue. £££.

BALLYWALTER
(STD 024 77)

Country Cake Shop
38 Main St. ☎ 38215.
0830-1730 Mon-Sat. Ulster fry, sandwiches, pastries.

Greenlea Farm
Dunover Rd. ☎ 58218.
Evening meals. Booking essential. Farmhouse cooking.

Pink Geranium 🍸
1 Harbour Rd. ☎ 58636.
1030-1800 Mon-Fri, until 2200 Sat, 1900 Sun. Scones, coffee, teas, grills. E£.

BANBRIDGE
(STD 082 06)

Bann Restaurant
43 Newry St. ☎ 24382.
0900-1700 Mon-Sat, until 1430 Thur. Breakfast, lunch, grills.

Banville House 🍷
174 Lurgan Rd. ☎ 24267.
1230-1400 & 1730-2130 Mon-Sun. Closed Good Fri, 25 Dec. Set lunch, high tea. Fresh salmon, duckling. A la carte. E££.

Belmont Hotel 🍷
Rathfriland Rd. ☎ 62517.
Last orders 2130 Mon-Fri, Sun 2030. Pub lunch. Scampi provençale, garnished steaks, melon in port wine.
A la carte. ££.

Coach Inn 🍷
13 Church Square. ☎ 22763.
1230-2300 Mon-Sat. Set meals. Beef stroganoff, duckling. E£.

Downshire Arms Hotel 🍷
95 Newry St. ☎ 62343.
Last orders 2030. A la carte. Set meals. E££.

First-Last 🍷
28 Scarva St. ☎ 22394.
1200-1500 Mon-Thur, 1200-1900 Fri & Sat. Lunch.

Gall Bog 🍷
4 Gall Bog Rd. ☎ (0846) 692546. 1130-2300 Mon-Sat, 1230-1430 & 1900-2200 Sun. Pub grub.

Golden Bloom
Scarva St. ☎ 25411. 0830-1730 Mon-Sat. Ulster fry, quiche, pastries.

Goodfellas 🍷
28 Scarva St. ☎ 62394.
1200-1500 Mon-Sat. Pub grub.

THE VISCOUNT of CLANDEBOYE

BANGOR

Where you'll find the liveliest entertainment all through the week

TUESDAYS	**The hottest Jazz!**
WEDNESDAYS	**Northern Ireland's most popular live bands!**
THURSDAYS	**Quality Country and Western!**
FRIDAYS	**Our very popular club night!**
SATURDAYS	**The biggest names in cabaret!**
SUNDAYS	**The best karaoke party night!**

plus a varied and mouth-watering menu of the finest food-
<u>LUNCH AND EVENING!</u>

SPRINGHILL SHOPPING CENTRE, BANGOR.
Telephone: (0247) 271545

Banbridge-Bangor **Co. DOWN**

Half Way House ♁
80 Half Way Rd. ☎ (0846) 692351. 1230-1430 & 1830-2100 Mon-Sat. Grills, snacks. Buffet.

Hallsmill Inn ♁
Banbridge Rd, Lawrencetown. ☎ 25565. 1130-2330 Mon-Sat. A la carte, high tea.

Harry's ♁ ⊗
7 Dromore St. ☎ 22794. 1200-1430 Mon-Sat. Pies, snacks.

Imperial Inn ♁
38 Bridge St. ☎ 22610. 1230-1430 Mon-Sat. Fish, omelettes, salads.

Jamies ♁
Peggy's Loaning, Scarva Rd. ☎ 26714. 1230-1430 Mon-Sat. Grills, salads.

Jinglers ♁
4 Rathfriland St. ☎ 22341. 1130-2300 Mon-Sat, 1230-1430 & 1900-2200 Sun. Toasties, burgers, stew.

Jockey Club ♁
21 Church Square. 1130-2300 Mon-Sat. Pub grub.

Lychee Garden ♁
42 Bridge St. ☎ 23523. 1200-1400 & 1700-2400 Tues-Sat, 1630-2400 Sun. Chinese & European.

Majestic Café
52 Newry St. ☎ 23602. 0900-2200 Mon-Sun. Fish, grills.

Patrisse Coffee Lounge
48 Newry St. 0800-1630 Mon-Sat, 0800-1330 Thur. Soup, burgers.

Rosamar
12 Bridge St. ☎ 22263. 0900-1730 Mon & Wed, until 1630 Thur, 1800 Fri & Sat. Fish & chips, grills. Self-service.

Strings ♁
41 Newry St. ☎ 62446. 1100-1430 Mon-Sat, 1730-2130 Tues-Thur, 1730-2200 Sat & Sun. A la carte. E£.

Ulster Bar ♁
72 Newry St. ☎ 22266. 1130-2300 Mon-Sat. Pub grub.

BANGOR
(STD 0247)

Anchor Lounge ♁
2 High St. ☎ 271178. 1130-1500 Mon-Sat in winter, until 2000 July & Aug. Pub grub.

Co. DOWN

Bangor

★ BACK STREET CAFÉ 🍷
14 Queen's Parade.
☎ 453990. 1900-2230
Tues-Sat. A la carte. Baked turbot, Barbary duck fillets, home-made bramble ice cream. E££.

Bamboo Tree 🍷
22 High St. ☎ 467826.
1200-1400 Mon & Wed-Sat, 1700-0030 Mon-Thur & Sun, until 0130 Fri & Sat.
Cantonese & European. E£.

Belfry 🍷
188 Rathgael Rd. ☎ 469212.
1200-1430 & 1800-2200
Mon-Sun. Lunch. A la carte. E£.

Bryansburn 🍷
151 Bryansburn Rd. ☎ 270173.
1200-1400 Mon-Sun, 1700-2130 Mon-Sat, 1700-1900 Sun. A. Home cooking.
A la carte. E£££.

Bunjy Jump 🍷
99 Main St. ☎ 461529.
1200-2300 Mon-Sat.
Tapas, canneloni, trout with stilton, vegetarian. E££.

Castle Arms 🍷 ⊘
1 Castle St. ☎ 465808. 1130-2300 & 1700-2200 Mon-Sat.
Set meals.

Castle Garden
Heritage Centre, Town Hall.
☎ 270371. 1100-1630
Tues-Sat, 1400-1630 Sun, until 1730 summer, earlier closing winter. Morning coffee, afternoon tea.

Charlie Heggarty's 🍷
17 High St. ☎ 271285.
1200-1500 Mon-Thur, until 2000 Fri & Sat. Set lunch, à la carte. E£.

Cineplex
1 Valentine Rd. ☎ 454729.
1000-1500 & 1700-2200
Mon-Sat, 1000-2130 Sun.
Lasagne, pies.

Coffee Pot
88a Groomsport Rd.
☎ 271765. 0930-1700
Mon-Sat. Soup, salads, sandwiches.

Donegan's 🍷
44 High St. ☎ 270362.
1230-1430 & 1700-2200
Mon-Sat, 1900-2100 Sun.
A la carte. E££.

Dragon House
76 High St. ☎ 459031. 1700-0030 Mon-Thur, 1700-0130 Fri & Sat, 1700-2400 Sun.
Chinese & European.
Vegetarian.

Bangor   **Co. DOWN**

Dragon Palace
5 Crosby St. ☎ 457817.
1200-1400 & 1700-2400
Mon-Thur, until 0100 Fri &
Sat, 1700-2330 Sun. Chinese
& European. E££.

Dutch Windmill
13 Bridge St. ☎ 452096.
1000-1900 Mon-Thur, until
2200 Fri & Sat. Pancakes.
A la carte. E££.

Esplanade
Esplanade, Ballyholme.
☎ 270954. 1215-1415 &
1830-2130 Mon-Sat,
1230-1400 Sun. Set meals.
A la carte. E£.

The Ganges
9 Bingham St. ☎ 453030.
1200-1400 & 1730-2330
Mon-Sat, 1700-2300 Sun.
Indian. E££.

★ **THE GEORGE**
10 Estate Rd, Clandeboye.
☎ 853311. 1200-1500 Mon-
Sat, 1900-2130 Fri & Sat,
1900-2200 Sun. Set meals.
A la carte. E££.

Gray's Bistro
20a Gray's Hill. ☎ 270339.
0900-1700 Mon-Sat,
1100-1900 Sun. Sandwiches,
toasties.

Green Bicycle
6 Hamilton Rd. ☎ 271747.
1000-1630 Mon-Sat.
Vegetarian, afternoon tea.

Gryphon
12 The Esplanade, Ballyholme.
☎ 473294. 1200-1415 Mon-
Sun, 1900-2115 Tues-Sat,
1700-1900 Fri & Sat. A la
carte. High tea. E££.

★ **HEATHERLEA TEA ROOMS**
94 Main St. ☎ 453157.
0900-1730 Mon-Sat. Quiche,
pies, salads, pizza, desserts.

Imperial
Central Avenue. ☎ 271133.
1200-1700 Mon-Sat,
1230-1430 & 1900-2200 Sun.
Pub grub.

Jenny Watt's
41 High St. ☎ 270401.
1130-2300 Mon-Sat,
1230-1430 & 1900-2200 Sun.
A la carte. Stir fry, ribs. £.

Jubilee Café
5 Bridge St. ☎ 454012.
1100-1900 Mon-Sat,
1400-1900 Sun. Fish & chips.

Kentucky Fried Chicken
1 Main St. ☎ 452686.
1100-2400 Sun-Thur, until
0200 Fri & Sat. Chicken,
barbecued ribs, coleslaw,
apple pie.

Co. DOWN — Bangor

King Jade 🍷
22 Dufferin Avenue.
☎ 270662. 1200-1400 &
1700-2330 Mon-Fri,
1200-2330 Sat, 1700-2330
Sun. Cantonese & European.
Chinese banquets. £££.

Knuttel's 🍴
7 Gray's Hill. ☎ 274955.
1200-1430 & 1730-2200
Mon-Sat. Pork in sherry &
cream sauce, duck with port &
redcurrant sauce. £££.

Leisure Centre
Castle Park. ☎ 270271.
0930-2200 Mon-Fri,
0930-1800 Sat, 1400-1800
Sun. Hamburgers, chips,
salads.

Loose Box 🍷
33 Main St. ☎ 467539.
1200-2200 Mon-Sat. Open
sandwiches, grills, sweets.

Mrs Bun's Coffee Shop
108 Abbey St. ☎ 466294.
0900-1730 Mon-Sat. Ulster
fry, stew, toasties, milk shakes.

★ **O'HARA'S ROYAL HOTEL** 🍷

26 Quay St. ☎ 271866.
Last orders 2130. Salads,
quiche. Sunday carvery, ££.
A la carte. Fresh prawns in
lobster sauce. £££.

Oriental Palace 🍷
2a King St. ☎ 452439.
1200-1430 & 1700-2400
Mon-Thur, until 0100
Fri & Sat, 1700-2330 Sun.
Chinese & European. £££.

Penguin Coffee Shop
5 King St. ☎ 271682. 0900-
1700. Pies, toasties, baked
potatoes.

Penny Whistle 🍷
13 High St. ☎ 473943.
1200-2130 Mon-Sat, 1230-
1430 Sun. Pub grub, scampi,
lasagne. £.

Pizza Hut 🍷
115 Main St. ☎ 271272.
1200-2400 Mon-Sat, until
2300 Sun. Pizza, pasta,
desserts. ££.

'Q'
188 Seacliff Rd. ☎ 274674.
1130-1500 & 1700-2130
Wed-Sat, 1230-1430 Sun.
Warm beef salad, pork marsala,
char-grilled swordfish. £££.

Sampan 🍷
2a Market St. ☎ 460470.
1200-1345 & 1700-2330
Mon-Sat, 1700-2300 Sun.
Cantonese. £££

Sands Hotel 🍷 ⌒
10 Seacliff Rd. ☎ 270696.
Last orders 2115, Sun 2000.
Garlic mushrooms, Portavogie
prawns. Set meals, à la carte.
£££.

Co. DOWN *Bangor-Carrowdore*

Silver Sea ♀
37 Queen's Parade.
☎ 452893. 1200-1400 Mon-Sat, 1700-2400 Mon-Thur, until 0100 Fri & Sat, 1700-2400 Sun. Chinese & European. Set lunch. E£.

Simas Indian Cuisine ♀
9 Crosby St. ☎ 271722. 1200-1400 Mon-Sat, 1700-2330 Mon-Sun, 1230-1430 Sun. Indian & European. ££.

Springers
Springhill Shopping Centre.
☎ 469802. 0900-1730 Mon-Sat, until 2100 Thur & Fri. Mince steak pie, quiche.

The Steamer Bar ♀
30 Quay St. ☎ 467699. 1200-1430 & 1730-2130 Mon-Thur, until 2200 Fri & Sat. Seafood, à la carte. E£.

Take Five ♀ ⊙
2a Castle Square. ☎ 272049. 0900-1700 Mon-Sat. Roast ham, stuffed chicken, home-baked cakes. Carvery. E£.

Tedworth Hotel ♀
Lorelei, Princetown Rd.
☎ 463928. Last orders 2115. Garlic prawns, snails, trout. A la carte. E££.

Victor's
6 Dufferin Avenue.
☎ 271088. 1100-2300 Mon-Sat. Fish & chips.

Viscount of Clandeboye ♀
Springhill Shopping Centre.
☎ 271545. 1200-1500 Mon-Sat, 1900-2200 Thur-Sat. Set meals. A la carte.

Warwick ♀
41 Queen's Parade.
☎ 271462. 1130-2300 Mon-Sat, 1230-1430 & 1900-2200 Sun. Pub grub.

★ **WHEATEAR** ⊙
108 Main St. ☎ 467489. 0830-1730 Mon-Sat. Lasagne, chicken special, Irish stew.

Windsor ♀
Quay St. ☎ 473943. 1200-2130 Mon-Sat, 1230-1430 Sun. Jazz Tues. A la carte. E££.

Winston Hotel ♀ ⊙
19 Queen's Parade.
☎ 454575. Last orders 2200, Sun 1900. A la carte. E£.

Wolsey's ♀
24 High St. ☎ 460495. 1200-2200 Mon-Sat, 1230-1430 & 1900-2200 Sun. Lasagne, pizza.

CARROWDORE

Tavern ♀
38 Main St. ☎ (0247) 861222. 1130-2300 Mon-Sat, 1230-1430 & 1900-2200 Sun. Pub grub.

The Villager Restaurant

3 Downpatrick Street, Crossgar. Tel: (0396) 830385

Fully Licensed Restaurant & Bars

*Exclusive High Class Restaurant
Specialising in Fresh Food & Good Service*

High Teas • Full à la carte
comprehensive wine list

★ Open Sundays ★

THE OLD SCHOOLHOUSE
RESTAURANT AND HOSTELRY

Open all year

Mon - Sat Dinner 7.00pm - 10.00pm

Sunday lunch fixed price menu

£12.95

Plus à la carte menu

Good food and a comfortable bed

A rural recipe for

pleasure and contentment

**100 Ballydrain Road,
Comber, Co. Down**

Telephone: (0238) 541182

DEANES on the SQUARE

Licensed Restaurant
HAYDN J.H. DEANE
and
MICHAEL DEANE
Chef
*Dorchester Hotel • Belfast Castle
Nick's • Santé*
Michael Deane Chef of the Year
Salon Culinare NIFEX 1993
ARE DELIGHTED TO INVITE YOU
TO ENJOY
SPLENDID FOOD
with
FINE WINES
in a
UNIQUE ATMOSPHERE
AT THEIR RESTAURANT IN
STATION SQUARE, HELEN'S BAY
(0247) 852841/(0247) 273155
FOR RESERVATIONS
Lunch by arrangement
Tuesday - Saturday Dinner from 7.00pm
Sundays with a difference
Mondays - Cookery Workshop

White Horse Inn ♀
39 Main St. ☎ (0247) 861212.
1230-1430 Mon-Sat, 1730-
2030 Mon-Fri & Sun, until
2230 Sat. Pub grub.

CARRYDUFF
(STD 0232)

★ **IVANHOE** ♀
556 Saintfield Rd. ☎ 812240.
1230-1400 & 1700-2130
Mon-Sat, until 2030 Sun. Set
meals. A la carte. E££.

Little Chef
Town & Country Shopping
Centre. ☎ 812097. 0930-2200
Mon-Sat. Chicken, salads,
sweets.

Old Saint Coffee House
5 Old Saintfield Rd.
☎ 815141. 1000-1800
Mon-Sat. Sandwiches, ice
cream parlour.

Oriental Garden ♀
Town & Country Shopping
Centre. ☎ 812755.
1700-2400 Mon-Sun. Chinese
& European. E££.

Pizza Hut
Town & Country Shopping
Centre. ☎ 815060. 1200-2400
Mon-Sat, 1200-2300 Sun.
Pizzas, garlic bread, salads. £.

Rick's
Carryduff Shopping Centre.
☎ 814558. 0900-1730
Mon-Sat, until 2100 Wed-Fri.
Breakfast, afternoon tea.
Home baking.

Royal Ascot ♀
Hillsborough Rd. ☎ 813477.
1200-2400 Mon-Sat,
1200-0100 Sun. Set meals,
à la carte. E££.

CASTLEWELLAN
(STD 039 67)

Chestnut Inn ♀
28 Lower Square. ☎ 78247.
1200-2100 Mon-Sat,
1200-1400 & 1700-2200 Sun.
Steak, scampi, pub grub. E££.

McElroy's ♀
151 Ballylough Rd. ☎ 78238.
1830-2130 Fri & Sat.
Soup, stew, pub grub.

Maginn Bros ♀
9 Main St. ☎ 78359.
1230-1430 Mon-Sat. Scampi,
chilli, salads.

Oak Grill ♀
45 Main St. ☎ 78616.
1000-0100 Mon-Sun.
Scampi, grills. A la carte. ££.

Rose Bar ♀
7 Upper Square ☎ 71500.
1200-1430 Mon-Sun. Pub
grub.

Co. DOWN — Castlewellan-Comber

Ulster Arms ♿
2 Moneyslane Rd.
☎ (082 064) 724. 1230-1430
& 1730-2200 Mon-Sat. Ulster
fry, open prawn sandwich.

CLOUGH

Clough Inn ♿
28 Main St. ☎ (039 687) 209.
1200-1400 & 1700-2200
Mon-Sat, 1230-1430 & 1900-
2200 Sun. A la carte.

CLOUGHEY

Kirkistown Castle Hotel ♿
206 Main Rd.
☎ (024 77) 72233.
Last orders 2130. A la carte,
high tea, Sunday lunch. E£.

COMBER
(STD 0247)

★ **CASTLE ESPIE**
78 Ballydrain Rd. ☎ 872517.
1030-1700 Mon-Sat, 1400-
1800 Sun. Coffee, home-made
soup, fisherman's pie, scones.

Castle Inn
40 Castle St. ☎ 872359. 1230-
1430 & 1900-2130 Mon-Sat.
Burgers, pies, Irish stew.

Country Fayre ⊙
Castle Arcade. ☎ 873728.
0900-1630 Mon-Sat.
Quiche, salads, pies.

Donnell's
12 The Square. ☎ 878307.
0900-1700 Mon-Thur, until
2100 Fri & Sat. Home baking.
Bistro.

Harry Fraser's
11 Castle St. ☎ 872546.
0830-2230 Tues-Fri, until
1900 Sat. Breakfast, set lunch,
fish & chips.

Kate's
47 Ballyhenry Rd. ☎ 874577.
1000-1700 Mon-Fri, 0930-
1730 Sat, 1230-1730 Sun.
Bistro, set meals. £.

Lisbarnett House ♿
Lisbane. ☎ (0238) 541589.
1200-1400 & 1830-2130
Mon-Fri & Sun. Garlic steak. E£.

McBride's
1 The Square. ☎ 878703.
1200-1430 Mon-Sat. Stuffed
steak, ham & parsley, stuffed
pork sultana.

Mayflower ♿
47 Castle St. ☎ 873254.
1200-1400 & 1700-2400
Mon-Thur, until 2430 Fri,
1200-2430 Sat, 1630-2330
Sun. Chinese & European. E£.

North Down House ♀
Belfast Rd. ☎ 872242.
1200-1400 Mon-Fri,
1900-2230 Mon-Sat. Pub
grub, prawn sandwiches,
baked potatoes.

★ **OLD SCHOOL HOUSE** ♀

100 Ballydrain Rd.
☎ (0238) 541182. 1900-2200
Tues-Sat, 1200-1500 Sun.
A la carte. £££.

Salems Gallery
29 Mill St. ☎ 873624.
1000-1630 Mon-Sat. Salads,
baked potatoes, daily specials.
Beside antiques gallery.

Ulster Arms ♀
3 The Square. ☎ 878703.
1200-1430 Mon-Sat. Pub grub.

CONLIG

Grapevine Restaurant ◠
105 Main St. ☎ (0247)
820219. 0930-1700 Mon-Sat.
Soup, lasagne, pies, salads.

CRANFIELD

Sandpiper
8 Lurganconary Rd.
☎ (069 37) 62384. 1030-1830
Mon-Sun July & Aug, 1400-
1800 Mon-Sun June & Sept.
Set lunch, coffee. Home baking.

CRAWFORDSBURN

Conservatory Restaurant ◠
Crawfordsburn Country Park.
☎ (0247) 852725. 1000-1830
in summer, earlier closing in
winter. Sandwiches, soup, coffee.

★ **OLD INN** ♀

15 Main St. ☎ (0247) 853255.
Last orders 2130, 2000 Sun.
Roast beef, sole, Portavogie
scampi, salmon, sherry trifle.
A la carte, 18th-century
minstrels' gallery. E££.

CROSSGAR
(STD 0396)

Hill House
53 Killyleagh Rd. ☎ 830792.
Steaks, home-made soups.
Pre-booking essential.

Hunter's Moon ♀
2 Downpatrick St.
☎ 831184. 1230-1430 &
1700-2100 Mon-Sat, 1900-
2100 Sun. Sunday lunch, high
tea, grills. £.

Magee's ♀
Downpatrick St. ☎ 830281.
1200-1400 Mon-Sat. Pub grub.

Co. DOWN — Crossgar-Donaghadee

★ ROSEMARY JANE TEA ROOM
20 Downpatrick St.
☎ 831335. 0930-1730 Mon-Sat. Home baking, afternoon tea.

Villager ☒
3 Downpatrick St.
☎ 830385. 1230-1430 Mon-Sun, 1700-2130 Wed-Sun. High tea, Sunday lunch. £. A la carte. £££.

CULTRA
(STD 0232)

★ CULLODEN HOTEL ☒
Craigavad. ☎ 425223.
Last orders 2145, Sun 2030. A la carte. ££££.

Cultra Inn ☒
Culloden Hotel, Craigavad.
☎ 425840. 1230-1415 & 1800-2145 Mon-Sat. Salmon, turkey, steak & kidney pie. Set lunch. A la carte. ££££.

Manor House ☒
Cultra Manor, Ulster Folk & Transport Museum. ☎ 428428. 1100-1700 Mon-Sat, 1400-1800 Sun. Open later in summer. Carvery Sun, snacks.

DONAGHADEE
(STD 0247)

Bow Bells
5 Bow St. ☎ 888612. 1000-1630 Mon-Sat. Home baking.

Bridewell ☒
19 High St. ☎ 882568.
1100-1500 & 1700-2030 Mon-Fri, until 2100 Sat, 1200-2000 Sun. A la carte. Salads, grills.

Captain's Table
22 The Parade. ☎ 882656.
1200-1400 & 1630-2100 Mon-Fri, closed Wed, 1200-2100 Sat & Sun. Fish & chips.

★ COFFEE PLUS
Market House, New St.
☎ 882641. 0930-1630 Mon-Sat. Pies, lasagne.

Copelands Hotel ☒
60 Warren Rd. ☎ 888189.
Last orders 2130. Sunday lunch. A la carte. £££.

Darlings
51 High St. ☎ 883674. 1200-1430 & 1700-1900 Mon-Sat. Omelettes, salads, baked potatoes.

The Deans
52 Northfield St. ☎ 882204.
Evening dinner. Booking essential.

Donaghadee-Downpatrick   Co. DOWN

Dunallan Hotel ♀
27 Shore St. ☎ 883569. Last orders 2030. Steaks, à la carte. E£.

Grace Neill's ♀
33 High St. ☎ 882553. 1130-2300 Mon-Sat. Pub grub, potted herrings. Beer garden at rear. 17th-century bar.

Harbour Inn ♀
36 The Parade. ☎ 883153. 1230-1500 & 1730-2200 Mon-Sun. High tea. A la carte.

Harlequin
5a Shore St. ☎ 883840. 1000-1730 Mon-Sat, 1400-1800 Sun. Tray bakes, sausage rolls, scones.

Moat Inn ♀
102 Moat St. ☎ 883297. 1230-1430 & 1730-2130 Mon-Sat, 1230-1400 & 1900-2100 Sun. Garlic steaks, curry, spaghetti. ££.

Moorings ◎
26 The Parade. ☎ 882239. 0930-1730 Mon-Thur, until 2100 Fri & Sat. Breakfast, set lunch, afternoon tea.

Old Pier Inn ♀
33 Manor St. ☎ 882397. 1230-2200 Mon-Sat, 1230-1430 & 1700-2200 Sun. Set lunch. A la carte. E£.

Tivoli Bar ♀
32 Manor St. ☎ 882961. 1230-1430 & 1630-2100 Mon-Sun. Roast lamb, steak & kidney pie, open sandwiches.

DOWNPATRICK
(STD 0396)

Abbey Grill
38 Market St. ☎ 613039. 0930-1730 Mon-Sat, 0930-1400 Wed. Grills.

Abbey Lodge Hotel ♀
Belfast Rd. ☎ 614511. Last orders 2130. Fresh oysters, trout, kebab, crêpe suzette. A la carte. M£, E££.

Aldo's Coffee Lounge
Downtown Shopping Centre. ☎ 615414. 0900-1730 Mon-Sat, until 1500 Wed. Stew, pastries, coffee.

Bon Appetit ♀
1c English St. ☎ 613364. 1200-1400 Mon-Sat, 1700-2400 Mon-Thur & Sun, 1700-0100 Fri & Sat. Chinese & European. E£.

Brendan's ♀
94 Market St. ☎ 615311. 1200-1430 & 1700-2130 Wed-Sun. Soup, stew, scampi.

Castle Inn ♀
109 Ballynoe Rd. ☎ 612116. 1230-1430 & 1800-2100 Mon-Sat. Basket meals.

Co. DOWN — Downpatrick-Dromara

Countryside Inn & Restaurant ♀
37 Mearne Rd, Saul.
☎ 615750. 1230-1430 Mon-Sun, 1700-2100 Mon-Sat, 1900-2130 Sun. Daily specials. A la carte, high tea.

De Courcy Arms ♀
14 Church St. ☎ 612522. 1200-1430 Mon-Sat, 1800-2000 Wed-Sat. A la carte. E££.

Dick's Cabin ♀
40 Church St. ☎ 612800. 1200-1500 Mon-Fri. Ulster fry, Irish stew.

Golden Dragon
21 Scotch St. ☎ 613364. 1200-1400 & 1700-2400 Mon-Thur, 1700-0100 Fri & Sat, 1700-2400 Sun. Chinese & European.

McMullen's ♀
55 Annacloy Rd. ☎ 831057. 1130-2300 Mon-Sat, 1230-1430 & 1900-2200 Sun. Pub grub.

Oakley Fayre ◌
Market St. ☎ 612500. 0930-1730 Mon-Sat. Quiche, lasagne, salads.

Pepper Pot
38 St Patrick's Avenue.
☎ 615165. 0900-1900 Mon-Sat, 1300-2000 Sun in summer. Set lunch, à la carte.

Portofino
Irish St. ☎ 612275. 1100-0100 Mon-Sat, closed Tues, 1400-0100 Sun. Lasagne, pizza, scampi.

Rea's ♀
78 Market St. ☎ 612017. 1200-1500 Mon-Sat. Fresh seafood. E££.

Russell ♀
7 Church St. ☎ 614170. 1230-1630 Mon-Fri. Soup, salads, savouries.

Slaney Inn ♀
Raholp. ☎ 612093. 1230-1430 & 1800-2100 Wed-Sun. Carvery. A la carte. £.

Tyrella House
Clanmaghery Rd.
☎ (039 685) 422. 2000-2200 Mon-Sat. Set meals. Booking essential. Parties of 6 plus only.

DROMARA
(STD 0238)

O'Reilly's ♀
7 Rathfriland Rd. ☎ 532209. 1130-2200 Tues-Sat, 1230-1430 & 1900-2100 Sun. Lobster, crab, salmon. Set meals. E£££.

DROMORE
(STD 0846)

Bayardo Inn ♘
16 Market Square. ☎ 692208. 1230-1430 Mon-Sun, 1900-2200 Thur-Sat. Grills, salads, pastries.

Castle Bar ♘
8 Castle St. ☎ 692378. 1130-2300 Mon-Sat, 1230-1430 & 1900-2200 Sun. Pub grub.

Red Hill ♘
41 Red Hill Rd. ☎ 692312. 1700-2300 Mon-Sat, 1230-1430 & 1900-2200 Sun. Pub grub.

Wendy's
36 Market Square. ☎ 693149. 0900-1700 Mon-Sat. Ulster fry, shepherd's pie, chicken, baguettes.

Winstaff
45 Banbridge Rd. ☎ 692252. 1900-2200 Mon-Sat. Set meals. Booking essential.

DUNDRUM
(STD 039 675)

Bay Inn ♘
169 Main St. ☎ 209. 1230-1400 & 1700-2200 Mon-Sat, 1230-1400 & 1900-2200 Sun. Snacks. A la carte.

The Bucks Head Inn ♘
77 Main St. ☎ 868/859. 1200-1430 & 1700-2130 Mon-Sat, 1200-1430 & 1700-2000 Sun. Seafood, steaks, vegetarian. High tea.

Marina Bar ♘
59 Main St. ☎ 284. 1130-2200 Mon-Sat, 1230-1430 & 1900-2200 Sun. Pub grub, steak, scampi.

Murlough Tavern ♘
143 Main St. ☎ 211. 1130-2300 Mon-Sun. Set lunch. Open sandwiches, quiche, lasagne, home-made soup.

GILFORD
(STD 0762)

★ **GILBERRY FAYRE** ⌒
92 Banbridge Rd. ☎ 832098. 0900-1630 Mon-Sat. Afternoon tea, quiche, salads, home baking.

Gilford Inn ♘
4 Dunbarton St. ☎ 831801. 1200-1400 Mon-Sun. Pub grub.

Pot Belly ♘
Banbridge Rd, Tullylish. ☎ 831404. 1830-2330 Tues-Sat, 1230-1430 Sun. A la carte. E££.

LA FONTAINE
RESTAURANT

(previously Whinney Knowes)

DONAGHADEE ROAD, GROOMSPORT
Telephone (0247) 883174
Proprietors: Kathleen & Tony Hughes

If you are looking for food that tastes as good as it looks then why not try dining in the intimate atmosphere of LA FONTAINE RESTAURANT

Open daily for LUNCH. 12.30 p.m. - 2.30 p.m.
HIGH TEA: 5-7 p.m. Full A LA CARTE 7 p.m.

Brook Cottage Hotel

58 Bryansford Road,
Newcastle, Co. Down, N.I.
Telephone: Newcastle
22204

Fully licensed. Open to non-residents. Registered grade 'B'

Brook Cottage is situated in spacious gardens at the very foot of the Mournes. After 25 years it retains its charm and atmosphere and is now well known for its food and interesting history.

Food is served in the dining room, bar and newly constructed conservatory and apart from the general clientele, it is very popular with anglers, golfers and mountain climbers.

Welcome to upstairs at

Bellamy's

(licensed restaurant)
& downstairs at

HUDSON'S

(cellar bistro bar)

For a unique dining out experience.
Lunch - high tea - a la carte and bistro (open 7 days a week)

**96-98 Frances Street,
Newtownards
(0247) 813480**

Gilford-Helen's Bay — Co. DOWN

Sarah Moon's ♀
Bridge St. ☎ 831543/831636.
1900-2200 Tues-Sat. Oysters, sherried mushrooms, garlic steak. ££.

GREYABBEY
(STD 024 774)

Boley Hill Farm
10 Cardy Rd. ☎ 252.
1000-2100 Mon-Sun July-Aug. Scones, biscuits, gateaux, home-made ice cream. On a fruit farm.

Hoops
7 Main St. ☎ 541.
0930-1730 Wed, Fri & Sat. Sandwiches, pizza, stew. Craft & antique shop.

Mount Stewart House
Ark Club tea room. ☎ 387. Open same times as National Trust house. Quiche, lasagne.

Poacher's Inn ♀
23 Main St. ☎ 330.
1200-1430 & 1700-2200 Mon-Sun. A la carte, seafood, duck with raspberries, venison. £££.

Wildfowler ♀
1 Main St. ☎ 260.
1200-1500 & 1700-2130 Mon-Sat, until 2200 Sun. High tea, pub grub. A la carte. £££.

GROOMSPORT
(STD 0266)

★ **ADELBODEN LODGE** ♀ ◠

38 Donaghadee Rd.
☎ (0247) 464288.
1700-2330 Tues-Sat. High tea, vegetarian. A la carte. ££.

Brown's ♀
49 Main St. ☎ (0247) 464335.
1200-1430 & 1800-2100 Mon-Sat, 1230-1430 & 1900-2000 Sun. Game, seafood, traditional Irish. £££.

La Fontaine ♀
81 Donaghadee Rd.
☎ (0247) 883174. 1230-1430 & 1700-2200 Mon-Sun. High tea, lunches, à la carte. £££.

★ **THE STABLES** ♀

26 Main St. ☎ (0247) 464229.
1230-1430 & 1700-2130 Mon-Sat, 1200-1400 & 1700-2100 Sun. Lasagne, steak. A la carte. ££.

HELEN'S BAY
(STD 0247)

★ **DEANE'S ON THE SQUARE** ♀

Station Square. ☎ 852841.
1900-2200 Tues-Sat & 1230-1430 Sun. A la carte. £££.

Co. DOWN — Hillsborough-Hilltown

HILLSBOROUGH
(STD 0846)

Carriage Restaurant ♙
Old Coach Rd. ☎ 689624.
1730-2130 Mon-Sun,
1230-1430 Sun. Pheasant,
trout, steak. E££.

Cornmill ♙
19 Lakeland Rd, Annahilt.
☎ (0238) 532818.
1700-2130 Wed-Sat,
1230-1430 & 1700-2030
Sun. A la carte, high tea. E££.

★ **HAMPTON'S COFFEE SHOP**
Harry's Rd. ☎ 682500.
0930-1700 Mon-Sat. Home-baking, cakes, scones.

★ **HILLSIDE** ♙ ⊙
21 Main St. ☎ 682765.
1200-1400 & 1900-2130
Mon-Sat, 1230-1400 & 1900-2045 Sun. Oysters, salmon and sole plait, duck breast in sweet brandy. E££.

Marquis of Downshire ♙
48 Lisburn St. ☎ 682095.
1200-1430 & 2000-2200
Mon-Sat. Pub grub.
Grills, salads.

Plough Inn ♙
The Square. ☎ 682985.
1200-1415 Mon-Sat,
1800-2030 Wed-Sat, 1230-1415 & 1900-2100 Sun.
Home-made soup, pies, seafood, steaks, sweets.

★ **RED FOX** ⊙
6 Main St. ☎ 682586.
1015-1400 & 1445-1700
Tues-Sat. Salads, quiche, sweets, coffee. Home baking.

★ **RITCHIE'S** ♙ ⊙
3 Ballynahinch St. ☎ 683601.
1230-1430 Mon-Sat. Club sandwiches, lasagne, pies.

Traveller's Kitchen
163 Dromore Rd. ☎ 683956.
0745-1900 Mon-Fri, until
1700 Sat. Ulster fry, gammon, fish.

★ **WHITE GABLES HOTEL** ♙ ⊙
14 Dromore Rd. ☎ 682755.
Last orders 2115, 2030 Sun.
Local vegetables, game in season. A la carte. M£, E££.

HILLTOWN

The Downshire Arms ♙
Main St. ☎ (082 06) 38899.
1230-2130 Mon-Sun. Salmon, chicken, steaks. Set meals, à la carte. E££.

Mourne Rambler ♙
22 Main St. ☎ (082 06) 30749.
1800-2300 Mon-Fri, 1130-2300 Sat, 1900-2200 Sun.
Pub grub.

Hilltown-Holywood — Co. DOWN

Shamrock 🍷
Main St. ☎ (082 06) 30045.
1130-2300 Mon-Sat, 1230-1430 & 1900-2200 Sun. Pub grub.

Village Inn 🍷
43 Main St. ☎ (082 06) 38649.
1230-1530 & 1800-2030 Mon-Sat, 1230-1430 & 1900-2200 Sun. A la carte.

HOLYWOOD
(STD 0232)

★ **BAY TREE COFFEE HOUSE** 🌿
Audley Court, 118 High St. ☎ 426414. 1000-1630 Mon-Sat. Cinnamon scones, vegetarian dishes, salmon plait. Restaurant open from 1930 last Fri each month. Booking essential. £££.

Bear Tavern 🍷
62 High St. ☎ 426837.
1230-1430 Mon-Sat, 2000-2400 Fri & Sat. Quiche, pies, burgers.

Bell's
8 Shore St. ☎ (023 17) 3203.
0900-1600 Mon-Fri. Home-made soup, pastries, set lunch. In bakery.

Bokhara 🍷
149 High St. 1700-2300 Mon-Thur & Sun, until 2330 Fri-Sat. Indian. £££.

★ **CARMICHAEL'S** 🍷
Hibernia St. ☎ 424759.
1230-1430 & 1730-2030 Mon-Sat. A la carte. £££.

Claudia's Patisserie 🍶
49B High St. ☎ 427552.
1900-2400 Tues-Sat. Salmon & spinach tart, stuffed pork rolled in smoked ham.

Clipper 🍷
2 Kinnegar Rd. ☎ 425533.
1200-2200 Mon-Sat. Grills.

Empress Oriental International 🍷
49 High St. ☎ 422333.
1200-1400 & 1700-2400 Mon-Sat, 1700-2300 Sun. Chinese & European. ££.

Herbert Gould & Co
Church Rd. ☎ 427916.
0915-1730 Mon-Sat, 1400-1730 Sun (Nov/Dec only). Scones, soup.

★ **IONA** 🍶
27 Church Rd. ☎ 425655.
1830-2400 Mon-Sat. Beef with garlic beans, pork with peppercorns, coffee ice cream with hazelnuts. ££.

Le Restaurant Santé 🍷
30 High St. ☎ 428880.
1230-1430 & 1830-2200 Tues-Fri & Sun, 1830-2200 Sat. Roast tomato soup, duck confit with fried polenta, sorbets, Irish cheeses. ££.

The Smuggler's Table

**Experience
The best in seafood**

Dining times

11am - 5pm Tues

11am - 10.30pm Wed - Sat

Sunday lunch from

12.30pm - 2.30pm

**The Harbour
Killyleagh, Co. Down
Telephone: (0396) 828778**

MARINE TAVERN
Orient Express

OPEN 7 DAYS
5.30 p.m. - 10.00 p.m.
Monday - Saturday

**SUNDAY-
CARVERY & LUNCH**
SUNDAY LUNCH
12.30 - 2.30 p.m.
Sunday, 4.30 p.m. - 9.00 p.m.

BAR SNACKS
12.30 - 2.30 p.m. and
5.30 - 9.00 p.m.

MARINE BAR
'Friends' each Wednesday nite

TELEPHONE
WARRENPOINT: (069 37) 54147

NEWRY & MOURNE

Enjoy

Hill Walking • Horseriding • Golfing

Windsurfing • Fishing • Caravanning

Camping and Exploring our Heritage

in the beautiful South Down,

South Armagh countryside:

For further information contact:
**Tourist Office
Newry & Mourne District Council**
Greenbank, Warrenpoint Road, Newry, Co. Down, Northern Ireland BT34 2QU
Telephone: (0693) 67226

Holywood-Kilkeel **Co. DOWN**

Old Priory Inn ♀
Main St. ☎ 428164.
1200-1430 & 1900-2200
Mon-Sat, until 2100 Sun.
Bistro: pâté, soup, salads. £.
Restaurant: steaks. ££.

Rayanne House ♀
50 Demesne Rd. ☎ 425859.
Pear stuffed with stilton in port
& redcurrant sauce, lamb with
roast peppers & rosemary.
A la carte. Booking essential.

Seaside Tavern ♀
19 Stewart's Place. ☎ 423152.
1200-1430 & 1700-2000
Mon-Fri, 1200-2000 Sat.
Home cooking. A la carte.

Silver City
124 High St. ☎ 428766.
1700-2400 Tues-Sun.
Chinese & European. ££.

Sullivan Coffee Shop
117 High St. ☎ 427467.
0900-1700 Mon-Sat.
Lasagne, pies.

Wilson's
58 High St. ☎ 427419.
0800-1630 Mon-Sat. Snacks,
coffee.

KATESBRIDGE
(STD 082 06)

Angler's Rest ♀
42 Aughnacloy Rd. ☎ 515.
1130-2300 Mon-Sat,
1230-1430 & 1900-2200 Sun.
Pub grub, baked potatoes.

KILKEEL
(STD 069 37)

Archways ♀
23 Newry St. ☎ 64112.
1230-1400 Mon-Sat. Pub
grub.

Captain's Table
24 Newcastle St. ☎ 64555.
1100-1800 Mon-Fri, until
2100 Sat. Fish, chicken, chips.

Coffee Shop
25a Greencastle St.
☎ 64370. 0930-1730
Mon-Sat, open 0830 in
summer. Quiche, pies,
lasagne.

Coffee Shop
Silent Valley. 1130-1830
Mon-Sun in summer. Home
baking.

Cranfield House Hotel ♀
57 Cranfield Rd. ☎ 62327. Last
orders 2045, Sun 2000. Set
lunch, high tea, pub grub. £££.

Fisherman ♀
68 Greencastle St. ☎ 62130.
1200-1430 Tues-Sun, 1730-
2130 Tues-Fri & Sun, 1800-
2230 Sat. Local prawns, clams,
lobster, salmon, turbot, stuffed
mushrooms. £££.

Harbour Café
5 Harbour Rd. ☎ 62207.
1030-1900 Mon-Wed,
1030-2000 Fri & Sat.
Fish, chicken.

Co. DOWN — Kilkeel-Killyleagh

Jacob Hall's
8 Greencastle St. ☎ 64751.
1200-1500 & 1700-2100
Mon-Sat. Starters, grills.

Kilmorey Arms Hotel
Greencastle St. ☎ 62220.
Last orders 2100, Sat 2200.
A la carte. £££.

Mourne Grange
169 Newry Rd. ☎ 62228.
1000-1230 Mon-Sat,
1400-1700 Mon-Sun. Scones,
cakes, coffee. Craft shop.

Old Mill
12 Knockchree Avenue.
☎ 62112. 1000-1830
Mon-Sat, until 2300 in
summer. Barbecued beef,
scampi, seafood platter.

Port Inn
3 The Square. ☎ 62453.
1130-2300 Mon-Sat. Pies,
burgers.

Port O Call
13 Bridge St. ☎ 62621.
0930-1730 Mon-Wed, until
1400 Thur, 1800 Fri, 2030 Sat.
Ulster fry, steaks, chicken.

Riverside Tavern
2 Bridge St. ☎ 64757.
1230-1400 Mon-Sat. Grills.

Silver Herring
4 The Square. ☎ 62491.
1200-1430 Mon-Sat. Pub
grub.

KILLINCHY
(STD 0238)

Balloo House
☎ 541210. 1230-2200
Mon-Sat, 1230-1430 & 1900-
2200 Sun. Grilled salmon. Hot
& cold buffet. A la carte. £££.

Daft Eddy's
Sketrick Island, Whiterock.
☎ 541615. 1230-1430
Mon-Sun, 1900-2130
Tues-Sat. Buffet lunch.
Salmon, steaks. Pub on island
across causeway. ££.

★ **PEPPERCORN COURT**
18 Kilmood Church Rd.
☎ 541472. 1900-2200
Tues-Sat. Mussels, goose,
lamb. ££.

KILLOUGH

Old Inn
36 Castle St. ☎ (0396) 841067.
1200-1430 Mon-Sun.
Ploughman's lunch, fish.

KILLYLEAGH
(STD 0396)

Anchor Inn
16 Catherine St. ☎ 828700.
1130-2300 Mon-Sat,
1230-1430 & 1900-2200
Sun. Pub grub.

★ DUFFERIN ARMS ☗

35 High St. ☎ 828229.
1230-1430 & 1900-2330
Mon-Sat, 1230-1400 Sun.
Steak, fish. A la carte. Live
music.

Siglu
Delamont Country Park.
☎ 821091. 1300-1700 Mon-
Sun Easter & June-Aug.
Weekends only rest of year.
Sandwiches, crepes, home-
made cookies.

Smuggler's Table ☗
2 Bridge St. ☎ 828778.
1100-1700 Tues, until 2230
Wed-Sat, 1230-1430 Sun.
Salmon, lobster, monkfish,
garlic prawns. E££.

KIRCUBBIN
(STD 024 77)

Saltwater Brig ☗
43 Rowreagh Rd. ☎ 38435.
1230-1430 Mon-Sun,
1700-2100 Mon-Sat,
1900-2100 Sun. Bistro menu.
£.

Village Inn ☗
34 Main St. ☎ 38382.
1130-1500 Mon-Sat. Toasties,
pies, grills.

LOUGHBRICKLAND

Road Chef
Dublin Rd. ☎ (076 286) 366.
0800-2000 Mon-Sat, 1230-
2130 Sun. Breakfast, lunch.
Grills, toasties, sweets. E£.

Seven Stars ☗
4 Main St. ☎ (082 06) 26461.
1230-1430 & 1800-2200
Mon-Sat, 1230-1430 & 1900-
2100 Sun. A la carte. Steak,
chicken, pavlova, gateaux. £.

MILLISLE
(STD 0247)

Dorothy's
53 Main St. ☎ 861852.
1130-2100 Mon-Sun in
summer. 1200-1400 & 1700-
2000 Mon-Fri, 1130-2030 Sat,
1400-2000 Sun in winter.
Fish, burgers, ice cream.

First Last ☗
37 Main St. ☎ 862644. 1130-
2300 Mon-Sat, 1230-1430 &
1900-2200 Sun. Roast beef,
pies, burgers.

Kingfisher ☗
26 Main St. ☎ 861304.
1200-1430 Fri-Sun in winter,
1800-2130 Tues-Sun in
summer. Seafood, steak. Set
meals. A la carte. E£.

Windmill Grill
Main St. ☎ 861461.
1000-2400 Mon-Sun. Grills.

Woburn Arms
69 Main St. ☎ 861272.
1200-2000 Mon-Sun.
Pub grub.

MOIRA
(STD 0846)

Ballycanal Manor
2 Glenavy Rd. ☎ 611923.
Traditional cooking, dinner.
Booking essential.

Bon Appetit
87 Main St. ☎ 619718. 1130-
2330 Mon-Wed, until 0030
Thur-Sat, 1700-2300 Sun.
Chicken, sausages.

Chestnut Lodge
6 Chestnuthill Rd.
☎ 611409. 1200-1430
Mon-Sat, 1700-2200
Wed-Sat, 1230-1430 &
1800-2100 Sun. A la carte. E£.

Cork & Cleaver
4 Rawdon Court, Main St.
☎ 611853. 0930-1630 Mon-
Sat, 1900-2130 Fri & Sat.
Steaks, lamb with apple &
cider sauce. A la carte. E£££.

Glenavy Road Restaurant
Glenavy Rd Service
Station, Airport Rd. ☎ 611909.
0830-1930 Mon-Sat, until
2130 Sun. Set lunch. Ulster
fry, chicken, fish.

Halfpenny Gate Inn
Halfpenny Gate Rd.
☎ 621280. 1130-2300
Mon-Sat, 1230-1430 &
1900-2200 Sun. Burgers,
scampi.

Maghaberry Arms
23 Maghaberry Rd.
☎ 611852. 1130-1430 &
1730-2130 Mon-Fri,
1130-1900 Sat. Scampi, pork
chops, salad.

Midnight Haunt
90 Main St. ☎ 611391.
1200-1400 & 1700-2400
Mon-Thur, until 2430 Fri &
Sat, 1500-2300 Sun. Chinese
& European. E£.

Nina's Pizzeria
74 Main St. ☎ 611185.
0900-1800 Mon-Sat. Pizzas,
soups, salads.

★ **NO. 1 GALLERY**
101 Main St. ☎ 619788.
0930-1730 Tues-Sat.
Casseroles, salads, sweet &
savoury pancakes.

Norman Inn
Main St. ☎ 611318.
1230-1430 Mon-Sat,
1800-2000 Wed-Fri. Pub
grub, snacks.

NEWCASTLE
(STD 039 67)

Anchor Bar ♀
9 Bryansford Rd. ☎ 23344.
1200-1430 Mon-Fri,
1200-1800 Sat. Curries,
lasagne.

Arkeen Hotel ♀
59 Central Promenade.
☎ 23473. Last orders 1930.
A la carte. £.

Armours Cove House
26 Ballagh Rd. ☎ 23814.
Dinner. Booking essential.

Avoca Hotel ♀
93 Central Promenade.
☎ 22253. Last orders 2100.
A la carte. £.

Brambles
4 Central Promenade.
☎ 26888. Winter 1000-1800
Fri-Sun. Summer 1000-1800
Mon-Fri, until 2300 Sat & Sun.
Apple pie, Canadian
cheesecake & pancakes.

Brook Cottage Hotel ♀
58 Bryansford Rd. ☎ 22204.
Last orders 2100, Sun 2030.
A la carte. ££.

★ **BURRENDALE HOTEL** ♀
51 Castlewellan Rd.
☎ 22599. Last orders 2100,
Sun 2000. A la carte. £££.

Central Park ♀
121 Central Promenade.
☎ 22487. 1230-1430 & 1900-2100 Mon-Sat, 1800-2100
Sun. Grills, salads, daily
specials.

Cookie Jar
Main St. ☎ 22427.
0900-1730 Mon-Sat.
Home-baked cakes.

Country Fried Chicken
119 Main St. ☎ 23900.
1100-2400 Mon-Fri & Sun,
until 0130 Sat. Chicken,
burgers.

Cup 'n' Saucer
87 Central Promenade.
☎ 22753. 1030-2000
Mon-Sun July-Sept, until 1700
Fri-Sun Easter-June. Open
sandwiches, snacks, sweets,
home baking.

The Cygnet
2 Savoy Lane. ☎ 24758.
Winter 1000-1700 Mon-Sat,
1100-1700 Sun. Summer
1000-1800 Mon-Sat, 1100-1800 Sun. Soup, stew, scones.

Donard Hotel ♀
27 Main St. ☎ 22203. Last
orders 2115. Closed Jan &
Feb. A la carte. ££.

Enniskeen Hotel ♀
98 Bryansford Rd. ☎ 22392.
Last orders 2030. Closed
Dec-Feb. A la carte. £££.

NEWCASTLE
IN THE HEART OF DOWN

FUN FOR ALL THE FAMILY IN THE NORTH'S PREMIER HOLIDAY SPOT

SPORT	SOME PLACES TO VISIT	ADVENTURE FOR CHILDREN	TOP CLASS ENTERTAINMENT
* Golf	* Mourne Mountains	* Tropicana Heated Outdoor Pools Complex	* Live Shows
* Fishing	* Delamont Country Park		* Drama
* Tennis	* Tollymore Forest Park	* Kiddies Club	* Cinema
* Swimming	* Castlewellan Forest Park	* Adventure Playground	* Pub Music
* Horse riding	* Seaforde Butterfly House	* Giant Slide	* Pipe Band Championships
* Windsurfing	* Murlough Nature Reserve	* Pitch and Putt	* Concerts
* Sailing	* Down County Museum	* Boating	* Exhibitions
	* Castleward	* Coco's Indoor Adventure Playground	* Festivals
	* Downpatrick/Ardglass Railway		

For a colour brochure and accommodation booking service contact:

**TOURIST INFORMATION OFFICE, NEWCASTLE CENTRE,
CENTRAL PROMENADE, NEWCASTLE, CO. DOWN.
Tel: (039 67) 22222**

*Enjoy excellent cuisine
in a warm country atmosphere*

*The restaurant is open daily from 7.00 p.m.
Now serving Sunday lunch 12.30 - 2.00 p.m.
Wine bar serves food from 12 noon (Sunday 12.30 p.m.)
Bar meals available every evening until 7.30 p.m.*

Bushmills Bar of the Year 1989

21 Main Street, Hillsborough
Telephone: (0846) 682765

Newcastle — Co. DOWN

Harbour House Inn
4 South Promenade. ☎ 23445.
1200-1500 & 1700-2130
Mon-Sat, 1230-1430 & 1700-
2200 Sun. Chicken curry,
pâté, rainbow trout. £.

Lunch Box Café
133a Main St. ☎ 68284.
1030-1700 Mon-Sun.
Burgers, fish.

McGlennon's Hotel
61 Main St. ☎ 22415. Last
orders 2200. A la carte. ££.

Mario's
65 South Promenade.
☎ 23912. 1830-2200 Tues-Sat,
1230-1430 & 1700-2130 Sun.
Italian. Minestrone, pasta,
zabaglione. A la carte.

Newcastle Centre
Central Promenade. ☎ 22222.
1100-1900 Mon-Sat, 1400-
1900 Sun summer only.
Sausage rolls, sandwiches.

Oaks
62 Main St. ☎ 26400.
1230-1500 Mon-Sat. Chicken,
lasagne, pork dishes.

Pavilion
36 Downs Rd. ☎ 26239.
Restaurant: 1900-2130
Wed-Sat, 1700-2030 Sun.
Salmon, steaks, gateaux. £££.
Pantry: 1000-1800 Mon-Sun.
Sandwiches, scones, lasagne,
plaice, salads.

Percy French
Downs Rd. ☎ 23175.
1230-1430 & 1730-2130
Mon-Sat, 1200-1400 &
1730-2100 Sun. Chicken
chasseur, poached haddock,
ploughman's lunch. A la carte.

Pizza Palazzo
98 Main St. ☎ 26444.
1700-2400 Mon-Thur & Sun,
until 0200 Fri & Sat. Pizzas,
fish, garlic bread.

Shimna Diner
14 Railway St. ☎ 23010. 1000-
1900 Mon-Sun. Kilkeel fish,
steaks, toasted sandwiches.

Slieve Donard Hotel
Downs Rd. ☎ 23681.
Last orders 2130. Booking
essential Sept-Feb. A la carte.
Dogs Head grill bar. £££.

Strand Coffee Shop
3 Main St. ☎ 23924. 0830-
1800 Mon-Sat July & Aug,
0900-1730 Mon-Sat rest of
year. Sandwiches, soup.

Strand Palace
53 Central Promenade.
☎ 23472. 1000-2300
Mon-Sun summer, limited
hours rest of year. Pancakes.
A la carte. Restaurant beside
bakery.

Co. DOWN — Newcastle-Newry

Tollymore Teahouse
Tollymore Forest Park.
☎ 24067. 0900-2030
Mon-Sun Mar-Sept,
1200-1800 Sat & Sun rest of
year. Scampi, chicken, grills.

Top of the Town
1 Main St. ☎ 24328.
1000-0030 Mon-Wed,
1000-0130 Thur-Sun.
Fish, burgers.

Toscano ♀
47 Central Promenade.
☎ 22263. 1100-2200
Mon-Sun, 1900-2130
Mon-Sun Easter-Oct. Ice
cream, snacks, high tea.
A la carte.

Wadsworths
42 Main St. ☎ 22626.
0930-1700 Mon-Sat, closed
Thur in winter. Snacks, lunch.
In department store.

NEWRY
(STD 0693)

Ambassador
81 Hill St. ☎ 65307.
0800-1900 Mon-Wed,
0800-2000 Thur-Sat. Set
meals. A la carte.

Arts Centre
1a Bank Parade. ☎ 61244.
1100-1600 Mon-Fri.
Sandwiches, coffee.

The Boulevard
1 Margaret Square, Hill St.
☎ 66555. 0800-1830 Mon-
Wed & Sat, until 2000 Thur &
Fri. Chicken curry, fish, roast
beef.

Boyd's
Hill St. ☎ 62424.
0900-1700 Mon-Sat. Snacks,
grills, lunch.

★ **BRASS MONKEY** ♀
Trevor Hill. ☎ 63176.
1130-2300 Mon-Sat.
Bar snacks, steaks, chicken.
M£. E££.

Brenda's Kitchen
Island Arcade, Sugar Island.
☎ 67987. 0900-1730
Mon-Sat. Set lunch.

Bridge Bar ♀
53 North St. ☎ 62240.
1200-1500 Mon-Sat. Pub
grub.

Cavern ♀
28 Church St. ☎ 62124.
1300-1400 Mon-Sat. Pub
grub.

Clarke's ♀
73 Kilmorey St. ☎ 63960.
1230-1500 Mon-Sat. Pub grub.

Crown Bar ♀
59 Lower North St. ☎ 62494.
1130-2300 Mon-Sat.
Hamburgers, pies.

Newry — Co. DOWN

Crusty Corner
22 Margaret St. ☎ 67708.
0830-1730 Mon-Sat. Quiche, snacks.

Cupids ⚰
25 Merchants Quay.
☎ 63221. 1230-1500 Mon-Sat.
Grills, pizzas. Set lunch, buffet.

**Dominic's &
 Hill Street Blues** ⚰
8 John Mitchell Place.
☎ 62413. 1230-2230
Mon-Sat. Grills, salad, pizzas.

Donnelly's ⚰
Silverbridge. ☎ 861410.
1130-2300 Mon-Sat,
1800-2400 Tues-Sat,
1230-1430 & 1900-2200 Sun.
Pub grub.

Friar Tuck's
3 Sugar Island. ☎ 69119.
1100-2400 Mon-Sat,
1500-2400 Sun. Burgers.

Glenside House
22a Tullynavall Rd. ☎ 861075.
1200-1430 & 1800-1930
Mon-Sat. Steaks, home baking.

Granville Arms ⚰
Mary St. ☎ 61785.
1200-2200 Mon-Sat,
1230-1430 & 1900-2200
Sun. Set lunch, Irish stew, sandwiches. A la carte. E£.

Hermitage Bar ⚰
1 Canal St. ☎ 64594.
1200-1500 Mon-Fri,
1800-2200 Thur & Fri,
1200-2200 Sat. Grills.

Hillside
1 Rock Rd. ☎ 65484/61430.
1630-1930 Mon-Sat. Set
meals. Booking essential.

Kylemore Café
10 Buttercrane Centre.
☎ 65555. 0900-1730
Mon, Tues & Sat, until 2100
Wed-Fri. Grills, snacks.

Lido
23 Hill St. ☎ 62626.
0930-1730 Mon-Sat, until
1400 Wed. Sandwiches, fried fish.

Lite 'n' Easy ⚰
Tullynavall Rd, Cullyhanna.
☎ 868262. 1230-1430 Sun,
1900-2300 Wed-Mon. Set
meals, pub grub.

Little Italy
Kildare St. ☎ 65111.
1130-2430 Mon-Wed, until
0100 Thur, 0230 Fri & Sat.
Pizzas, burgers.

★ **McLOGAN'S** ⚰

55 Merchant Quay.
☎ 62143. 1230-1500 & 1830-
2215 Mon-Sun. Carvery,
steaks. A la carte. E£.

Mall View
60 Lower Mill St. ☎ 66236.
0900-1800 Mon-Sat. Snacks.

ADELBODEN LODGE COUNTRY HOUSE INN

FULLY LICENSED

Open Tuesday to Saturday for:
Lunches 12-2.30pm, High Tea 5-7pm,
Dinner 7-9pm

Bar snack menu also served
Excellent facilities for wedding receptions,
conferences and functions

Bangor 464288   Fax: 0247 270053

38 Donaghadee Road, Groomsport,
Co. Down BT19 2LH

 # The Bucks Head Inn

77 MAIN STREET : DUNDRUM

Enjoy a friendly drink in a relaxing atmosphere and dine in convivial surroundings choosing from an extensive menu which includes Vegetarian and Seafood Dishes, Steaks etc.

Lunches and snacks: 12.00 noon - 2.30 pm Mon to Sat.
Evening meals: 6.00 pm - 9.30 pm Mon to Sat.
Sunday lunch: 12.00 noon - 2.30 pm.
High teas: until 7 pm Mon to Sat
Sundays until 8pm.

**We can also cater for small weddings,
cocktail parties and christening parties etc.
(up to 50 persons)**

Please call for reservations
DUNDRUM (039 675) 868 or 859

Newry — Co. DOWN

Mister B's
8 Water St. ☎ 62193.
1200-1500 & 1800-2130
Mon-Sat. Pub grub.

Mourne Country Hotel
52 Belfast Rd. ☎ 67922.
Last orders 2115. Carvery.
A la carte. M£, E£££.

Murtaghs
25 Bridge St. ☎ 62558.
1230-1430 Mon-Sat. Baked
potatoes, toasties, grills.

Newry Golf Inn
11 Forkhill Rd. ☎ 63871.
1230-1400 & 1700-2100
Mon-Fri, 1130-2300 Sat.
A la carte. E£.

Orchard Bar
114 Rathfriland Rd. ☎ 64911.
1200-1400 & 1800-2100
Mon-Sat. Pub grub.

Red Baron
58 Mill St. ☎ (0693) 61785.
1130-1600 Mon-Sat, bar
snacks to 2330. Soup, fish,
grills.

Riverside
3 Kildare St. ☎ 2170.
1200-1400 Mon-Sat,
1700-2330 Mon-Thur,
1700-2430 Fri & Sat,
until 2315 Sun. Cantonese
& Peking.

Rose Garden
3 Sugar Island. ☎ 68702.
1200-1400 Mon-Fri,
1700-2330 Mon-Thur, until
2430 Fri & Sat, 1700-2315
Sun. Chinese & European. E£.

Satellite
13 Kilmorey St. ☎ 62657.
1200-2330 Mon-Sat,
1700-2430 Sun. Fish, chicken,
pies.

Shakespeare
48 Monaghan St. ☎ 60006.
1130-2300 Mon-Sat. Pub
grub.

Sheepbridge Inn
143 Belfast Rd. ☎ 60000.
1800-2200 Wed-Sat,
1230-1430 & 1800-2200 Sun.
High tea, fish, steaks, pub grub.

Shelbourne
69 Hill St. ☎ 62006.
0900-1730 Mon-Sat, closed
Wed. Soup, stews, pies.

Snaub's Coffee Shop
15 Monaghan St. ☎ 65381.
0930-1730 Mon-Sat. Home
cooking, salads. Hot & cold
buffet. A la carte.

Speakeasy
5 Cornmarket. ☎ 68614.
1130-2230 Mon-Sat.
Grills, baked potatoes, sweets.

Sports Centre
61 Patrick St. ☎ 67322.
0900-2200 Mon-Fri. Snacks.

Co. DOWN — Newry-Newtownards

Tall Man ♷
2 Water St. ☎ 68654.
1130-2030 Mon-Sat. Pub grub.

Terrace
6 Marcus St. ☎ 65396.
0900-1730 Mon-Sat.
Breakfast, lunch.

Texas Pantry
Merchant Quay. 1000-1900 Mon-Tues, until 2000 Wed-Fri. Limited hours at weekend. Scones, pizzas, baked potatoes.

Three Steps ♷
75 Finegan's Rd, Drumintee.
☎ 888543. 1130-2300 Mon-Sat, 1230-1430 & 1900-2200 Sun. Pub grub.

Timoney's
6 Canal St. ☎ 67189.
0900-2100 Mon-Sun. Ice cream parlour.

Yewtree ♷
1 Trevor Hill. ☎ 64888.
1230-1800 & 1800-2200 Mon-Sat. Burgers, lasagne, plaice. £

NEWTOWNARDS
(STD 0247)

Ballyharry Roadhouse ♷
151 Donaghadee Rd.
☎ 820808. 1200-2300 Mon-Sat, 1230-1430 & 1700-2200 Sun. Ribs, garlic bread, garlic shrimps, mushroom & pepper stroganoff. E££.

Beechill Farm
10 Loughries Rd. ☎ 818404.
Home grown produce, dinner. Booking essential.

Bellamy's ♷
96 Frances St. ☎ 813480.
1200-1430 Mon-Sun, 1730-2200 Tues-Sun. Seafood, lamb. E£.

Cafolla
15 Conway Square. ☎ 812185.
0800-1730 Mon-Sun. Fish & chips, ice cream parlour.

Castle Garden ♷
90 Upper Greenwell St.
☎ 818577. 1200-1500 Tues-Thur, until 1900 Fri & Sat. Basket meals.

Castle Palace ♷
17 Castle St. ☎ 813903.
1200-1400 & 1700-2400 Mon-Sat, 1630-2300 Sun.
Chinese & European. E££.

Eastern Tandoori ♷
16 Castle St. ☎ 819541.
1200-1400 & 1700-2330 Mon-Sat, 1700-2230 Sun.
Indian & European. E£££.

Newtownards   Co. DOWN

Edit Smyth's Café
134 Frances St. ☎ 810655.
1200-1400 & 1600-2400
Mon-Sat. Fish & chips, scampi.

Gallery ⊘
5 South St. 0900-1700
Mon-Sat. Set lunch, grills, salads.

Ganges ♀
69 Court St. ☎ 811426.
1200-1400 & 1730-2330
Mon-Thur, until 2400 Fri & Sat, 2300 Sun. Indian. E££.

★ **GASLAMP** ♀
47 Court St. ☎ 811225.
1830-2200 Tues-Sat, 1230-1500 Sun. Rack of lamb with red wine, trout in lime & walnut sauce, langoustine in cream & chablis. E£££.

Guiseppe's Ristorante ♀ ⊘
31a Frances St. ☎ 812244.
1700-2300 Mon-Sat. Italian. E£.

Huntsman ♀
10 Castle St. ☎ 813073.
1200-1430 Mon-Sat,
1800-2200 Sun. Pub grub, curry, plaice.

Ivy Bar ♀
14 Castle St. ☎ 813063.
1230-1500 & 1900-2100
Mon-Sat. Grills, savouries.

Jack Murphy's ♀
Ards Shopping Centre.
☎ 817211. 1200-1430
Mon-Sat. Pub grub.

Jolly Judge ♀
54 Regent St. ☎ 819895.
1200-1415 Mon-Sun,
1700-2130 Mon-Sat. High tea, à la carte.

Knightsbridge Inn ♀
Scrabo Rd. ☎ 813221.
1200-2230 Mon-Sat,
1230-1500 & 1900-2200 Sun.
A la carte. Sunday carvery. ££.

★ **KNOTT'S COFFEE SHOP** ⊘
45 High St. ☎ 819098.
0900-1700 Mon-Sat, closed Thur. Coffee, quiche, salads, pastries, home baking.

Menary's Café
99 East St. ☎ 812870.
1200-1400 & 1600-2400
Mon-Thur, 1600-0100 Fri & Sat, 1230-2300 Sun. Fish & chips.

★ **MING COURT** ♀
63 Court St. ☎ 815073.
1200-1400 & 1730-2330
Mon-Fri, 1200-2400 Sat,
1230-2300 Sun. Chinese. E££.

Minstrels
7 Lower Mary St. ☎ 811760.
0900-1645 Mon-Sat. Set lunch, baked potatoes, open sandwiches.

Mount Stewart Ark Tea Rooms
Mountstewart. ☎ (024 774) 387. 1200-2000 Tues-Sun in summer. Coffee, cakes.

Co. DOWN — Newtownards

Old Cross Inn ♀ ⊙
3 Castle Place. ☎ 811320.
1200-1500 Mon-Wed, until
1900 Thur-Sat. Steaks, fish.
A la carte. E££.

Peach Tree ♀
4 North St. ☎ 822185.
1130-2200 Mon-Sat.
Ulster fry, lasagne, burgers. £.

Pied Piper
11 High St. ☎ 818140.
0930-1730 Mon-Sat. Pies,
lasagne.

Regent Court ♀
54 Regent St. ☎ 819895.
1130-2300 Mon-Sat,
1230-1430 & 1900-2200 Sun.
Bar lunches, high tea. A la
carte.

★ **ROMA'S** ♀
4 Regent St. ☎ 812841. 1200-
1430 & 1730-2130 Mon-Sun.
A la carte. Sunday lunch. E££.

Scrabo Café
187 Mill St. ☎ 810963.
1230-1430 & 2000-2300
Mon-Sat. Fish & chips.

Scrabo Inn ♀
3 West St. ☎ 811431.
1230-1430 & 2000-2300
Mon-Sat. Pub grub.

Smyth's
31 West St. ☎ 812732.
1130-2300 Mon-Thur,
1130-0030 Fri & Sat. Fish &
chips, Ulster fry, chicken.

Steeplechase Inn ♀
48 South St. ☎ 812019.
1130-1430 Mon-Sat,
1730-2200 Fri & Sat. Set
lunch, high tea. £.

Strangford Arms Hotel ♀
92 Church St. ☎ 814141.
Last orders 2130, Sun 2030.
Oysters. Set lunch, Sunday
carvery. A la carte. E£££.

T Bone Kelly's ♀ ⊙
South St. ☎ 820960.
1700-2230 Mon-Sun. Steaks,
chicken. £.

Take Five ⊙
25 High St. ☎ 819591.
0815-1700 Mon-Sat. Full
lunch menu, home-cooked
hams, chocolate & mandarin
gateau.

Temptations ⊙
31b Frances St. ☎ 882565.
0930-1700 Mon-Sat. Baked
potatoes, seafood vol-au-vents,
home-made sweets.

Toby Jug ♀
9 High St. ☎ 815041.
1200-1430 Mon-Sat, 1900-
2200 Thur-Sat. Soup,
sandwiches, grills.

Tower Court
8 Court St. ☎ 815332.
0900-1730 Mon-Sat,
1200-1800 Sun. Ulster fry,
set lunch.

Newtownards-Rathfriland — Co. DOWN

Tudor Tavern ⌛
6 Georges St. ☎ 815453.
1130-2300 Mon-Sat,
1230-1430 & 1900-2200
Sun. Pub grub.

Wellworths
Ards Shopping Centre.
☎ 815577. 0900-1730
Mon-Sat, until 2100 Wed-Fri.
Ulster fry, liver & onion,
stuffed sausage & bacon, fish.
Restaurant in chainstore.

The Willows
101b Victoria Avenue.
☎ 812116. 0900-1700 Tues-
Thur Sept-June. Lasagne, pies.
College training restaurant.

PORTAFERRY
(STD 024 77)

Cleary's Bar ⌛
26 High St. ☎ 28215.
1130-2300 Mon-Sat. Pub
grub.

Coach Inn ⌛
1 Ann St. ☎ 28409.
1130-2300 Mon-Sat,
1230-1430 & 1900-2200 Sun.
Sausage rolls, hamburgers.

Coffee Pot
3 The Square. ☎ 28971. 0945-
1700 Mon-Sat, later opening
in summer. Ulster fry, home-
baked pastries, teas.

Elaine's
22 Church St. ☎ 28915.
1000-1800 Mon-Sun. Lunch.
A la carte.

Exploris
Rope Walk, Castle St.
☎ 28062. 1200-1700
Mon-Sun in summer,
1200-1700 at weekends.
Snacks.

Ferry Grill
3 High St. ☎ 28448.
1200-2400 Mon-Sat,
1700-2230 Sun in summer,
limited hours in winter. Fish
& chips.

★ **PORTAFERRY HOTEL** ⌛
10 The Strand. ☎ 28231.
Last orders 2100, 2030 Sun.
Bar lunches. Stuffed mussels,
fried oysters, turbot. A la carte.
£££.

Scotsman ⌛
156 Shore Rd. ☎ 28024.
1730-2130 Mon-Sun in
summer, Wed-Sun in winter.
High tea, à la carte.

RATHFRILAND
(STD 082 06)

Harp & Crown ⌛
The Square. ☎ 30369.
1130-2300 Mon-Sat. Soups,
pies, burgers.

Home Cooking
19 Downpatrick St.
☎ 30530. 0930-1730
Mon-Wed, until 1400 Thur,
2200 Fri & Sat. Lunch,
afternoon tea, snacks.

4 NORTH STREET, NEWTOWNARDS
Telephone: (0247) 822185

Serving delicious food
from 11.30 a.m. - 10 p.m.
VERY GOOD PRICES. WE'LL SEE YOU THERE

DAFT EDDY'S LTD
SKETRICK ISLAND, KILLINCHY
Unique island setting

Hot & cold buffet Mon-Sat 12.30 pm - 2.30 pm
A la carte Tues-Sat 7.00 pm - 9.30 pm
Special Sunday lunch 12.30 pm - 2.00 pm

Tel: Killinchy (0238) 541615

The Half Way House
(Fully Licensed)

*For an enjoyable meal in a quiet
relaxing atmosphere*

OPEN: Mon.-Sat. 11.30 a.m.-2.30 p.m. and 6.00 p.m.-9.30 p.m.

Half Way Road, Banbridge

Tel: Dromore (0846) 692351 for reservations

Rathfriland-Rostrevor — Co. DOWN

Maple Leaf Café
4 John St. ☎ 30788.
1130-2300 Tues-Sat. Fish,
chicken, scones, pastries.

Monterey ♀
10 Downpatrick St. ☎ 30286.
1230-1430 Mon-Sat. Pies,
burgers.

Mourne Sauna
37 Downpatrick St.
☎ 30808. 0900-2100 Mon-Fri.
0900-2400 Sat. Salads, coffee.
In health club.

Old George ♀
Caddell's Lane. ☎ 30836.
1230-1900 Mon-Sat. Set
lunch. A la carte. £.

Pat's Bar ♀ ⊙
Lenish. ☎ 30439. 1900-2130
Tues-Fri, 1800-2100 Sat,
1700-2130 Sun. A la carte. E£.

Rafferty's Bar ♀
1 Caddell's Lane. ☎ 30575.
1700-2300 Mon-Thur, 1130-
2300 Fri & Sat, 1900-2200
Sun. Pub grub.

Ye Olde Bar ♀
40 Downpatrick St. ☎ 30395.
1130-2300 Mon-Sat, 1230-
1430 & 1900-2200 Sun. Pub
grub.

ROSTREVOR
(STD 069 37)

Cloughmor Inn ♀
2 Bridge St. ☎ 38007. 1230-
1430 Mon-Sat. Pub grub.

Corner House ♀
1 Bridge St. ☎ 382236.
1200-1430 & 1830-2200
Mon-Sun. Pub grub.

Kilbroney Park
☎ 38026. May-Oct 1100-1730
Mon-Fri, until 1900 Sat & Sun.
Earlier closing rest of year.
Café in forest park.

Patrick K ♀
The Square. ☎ 38969. 1230-
1530 & 1900-2130 Tues-Sun.
Buffet lunch. Grilled duck &
walnut sausage, monkfish
gratinée with fresh prawns.
E£££.

Top of the Town
31 Church St. ☎ 38276. 1130-
2200 Mon-Sat, 1230-1400 &
1900-2030 Sun. Steak, scampi.

Ye Olde Corner House ♀
The Square. ☎ 38236.
1900-2200 Mon-Sun. Salads,
baked potatoes.

Co. DOWN — Saintfield-Strangford

SAINTFIELD
(STD 0238)

★ BARN ♀

120 Monlough Rd. ☎ 510396. 1900-2200 Tues-Sat. Salmon & prawn mousse, roast duck in orange & vermouth sauce, honey & walnut flan. £££.

Caroline's Parlour
66 Main St. ☎ 511108. 0900-1700 Mon-Sat. Set lunch, afternoon tea.

Rosy Bar ♀
14 Main St. ☎ 510388. 1900-2300 Mon-Thur, 1130-2300 Fri & Sat, 1900-2200 Sun. Pub grub.

Rowallane Gardens
Rowallane. ☎ 51013. May-Aug 1400-1800 Mon-Sun, closed Fri. April & Sept 1400-1800 Sat & Sun. Cream teas. Edwardian tea parlour.

Rowallane Inn ♀
Belfast Rd. ☎ 510466. 1130-1400 & 1800-2200 Mon-Sat, 1730-2100 Sun. Pub grub. A la carte. E£.

White Horse Inn ♀
49 Main St. ☎ 510417. 1130-2230 Mon-Sat. Garlic steaks, home-baked gammon.

SEAFORDE
(STD 039 687)

Seaforde Butterfly House
☎ 225. Summer & Easter 1200-1700 Mon-Sun, weekends only May, Sept & Oct. Afternoon tea, snacks.

Seaforde Inn ♀
24 Main St. ☎ 232. 1230-1730 & 1900-2145 Mon-Sat. Cold buffet, garnished steaks. A la carte. ££.

STRANGFORD
(STD 0396)

Castleward Tea Rooms
Strangford. ☎ 881204. Open during Castle Ward House viewing hours (National Trust). Lunch, scones, cakes.

Cuan Bar & Restaurant ♀ ⌂
6 The Square. ☎ 881222. 1200-1430 & 1730-2130 Mon-Sun. Hot & cold buffet lunch, daily specials. E£.

★ LOBSTER POT ♀
9 The Square. ☎ 881288. 1230-2130 Mon-Sat, 1230-1430 & 1800-2100 Sun. Lobster, clams, fresh salmon. ££.

TEMPLE

Laurel House ♣
99 Carryduff Rd. ☎ (0846) 638422. 1230-1430 & 1730-2000 Mon-Sun. Lunches & high tea. £.

WARINGSTOWN
(STD 0762)

★ THE GRANGE ♌
Mill Hill, Main St. ☎ 881989.
1930-2230 Tues-Sat,
1230-1430 Tues-Fri & Sun.
Baked salmon, whiskey steak,
chocolate mousse. A la carte.
Booking essential. £££.

Grange Restaurant ♌
☎ 881232. 1230-1430
Mon-Sat. Pub grub.

Joy's Kitchen
51 Main St. ☎ 882557.
1100-2200 Mon-Sat. Chicken,
fish, ice cream.

Planters Tavern ♌
4 Banbridge Rd. ☎ 881510.
1200-1430 Mon-Sun,
1730-2030 Thur-Sat,
1900-2100 Sun. Burgers,
curry, salads, scampi.

The Village Inn ♌
51 Main St. ☎ 881495.
1200-1400 Mon-Sat. Pub
grub.

WARRENPOINT
(STD 069 37)

★ AYLESFORTE HOUSE ♌
44 Newry Rd. ☎ 72255.
1230-1430 & 1800-2200
Mon-Sat, 1730-2030 Sun.
Carvery. A la carte. £££.

Balmoral ♌
13 Seaview. ☎ 54093.
1230-1430 & 1700-2100
Mon-Sat, 1230-1430 Sun.
Pub grub, pies.

Bennett's ♌
21 Church St. ☎ 52314.
1200-1430 & 1700-2130
Mon-Sun. Seafood, steaks.

Carlingford Bay Hotel
Osborne Promenade.
☎ 73521. Last orders 2130. £.

Central Café
32 Church St. ☎ 72693.
0930-1800 Mon-Sat,
0930-1400 Wed. Set lunch,
sweets.

Coffee House
40 Church St. ☎ 72718.
0930-1800 Mon-Sat,
1430-1800 Sun. Closed Wed.
Coffee, cakes.

The Crown ♌
7 The Square. ☎ 52917.
1200-1500 & 1700-2100
Mon-Sun. Steaks, afternoon
tea. A la carte. ££.

The Diplomat ♌
6 Seaview. ☎ 53629.
1215-1415 & 1715-2130
Mon-Sun. A la carte, pub grub.

Donmir Inn ♌
The Square. ☎ 52001. 1230-
1500 & 1730-2200 Mon-Sat,
1200-1500 & 1730-2200 Sun.
Bar lunch. A la carte, set
menu.

Co. DOWN — Warrenpoint

Duke of Mourne
7 Duke St. ☎ 73149.
1700-2300 Tues-Thur,
1700-2200 Sun. Grills, daily specials.

Mac's Bar
1 Marine Parade. ☎ 72082.
1200-1500 & 1700-2130
Mon-Sat, 1230-1430 &
1900-2200 Sun. Pub grub.

Marine Tavern
4 Marine Parade. ☎ 54147.
1800-2200 Mon-Sun. Set meals, à la carte, high tea. £££.

Ship Lounge
14 The Square. ☎ 72685.
1230-1430 Mon-Sat. Pub grub.

Silvana
29 Church St. ☎ 72714.
1000-2200 Mon-Sun. Grills, salads. A la carte.

Ulster Bar
The Square. ☎ 72892. 1200-2200 Mon-Sat, 1230-1430 & 1730-2100 Sun. A la carte.

The Halfway House

138 Glassdrumman Road
Annalong, Co. Down
Tel: (039 67) 68224

Bar Snacks - daily
Lunches - 12.30 p.m. to 2.30 p.m.
High Tea - 7.00 p.m. to 9.00 p.m.
Sunday Lunch - 12.30 p.m. - 2.30pm
Special Evening Meal
Fri-Sat-Sun - 7.00 p.m. to 9.00 p.m.

Located in the heart of the Mournes, this 18th-century pub & restaurant offers a a wide range of ales and a selection of fine wines, beers & spirits. The front bar is known for its traditional music. In the restaurant we serve excellent home cooked meals with fresh vegetables and a selection of fresh fish. Come along and enjoy anything from a bar snack to full à la carte.

Four Roads Inn

Friendly atmosphere
Situated 1 mile approx from Tyrella beach

★ **Open all day for pub grub** ★

Tel: (039 685) 267

15 Carricknab Road, Ballykinler

COUNTY FERMANAGH

BALLINAMALLARD
(STD 036 581)

Encore Steak House ♆
Main St. ☎ 606. 1730-2200 Tues-Sun. Open bank hols, closed Mon Oct-Easter. Steak, Italian beef, duck, trout. E££.

BELCOO
(STD 036 586)

Border Diner
11 Main St. ☎ 464. 0900-0100 Mon-Sat, 1400-2400 Sun. Grills.

Leo's ♆
Main St. ☎ 228. 1930-2200 Thur-Sat. Pub grub.

BELLANALECK

The Moorings ♆
☎ (036 582) 328. 0930-2130 Mon-Sun. Lunch, snacks, à la carte, children's menu. £.

★ **THE SHEELIN** ♆
☎ (036 582) 232. 1000-1800 Mon & Tues, until 2130 Wed-Sat summer, 1000-1800 Mon-Sat winter. Set dinner Sat. Booking essential. Gourmet. E£££.

BELLEEK
(STD 036 56)

Belleek Pottery Tea Rooms
☎ 58501. 0930-1800 Mon-Sat, 1400-1800 Sun. Lasagne, quiche, baked potatoes.

Carlton Inn ♆
Main St. ☎ 58282. 1230-2200 Mon-Sun. Set lunch. A la carte. Irish stew, local trout, salmon. £.

Cleary's Corner Bar ♆
5 Main St. ☎ 58403. 1200-2200 Mon-Sat. Pub grub.

Fiddlestone Café
Castle Caldwell Forest Park. ☎ 58236. 1000-1900 Mon-Sun Easter-Sept. Quiche, vol-au-vents, salads. Craft shop.

Rooney's Bar ♆
Main St. ☎ 58279. 1200-1500 Mon-Sat. Pub grub.

BROOKEBOROUGH
(STD 036 553)

Castle Hill Bar ♆
58 Main St. ☎ 424. 1200-2200 Mon-Sat, 1230-1400 & 1900-2200 Sun. Pub grub.

Co. FERMANAGH — Brookeborough-Enniskillen

Forest Inn ♀
Main St. ☎ 636. 1200-1430
& 1900-2200 Mon-Sat,
1230-1430 Sun. Pub grub.

DERRYGONNELLY
(STD 036 564)

Bond Store ♀
Main St. ☎ 254. 1230-1430 &
1900-2200 Mon-Sun. Pub
grub.

Cozy Bar ♀
Main St. ☎ 636. 1130-2300
Mon-Sat, 1900-2200 Sun.
Pub grub.

Drumary Farm
Glenasheever Rd. ☎ 420.
0800-2000 Mon-Sun.
Breakfast, scones. Dinner -
booking essential. E£.

Linett Inn ♀
Boho. ☎ (036 589) 218.
1130-2330 Mon-Sat. Snacks,
burgers, pies.

McGovern's ♀
66 Main St. ☎ 212.
1230-1430 & 1800-2300
Mon-Sun. Pub grub.

DERRYLIN
(STD 036 57)

Blake's ♀
Main St. ☎ 48203. 1230-1430
& 1830-2130 Mon-Sat.
Burgers, scampi.

Knockninny Restaurant
Corraclare. ☎ 48339.
0930-2200 Mon-Sun. Home
cooking, lunches, à la carte.
E££.

Mountview Inn ♀
☎ 48226. Last orders 2100. Set
meals. A la carte. M£. E££.

EDERNEY

Gallen's Café
Market St. ☎ (036 56) 31506.
1230-2400 Mon-Sat,
1230-2200 Sun, closed
Wed. Fries, burgers, fish.

ENNISKILLEN
(STD 0365)

Ardhowen Theatre ⊗
Dublin Rd. ☎ 325254.
1100-1600 Mon-Sat.
Coffee, lunches, salads.

Barbizon
5 East Bridge St. ☎ 324456.
0800-1800 Mon-Sat. Home
baking.

Blake's of the Hollow ♀
6 Church St. ☎ 322143.
1130-2300 Mon-Sat.
Sandwiches, soup in Victorian
pub. Live music.

Bush ♀
26 Townhall St. ☎ 325210.
1200-1500 Mon-Sat.
Pub grub.

Enniskillen — Co. FERMANAGH

Concorde
Tempo Rd. ☎ 322955.
1000-2400 Mon-Sat, 0900-2230 Sun. A la carte. Set lunch. £££.

County Bar
14 Forthill St. ☎ 327484.
1130-2300 Mon-Sat, 1200-1400 & 1900-2200 Sun. Toasted sandwiches, hamburgers.

Crow's Nest
12 High St. ☎ 325252.
1130-2100 Mon-Sat, 1230-1430 Sun. A la carte. £.

Devenish Bar
24 Darling St. ☎ 325350.
1130-2300 Mon-Sat. Toasted sandwiches, hamburgers, salads.

Fort Lodge Hotel
72 Forthill St. ☎ 323275.
Last orders 2100 Mon-Wed, until 2200 Thur-Sun.
A la carte. £££.

★ **FRANCO'S**
Queen Elizabeth Rd.
☎ 324424. 1200-2330 Mon-Sat, 1700-2200 Sun. Pasta, pizza, kebabs. Italian. ££.

Golden Arrow
23 Townhall St. ☎ 322259.
1000-1800 Mon-Sat, closed Wed. Fish & chips, snacks.

Harp & Crown
33 Darling St. ☎ 322059.
1200-1430 Mon-Sat.
Irish stew, pub grub.

Johnston's
6 Townhall St. ☎ 322277.
0900-1730 Mon-Sat. Sandwiches, lasagne, home-made pastries.

Killyhevlin Hotel
Dublin Rd. ☎ 323481.
Last orders 2100, Sun 2000.
A la carte. £££.

Lakeland Forum
Broad Meadow. ☎ 325534.
Same hours as sports centre. Health food bar, main meals.

★ **LE BISTRO**
Erneside Centre. ☎ 326954.
0900-1730 Mon-Sat, until 2100 Thur & Fri. Breakfast, coffee, grills.

Leslie's
10 Church St. ☎ 324902.
0830-1700 Mon-Sat. Coffee, savouries, cakes.

Lough Erne House
St Catherines, Blaney.
☎ (036 564) 216. 1200-2200 Mon-Sun. Snacks, afternoon tea. Home cooking.

McCartney's Inn
17 Belmore St. ☎ 320122.
1230-1430 & 1900-0100 Mon-Sat. Home-made broth, Irish stew. Dinner. Booking essential.

**Welcome to
Saddlers Restaurant
Bars and Lounge • Off Sales**
66 BELMORE ST., ENNISKILLEN,
CO. FERMANAGH

Relax and enjoy a refreshing drink in our
traditional bar or lounge

'The Horseshoe', 'Saddlers' and 'The Coachman'
are centrally located and ideal for any occasion

Savour the freshly prepared food in Enniskillen's
Award-winning Restaurant

Light Meals and Full Children's Menu available
Full à la Carte, Lunch and Bar Grill Menus

OPEN 7 DAYS A WEEK • LAST FOOD ORDERS 10.45 P.M.

**Telephone (0365) 326223
Live entertainment each weekend**

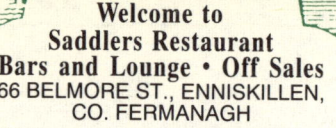

FRANCO'S !

A warren of nooks and crannies
serving authentic Mediterranean
food, warm and atmospheric.
Regular live music sessions - Jazz,
Traditional, etc.
Mentioned in Bridgestone Guide,
Routiers, Daily Telegraph,
The Independent and other local and national press.
Fresh fish, shell fish including oysters,
mussels and lobster from west
coast of Ireland daily.

**Queen Elizabeth Road, Enniskillen,
Co. Fermanagh. Tel: (0365) 324424**

Enniskillen   Co. FERMANAGH

Manor House Hotel
Killadeas. ☎ Irvinestown
(036 56) 21561. Last orders
2200. M£, E£.

Melvin Bar
Townhall St. ☎ 327462.
1200-1800 Mon-Sat.
Salad, toasties. Bar lunches.

★ **MELVIN HOUSE**
Townhall St. ☎ 322040.
0930-1800 Mon-Thur, until
2130 Fri, 2200 Sat. Coffee, set
lunch, teas. A la carte. E££.

Oscar's
29 Belmore St. ☎ 327037.
1100-2300 Tues-Sat, until
1700 Mon, 1800-2230 Sun.
Curries, baked potatoes,
seafood. £.

Pat's Bar
Townhall St. ☎ 327462.
1200-1500 & 1900-2200
Mon-Sun. Salads, grills. Live
music Sun pm.

Peppercorn
15 Townhall St. ☎ 324834.
0930-1730 Mon-Sat. Fish,
chicken, lasagne.

Railway Hotel
34 Forthill St. ☎ 322084.
Last orders 2100. A la carte.
E£.

Rebecca's
Buttermarket, Down St.
☎ 324499. 0930-1730
Mon-Sat. Sandwiches, salads,
pastries.

Round 'O' Tea Room
Brooke Park. ☎ 322882.
0900-1900 Mon, Wed, Fri &
Sat, until 2200 Tues, Thur &
Sun. Pancakes, sandwiches,
pastries.

Saddler's Restaurant
66 Belmore St. ☎ 326223.
1200-1430 & 1730-2300
Mon-Sun. Pub grub. Sunday
lunch. A la carte. E£.

Silver Lough
64 Belmore St. ☎ 325243.
1200-1400 Mon-Sat,
1700-2400 Mon-Sun.
Chinese & European. E£.

Silver Swallow
Drumawill, Sligo Rd.
☎ 322051. 1130-2300
Mon-Sat, 1200-1400 &
1900-2200 Sun.
Hamburgers, rolls, pies.

Three Way Inn
Ashwoods, Sligo Rd.
☎ 327414. 1130-2100
Mon-Sat. Soup, plaice, salads.

Tippler's Brook
1 The Brook. ☎ 32204.
1130-2300 Mon-Sat,
1230-1430 & 1900-2200
Sun. Pub grub.

Tippler's Inn
Skea, Arney. ☎ 82492.
1130-0100 Mon-Sat. Light
grills, fried foods.

Co. FERMANAGH — *Enniskillen-Irvinestown*

Village Inn ♀
Sligo Rd. ☎ 323132.
1130-1700 Mon-Sat.
Chicken, plaice, roast beef.

Vintage ♀
13 Townhall St. ☎ 324055.
1200-1900 Mon-Sat. Set
lunch, high tea, self-service
buffet. E£.

Waterfront ♀
Rosigh, Killadeas.
☎ (036 56) 21938. 0900-1800
Mon-Sat, 0900-2030 Sun
summer, closed winter. Soup,
sandwiches.

Watergate ♀
1 Ann St. ☎ 327447.
1130-1800 Mon-Fri.
Hamburgers, sandwiches, pies.

Welcome Inn ♀
10 Sligo Rd. ☎ 323734.
1700-2430 Mon-Thur, until
0130 Fri & Sat, 0100 Sun.
Chinese & European. E££.

FLORENCECOURT
(STD 0365)

Florence Court House
☎ 348249. 1200-1800 Mon &
Wed-Sun July & Aug. 1400-
1800 April-Sept. Quiche, meat
loaf, stew, wheaten bread.

Le Bistro
Marble Arch Caves.
☎ 348855. 1100-1630
Mon-Sun Mar-Sept. Coffee,
sandwiches, pastries.

Regal Bar ♀
2 Mullanaveay Rd. ☎ 348264.
1130-2300 Mon-Sat.
Grills, salads.

★ **TULLYHONA** 🍾
59 Marble Arch Rd.
☎ 348452. 1000-1900 Mon-
Sun Easter & June-Aug only.
Buffet salad, snacks, coffee,
home baking. A la carte.

GARRISON

Heather Grove
Meenacloybane. ☎ (036 56)
58362. Dinner. Booking
essential. Lough Melvin trout. £.

**Lough Melvin Holiday
 Centre** ⓐ
☎ (036 565) 8142. 1200-2100
Mon & Wed-Fri, 1000-2100
Sat & Sun. Set lunch,
afternoon tea, evening
meal. Fresh fish.

IRVINESTOWN
(STD 036 56)

Ann's Coffee Shop
Main St. ☎ 28089.
0900-1730 Mon-Sat, closed
Thur. Quiche, cakes.

Castle Archdale Café
☎ 21345. 0900-2230
Mon-Sun July & Aug, earlier
closing June & Sept.
Lasagne, quiche, scampi.

Irvinestown-Kesh   **Co. FERMANAGH**

★ CEDARS

Drumal, Castle Archdale.
☎ 21493. 1800-2400
Wed-Sun. Set meals,
à la carte.

Central Bar
Main St. ☎ 21249.
1230-1530 & 1800-2130
Mon-Sat. Basket meals.

Corner Café
Church St. ☎ 21696.
0900-1900 Mon-Sat, closed
Thur. Fish & chips, chicken.

★ HOLLANDER
5 Main St. ☎ 21231.
1130-2300 Mon-Sat, 1900-
2200 Sun in summer. 1230-
1430 Mon-Sat, 1730-2200
Sun in winter. Bar lunches.
A la carte. E££.

Lily House
54 Main St. ☎ 21880.
1700-2400 Mon & Wed-Sat,
until 0100 Fri & Sat,
1600-2400 Sun. Chinese &
European. E££.

Mahon's Hotel
Enniskillen Rd. ☎ 21656.
Last orders 2100. Garlic steak,
stuffed mushrooms. E£.

Robinson's Corner Bar
Church St. ☎ 21572.
1130-2300 Mon-Sat.
Pub grub.

Woodhill Hunting Lodge
Derrynanny. ☎ 21863.
1700-2300 Wed-Sun, until
0100 Sat. A la carte. E££.

KESH
(STD 036 56)

Drumrush Lodge
Boa Island Rd. ☎ 31578.
1730-2130 Mon-Sun,
1230-1430 Fri-Sun June-Sept.
Grills, à la carte.

Hunting Lodge
Lusty Beg, Boa Island.
☎ 31342. 1100-2400
Mon-Sat, 1230-1430 &
1830-2100 Sun Mar-Sept.
Grills.

Irene's Café
23 Main St. ☎ 31014.
1100-0100 Mon-Thur,
1800-2400 Sun, until
0200 Fri, 0300 Sat. Shorter
hours in winter. Snacks.

Lough Erne Hotel
Main St. ☎ 31275. Last orders
2100. A la carte. E££.

May Fly
Main St. ☎ 31281.
1200-1430 Mon-Sat,
1800-2200 Fri-Sun.
Pub grub. A la carte. E£.

Mullynaval Lodge
Boa Island. ☎ 31995.
Home-baked bread, dinners.
Booking essential.

Concorde

Family run restaurant

Specialising in
French and country cuisine
West coast seafood
Morning coffee, carvery lunch
light meals

Full à la carte & chef's specials
Extensive wine list.

**Tempo Road, Enniskillen,
Co. Fermanagh.
Telephone: (0365) 322955**

McCartney's Inn

Fermanagh Locals - Visitors

Enjoy yourself at
McCartney's Inn
17 Belmore Street • Enniskillen

Good food served daily at very keen prices

Lots of entertainment in our traditional Public Bar or Cellar

Lounge Disco Music -
Live Bands

Karaoke Nights -
Special Promotion Nights

Late Bar nightly. Happy hour every Thursday night
8.30pm - 9.30pm

POOL competitions every Saturday.

Forthcoming attractions will be advertised in the bar.

Give us a call-you'll enjoy it
TEL: (0365) 320122

GLENCAR BAR

Extensive à la carte menu
bar snacks served daily

For the best in food
and entertainment
every Friday & Saturday

Now open Sat & Sun
6.00pm. - 9.30pm.

Booking essential

**Main Street, Lisbellaw
Telephone:
(0365) 87818**

Sarah Jane's
41 Main St. ☎ 31940.
1030-1700 Mon-Sat,
1200-2000 Sun. Home baking.

Willow Pattern Pantry
Clareview House, Crevenish
Rd. ☎ 31278. 1030-2000
Mon-Sat July & Aug,
1100-1700 Sat Easter-June.
Irish stew, pavlova, coffee.

KINAWLEY

Corrigans ♀
39 Main St. ☎ (036 582) 285.
1230-1430 & 1800-2200
Mon-Sat. Pies, grills.

LETTERBREEN

Half Way Inn ♀
☎ (036 589) 367. 1200-2200
Mon-Sat. Grills, curries,
salads.

LISBELLAW
(STD 0365)

Carrybridge Hotel ♀
☎ 87282. Last orders 2200.
A la carte. E£.

Glencar Bar ♀
Main St. ☎ 87818.
1230-1430 Mon-Sat,
1800-2130 Fri-Sun.
A la carte. Booking essential.

Wild Duck Inn ♀
Main St. ☎ 87258.
1130-2300 Mon-Sat,
1230-1430 & 1900-2200
Sun. Pub grub.

LISNARICK

★ **DRUMSHANE HOTEL** ♀

☎ (036 56) 21146. Last orders
2000. Lamb kebab Drumshane,
shark steaks, flambéd Irish
coffee. A la carte. E£.

LISNASKEA
(STD 036 57)

Corner House ♀
169 Main St. ☎ 21172.
1200-1900 Mon-Sat.
Pub grub.

FDH Coffee Shop ⊗
Main St. ☎ 21276. 1000-1700
Mon-Wed & Sat, until 2030
Thur & Fri. Quiche, pizza,
desserts.

Horse & Hound ♀
133 Main St. ☎ 21298.
1230-1430 & 1900-2230
Mon-Sat. Pub grub.

Moate
78 Lower Main St. ☎ 22598.
1000-2200 Mon-Sat,
1800-2200 Sun.
Breakfast, set lunch.

Co. FERMANAGH — *Lisnaskea-Tempo*

Ortine Hotel ♢
Main St. ☎ 21206. Last orders 2130. Pub lunch, gateaux. A la carte. £££.

Stag's Head ♢
112 Main St. ☎ 21968. 1130-2300 Mon-Sat, 1230-1430 & 1900-2200 Sun. Pub grub.

Teach a' Ceili
Inishcorkish. ☎ 21360. Booking essential for hot meals. Grills & snacks for holidaymakers on boats. On island.

Wyvern Inn ♢
Main St. ☎ 21248. 1230-1430 Mon-Sat. Pub grub, buffet.

NEWTOWNBUTLER
(STD 036 573)

★ **RAFTERS**

30 High St. ☎ 8165. 0800-2000 Mon-Sat. Traditional Irish cooking.

ROSLEA
(STD 036 575)

Roslea Arms ♢
Main St. ☎ 343. 1230-1430 & 1900-2300 Mon-Sat, 1900-2200 Sun. Daily specials.

Roslea Heritage Centre
Monaghan Rd. ☎ 750. 0900-1700 Mon-Fri, April-Sept 1600-1800 Sat & Sun. Scones, pastries, coffee.

TEMPO
(STD 036 554)

Milltown Manor ♢
61 Main St. ☎ 779. 1230-1430 Mon-Sat. Toasties, grills, daily specials, à la carte.

COUNTY LONDONDERRY

AGHADOWEY
(STD 0265)

★ **BROWN TROUT GOLF & COUNTRY INN** ♀

209 Agivey Rd, Mullaghmore. ☎ 868209. 0700-2130 Mon-Sun June-Sept, 0700-1500 & 1700-2130 Mon-Sun rest of year. Grills, steaks. A la carte, set lunch. E£.

BALLYKELLY

Drummond Hotel ♀
481 Clooney Rd. ☎ (050 47) 22121. Last orders 2130. A la carte. E£.

Helen's Restaurant ♀
440 Clooney Rd. ☎ (050 47) 62098. 1700-2330 Sun-Thur, until 0030 Fri & Sat. Chinese & European. ££.

Marmadukes ♀
63 Main St. ☎ (050 47) 63266. 1230-1430 & 1900-2130 Mon-Sat. Baked crab & prawn soufflé, beef with green peppercorn & mushroom cream sauce, seasonal fruit pie. E££.

Weavers ♀
450 Clooney Rd. ☎ (050 47) 62999. 1230-1430 & 1900-2130 Mon-Sat. Steak, curry, lasagne.

CASTLEDAWSON
(STD 0648)

Ditty's Home Bakery ⌒
44 Main St. ☎ 68243. 0900-1730 Mon-Sat. Vegetarian pies, lasagne, sandwiches.

Moyola Lodge ♀
9 Broagh Rd. ☎ 68224. 1700-2130 Mon, Thur & Fri, 1600-2130 Sat & Sun. Set meals. A la carte. E£.

Shillgray Lounge ♀
1 Bridge St. ☎ 68951. 1230-1330 Mon-Fri. Lunches, scampi, chicken.

Thatch Inn ♀
116 Hillhead Rd. ☎ 68322. 1230-1430 & 1800-2200 Wed-Sun. Steak, fish. £.

Co. LONDONDERRY — Castlerock-Coleraine

CASTLEROCK
(STD 0265)

Copper Kettle
4 Main St. ☎ 848229.
1000-1730 Tues-Sat in summer, 1000-1700 Thur-Sat Easter-Sept. Home baking.

Golf Hotel ♀
17 Main St. ☎ 848204. Last orders 2030. A la carte. £££.

Marine Inn ♀
9 Main St. ☎ 848456.
1230-1930 Mon-Sat,
1230-1500 & 1700-2200 Sun. £.

Pool Café
Main St. ☎ 42232. 1030-2200 Mon-Sun Easter-Sept. Fish & chips, chicken.

Temple Lounge ♀
17 Sea Rd. ☎ 848423.
1130-2300 Mon-Sat,
1230-1430 & 1900-2200 Sun. Roast meat, fish, chicken.

CLAUDY
(STD 0504)

Beaufort House ♀
☎ 338248. 1230-2030 Mon-Sat. Snacks.

Claudy Inn ♀
Main St. ☎ 338515.
1130-2300 Mon-Sat,
1230-1430 & 1900-2200 Sun. Pies, burgers.

Connolly's ♀
68 Main St. ☎ 338546.
1130-2300 Mon-Sat,
1230-1430 & 1900-2200 Sun. Grills, pies, hamburgers.

McGonigle's
64 Main St. ☎ 338819.
1200-1400 & 1700-2400 Mon-Thur, 1200-0100 Fri & Sat, 1700-2200 Sun. Sandwiches, grills, Ulster fry.

Rio Grande ♀
Park. ☎ (050 47) 81210.
1430-2300 Mon-Fri,
1130-2300 Sat. Pub grub.

COLERAINE
(STD 0265)

Beau Brummel
18 Bridge St. ☎ 55145.
1000-1730 Mon-Sat. Pizzas, burgers, grills.

Belfry Restaurant
Church Lane. ☎ 44646.
0900-1730 Mon-Sat. Quiche, salad.

Bertie's ♀
108 Long Commons. ☎ 42874.
1200-1430 Mon-Sat. Pub grub, stew, pies.

Big 'O'
11 New Row. ☎ 44777.
0900-1700 Mon-Sat. Hamburgers, pizzas. Set lunch.

Coleraine — Co. LONDONDERRY

Blackthorn Inn ♇
16 New Market St. ☎ 44514.
1200-1430 Mon-Sat. Stew, lasagne.

Bohill Hotel & Country Club ♇
69 Cloyfin Rd. ☎ 44406.
Last orders 2100, Sun 2000. Grill bar, poached salmon. ££.

Brook's Wine Bar ♇
21 Park St. ☎ 42552.
1200-1430 Mon-Sat. Burgers, steaks, baked potatoes.

Bull's Eye ♇
Lime Market St. ☎ 43485.
1200-1500 Mon-Sat, 1730-2200 Wed-Sat, 1900-2130 Sun. Savoury pies, open sandwiches.

Bushtown House Hotel ♇
283 Drumcroone Rd.
☎ 58367. 1200-2130 Mon-Sun. Set lunch. A la carte. £££.

The Buttery ☺
31 Kingsgate St. ☎ 52127.
0745-1745 Mon-Sat. Carvery, casseroles, quiche, lasagne, salads. Home baking.

Charly's ♇
34 Newbridge Rd. ☎ 52020.
1200-2200 Mon-Sun. Closed 1500-1700 in winter. Beef, pork, chicken, lamb.

Chew Chews
21 Railway Rd. ☎ 55504.
1030-1900 Mon & Tues, until 2400 Wed-Fri, 0200 Sat, 1300-2400 Sun. Hot dogs, burgers.

Clyde Bar ♇
40 Railway Rd. ☎ 42791.
1200-1430 Mon-Fri. Pub grub.

Coffee Cup
Queen St. ☎ 43810.
0900-1715 Mon-Sat, until 1600 Thur. Home-made pies, scones, gateaux, milk shakes.

Coffee Dock
20 New Row. ☎ 52565.
0900-1700 Mon-Sat. Baked potatoes, salads. Home baking.

Copper Room
4 Railway Rd. ☎ 53184.
1000-1700 Mon-Sat, closed Thur. Pizza, pies.

Dolphin
26 Railway Rd. ☎ 56247.
1200-2300 Mon-Sat. Set lunch. Steak, hamburgers, scampi.

Eileen's Diner
Station Square. ☎ 57386.
0830-1730 Mon-Sat. Quiche, salads, toasties.

Erin Eating House
5 Long Commons. ☎ 43612.
1000-1730 Mon-Sat, 0900-1400 Thur. Set lunch. Salads, curry, baked potatoes.

Co. LONDONDERRY — *Coleraine*

Forum
15 Church St. ☎ 52638.
0930-1700 Mon-Sat. Coffee shop in department store.

Grandma Smyth's
9 Railway Rd. ☎ 51150.
0900-1700 Mon-Sat. Lunch, snacks.

★ **KITTY'S OF COLERAINE**
3 Church Lane. ☎ 42347.
0900-1730 Mon-Sat, closed Thur. Sandwiches, sausage rolls, coffee.

Lacy's Wine Bar
Beresford Rd. ☎ 43755.
1200-1500 & 1700-2300 Mon-Sat. Lasagne, chicken kiev.

Lily Lecky Bistro
2 The Diamond. ☎ 42996.
0900-1730 Mon-Sat. Home baking.

★ **LITTLE TEA ROOM**
Diamond Arcade.
1000-1730 Mon-Sat. Afternoon tea, set lunches.

Lodge Hotel
Lodge Rd. ☎ 44848. Last orders 2100, Sun 1930. A la carte. £££.

Lombard Café
Queen St. ☎ 43041.
0900-1730 Mon-Sat. Set lunch. Soup, sandwiches, scones.

★ **MACDUFF'S**
112 Killeague Rd, Blackhill.
☎ 868433. 1900-2130 Tues-Sat. Game in season, seafood, local country produce. £££.

Mandarin Palace
30 Railway Rd. ☎ 54012.
1200-1400 & 1700-2400 Mon-Sat, 1600-2300 Sun. Chinese & European. £££.

Mary Craig's
30 New Market St. ☎ 52461.
1200-1400 Mon-Sat. Pub grub.

Old Forge Inn
6 New Market St. ☎ 52931.
1200-1430 & 1730-2200 Mon-Sat. Grills, à la carte. ££.

The Pantry
Right Price Carpets, Bushmills Rd. 0900-1700 Mon-Sat. Lasagne, Sheperd's pie, salads.

Pine Tree Country Club
1 Somerset Rd. ☎ 58002.
1200-1430 Mon-Sat. Snacks.

Racquets
Leisure Centre, Railway Rd.
☎ 56432. 1000-2130 Mon-Fri, until 1800 Sat, 1400-1800 Sun. Soup, sandwiches, rolls.

Red Cross Café
43 Kingsgate St. ☎ 58250.
1000-1600 Mon-Sat. Lasagne, pies, high tea.

Coleraine-Dungiven — **Co. LONDONDERRY**

Restaurant Twenty Two
22 Church St. ☎ 43761.
0900-1730 Mon-Sat. Salads,
quiche, lasagne.

Roost ⚲
2 Shuttle Hill. ☎ 42516.
1130-2300 Mon-Sat,
1230-1430 & 1900-2200
Sun. Pies, burgers.

Salmon Leap ⚲
53 Castleroe Rd. ☎ 52992.
1130-2300 Mon-Sat, 1230-
1430 & 1730-2130 Sun. Buffet
lunch, game in season, smoked
fish. A la carte. M£, E££.

Sun Do
66 New Row. ☎ 53022.
1200-1400 & 1700-0030
Mon-Sat, 1700-2400 Sun.
Chinese & European.

Teady & Son
12 Railway Rd. ☎ 53211.
0900-1700 Mon-Sat.
Sandwiches, snacks.

Wellworths ⊙
2 Ring Rd. ☎ 58446.
0900-1730 Mon, Tues & Sat,
until 2100 Wed-Fri. Afternoon
tea, salad bar.

DRAPERSTOWN
(STD 0648)

Corner House ⚲
2 St Patrick St. ☎ 28051.
1200-1430 Mon-Sun,
1800-2130 Sun. A la carte.

Market Inn ⚲
27 St Patrick St. ☎ 28250.
1200-1430 Mon-Sat.
Pub grub.

Shepherds ⚲
220 Sixtowns Rd. ☎ 28517.
1200-1430 Mon-Sat. Snacks.

DUNGIVEN
(STD 050 47)

Carraig Rua ⚲
40 Main St. ☎ 41682.
1200-1430 Mon-Sat,
1800-2130 Mon-Sun. E££.

Castle Inn ⚲
Upper Main St. ☎ 41369.
1230-2200 Mon-Sat,
1230-1430 & 1900-2100
Sun. Lunch, snacks.
A la carte.

Cosy Inn ⚲
84 Main St. ☎ 41781.
1230-1430 & 1800-2200
Mon-Sat. Pub grub.

Dolphin Bar ⚲
Gortnaghey Rd. ☎ 41289.
1000-0100 Sat, 1800-2200
Sun. Pub grub.

Ponderosa ⚲
Glenshane Rd (top of
Glenshane Pass). ☎ 41987.
1130-1900 Mon-Thur, until
2100 Fri & Sat, 1230-1430 &
1900-2100 Sun. A la carte.
Steak, seafood.

Co. LONDONDERRY — Eglinton-Kilrea

EGLINTON
(STD 0504)

Glen House Hotel ♀
9 Main St. ☎ 810527.
Last orders 2200, Sun 2100.
Scallops in bacon, veal.
A la carte. E£££.

Longfield Inn ♀
Longfield Rd. ☎ 810211.
1230-1430 Mon-Sun. Pub
grub, chicken, fish, pies.

Station Inn ♀
37 Station Rd. ☎ 810470.
1200-1400 Mon-Sat, 1730-
2200 Tues & Wed, until 2300
Thur-Sat, 1230-1430 & 1900-
2100 Sun. Grills, set meals.

The Villager ♀
4 Main St. ☎ 810206.
1230-2100 Mon-Thur,
1230-2200 Fri-Sun. Pub grub.
A la carte. E£.

GARVAGH
(STD 026 65)

The Café
Main St. ☎ 58374.
1000-1700 Mon-Sat. Café in
grocery shop. Set lunch.

Imperial Hotel ♀
38 Main St. ☎ 58218. Last
orders 2200. Trout. £.

Tasty Bite
37 Main St. ☎ 58262.
0800-2300 Mon-Wed,
until 0100 Thur-Sat. Fish &
chips.

Turn Inn ♀
33 Main St. ☎ 58257.
1130-2300 Mon-Sat,
1900-2200 Sun. A la carte.

GREYSTEEL

Foyle View Bar ♀
161 Clooney Rd. ☎ (0504)
810560. 2000-2200 Mon-Sun.
Pub grub.

McEleney's ♀
265 Clooney Rd. ☎ (0504)
810220. 1200-1430 Mon-Sat,
1230-1430 Sun. Grills, carvery.

Rising Sun ♀
105 Killylane Rd. ☎ (0504)
810959. 1200-2100 Mon-Sun.
Pub grub. A la carte.

KILREA
(STD 026 65)

Bridge Way Café
4 Bridge St. 1000-1800
Mon-Wed, until 2130
Thur-Sat. Ulster fry,
sandwiches, pies.

Kilrea-Limavady   **Co. LONDONDERRY**

The Manor ♁
69 Bridge St. ☎ 40205.
1200-1500 Mon-Sun, 1600-2100 Mon-Thur, 1900-2100 Sun. Garlic mushrooms, curry, lasagne, home-made apple pie.

New Point Inn ♁
The Diamond. ☎ 40404.
1200-1500 Mon-Sat. Bar snacks.

Old Point Inn ♁
80 Drumagarner Rd.
☎ 40330. 1200-1400 & 1800-2130 Tues-Sat, 1230-1430 & 1900-2130 Sun. Pies, hamburgers.

KNOCKCLOGHRIM

Fireside Inn ♁
☎ (0648) 42635. 1200-2000 Thur-Sat. Pub grub.

Fox & Pheasant Inn ♁
69 Glenmaquille Rd.
☎ (0648) 69463. 1300-1400 & 1800-2100 Thur-Sun. Grills, set meals. A la carte.

LIMAVADY
(STD 050 47)

Alexander Arms ♁
Main St. ☎ 63443. 0800-1000, 1200-1430 & 1700-2230 Mon-Sat. A la carte.

Beehive
21 Market St. ☎ 63692.
0900-1800 Mon-Sat. Grills, snacks, chicken, steak.

Belmont ♁
24 Linenhall St. ☎ 64172.
1130-2300 Mon-Sat. Pub grub.

Coast Road Inn ♁
144 Seacoast Rd. ☎ 63562.
1230-1430 & 1900-2200 Mon-Sun in summer, 1900-2200 Thur-Sat in winter. Steak, pizza.

Crown Bar ♁
24 Irish Green St. ☎ 62402.
1230-1430 & 1900-2300 Fri & Sat. Pies, hamburgers.

Crumpet ☕
43 Market St. ☎ 22886.
0900-1730 Mon-Sat, until 1400 Thur. Breakfast, grills, salads, pastries.

Gentry's ♁
18 Main St. ☎ 22017.
1230-2230 Sun-Wed, 1200-2400 Thur-Sat. Indian, European. E££.

Gorteen House ♁
Deerpark, 187 Roe Mill Rd.
☎ 22333. Last orders 2230, 2100 Sun. A la carte. E£££.

Lucille's Kitchen ☕
17c Catherine St. ☎ 68180.
0900-1730 Mon-Sun. Curries, soup, scones.

The Galvey Lodge

LICENSED RESTAURANT

158 Station Road, Portstewart, Co. Londonderry

Telephone: Portstewart 832218

The Galvey Lodge

Restaurant & Grill Bar, with upstairs lounge bar
We specialise in weddings, birthday parties, anniversaries.
Full à la carte and grill bar menus.

Opening times as follows

Monday to Sunday 12.00 until 2.30 5.00 until 9.30

Special 4 course Sunday lunch also available
We are fully licensed and have late bar with entertainment on Friday and Saturday nights.

BROWNS RESTAURANT

CLOSED MONDAY
1 VICTORIA ROAD, DERRY.
TEL: 0504 45180

'From a re-furbished railway station Browns offers an eclectic mix of modern and traditional European cooking, complemented by a list of wines from Europe, the New World and the Americas.

With live (not loud!) music on Saturdays, Browns is altogether a different place!'

Coach Parties (by arrangement)

MOYOLA LODGE

A LA CARTE MEALS — Pleasant surroundings
WEDDINGS — Warm welcome
FUNCTIONS
PRIVATE PARTIES — Relaxing atmosphere
CONFERENCES
ACCOMMODATION — High standard of food & service

RESTAURANT-GUESTHOUSE

Castledawson, Magherafelt, Co. Londonderry.
Tel: (0648) 68224

Limavady-Londonderry — **Co. LONDONDERRY**

Oven Door ♀
Hunter's Bakery, 5 Market St.
☎ 63411. 0800-1730
Mon-Sat, closed 1630 Thur
Oct-May. Beef & pepper
casserole, wheaten bread,
coffee cake.

Rivolli Pizzeria ♀
4a Ballyclose St. ☎ 66663.
1700-2300 Mon-Sun. Pizza,
pasta, salads.

Rendezvous
15 Catherine St. ☎ 22272.
0900-1830 Mon-Sat. Grills,
fish & chips, Ulster fry.

Roe Valley Country Park
Dog Leap Café. ☎ 22074.
1030-1700 Mon-Fri, until
2000 Sat & Sun. 1000-1800
Sun in winter. Snacks.

Roe View Inn ♀
160 Ballyquin Rd. ☎ 62550.
1230-1430 Mon-Sat,
1900-2100 Sun. Snacks.

Roebuck Inn ♀
25 Main St. ☎ 68558.
1200-1430 Mon-Sat. Fish,
chicken, salads.

Shanvey ◌
109 Aghanloo Rd. ☎ 50229.
1200-1400 & 1700-2300
Fri-Sat. Salmon steak, trout.
A la carte.

Shenandoah ♀
88 Main St. ☎ 64366.
1200-1430 Mon-Sun.
Pub grub.

Thatch Bar ♀
10 Catherine St. ☎ 64876.
1200-2200 Mon-Sat,
1230-1430 & 1900-2200
Sun. Pub grub. A la carte.

LONDONDERRY
(STD 0504)

Abrakebabra
Strand Rd. ☎ 264407.
2400-0200 Mon-Wed & Sun,
until 0300 Thur & Fri, until
0400 Sat. Turkish kebabs,
burgers.

Acorn
3 Pump St. ☎ 262539.
1000-1730 Mon-Sat. Soup,
stew, home-made savouries,
salads, pastries.

Andy Cole's Bar ♀
125 Strand Rd. ☎ 265308.
1230-1430 Mon-Sat. Pub
grub.

★ **BEECH HILL COUNTRY
HOUSE HOTEL** ♀
32 Ardmore Rd. ☎ 49279.
Last orders 2145. M££. E£££.

Beechtree Bar ♀
106 Beechwood Avenue.
☎ 268568. 2000-2200
Mon-Sat. Pub grub.

Beehive
101 Richmond Centre.
☎ 264661. 0900-1730
Mon-Sat, until 2100 Thur &
Fri. Soup, stew, salads.

Co. LONDONDERRY — Londonderry

Bengal Tandoori ♆
59 Strand Rd. ☎ 365287.
1200-1430 & 1800-2400
Mon-Wed & Sun, until 0300
Thur-Sat. Indian & European.
E£.

Bogside Inn ♆
21 Westland St. ☎ 269300.
1130-2300 Mon-Sat,
1230-1430 & 1900-2200
Sun. Pub grub.

Boston Tea Party
42 Shipquay St. ☎ 263326.
0900-1730 Mon-Sat.
Sandwiches, pies.

Brendan's Diner ♆
164 Spencer Rd. ☎ 44875.
0900-2400 Mon-Sat,
1630-2300 Sun. Hamburgers,
fish & chips, duck, salmon.

Brewster's Bistro ♆
Little James St. ☎ 264768.
1200-2200 Mon-Sat,
1230-1500 & 1900-2130 Sun.
A la carte.

Broomhill House Hotel ♆
Limavady Rd. ☎ 47995.
Last orders 2130. ££.

★ **BROWN'S** ♆
1 Victoria Rd. ☎ 45180.
1230-1430 Tues-Fri,
1730-2330 Tues-Sat,
1230-1430 & 1730-2130 Sun.
Modern European. Irish lamb,
Kilkeel fish, vegetarian. E££.

Carraig Bar ♆
121 Strand Rd. ☎ 267529.
1200-1430 & 1900-2300
Mon-Sat. Soup, grills,
sandwiches.

Caspers Bar & Lounge ♆
Waterloo St. ☎ 263278.
1200-1500 Mon-Sat.
Pies, burgers, stews.

Castle Bar ♆
26 Waterloo St. ☎ 263118.
1230-1430 Mon-Sat. Lunch,
grills. Live traditional music
Fri & Sat.

Chat & Chew
23 William St. ☎ 269376.
0900-1700 Mon-Sat, until
1400 Thur. Soup, stew, rolls.

Churn
37 Great James St.
☎ 268001. 0930-1730
Mon-Fri, until 1500 Sat.
Home baking.

City Restaurant ♆
27 Shipquay St. ☎ 271011.
1200-0100 Mon-Thur, until
0200 Fri & Sat, until 2400 Sun.
Chinese & European.

Claddagh Bar ♆
5 Chamberlain St. ☎ 265877.
1200-1500 Mon-Sat. Fish,
chicken.

Clarendon Bar ♆
44 Strand Rd. ☎ 263705.
1200-1430 & 1700-2000
Mon-Sat. Pub grub.

Londonderry

Co. LONDONDERRY

Clarendon Café
3 Lower Clarendon St.
☎ 267165. 0900-1600
Mon-Sat. Breakfast, lunch, grills.

The Coffee Shop
32 Waterloo St. ☎ 266612.
0900-1700 Mon-Sat. Ulster fry, sandwiches, home-made pastries.

Coffee Stop
Drumahoe Shopping Centre.
☎ 301068. 0900-1700
Mon-Sat. Lasagne, quiche.

Crusty Kitchen ⊛
304 Richmond Centre.
☎ 260637. 0900-1730
Mon-Sat, until 2100 Thur & Fri. Coffee, cakes.

Curry King
8 Campsie Rd. ☎ 46502.
1200-2400 Mon-Sun. Burgers, pizza, American chicken.

Da Vinci ♀
Culmore Rd. ☎ 264507.
1230-1430 Mon-Sat.
Pub grub.

Delacroix ♀
Buncrana Rd. ☎ 262990.
1200-1430 & 1800-2200
Mon-Sat, 1230-1430 Sun.
Toasties, soup. A la carte.

The Diamond
13 Ferryquay St. ☎ 263795.
1030-1800 Mon-Sat. Chicken, burgers.

Doherty's Bar ♀
10 Magazine St. ☎ 360177.
1200-1400 Mon-Sat. Burgers, salads, grills.

Don Vincenzo's ♀
45a Carlisle Rd. ☎ 263512.
1200-2400 Mon-Sat. Italian.

Duffy's No.17 ♀
17 Foyle St. ☎ 361362.
1200-1500 Mon-Fri. Set lunch.
Fish dishes, salads, pies.

Dungloe Bar ♀
41 Waterloo St. ☎ 267716.
1200-1500 Mon-Sat.
Pub grub.

Ebrington House ♀
6 Ebrington Terrace.
☎ 44692. 1200-1430
Mon-Sat, 2100-2400
Wed-Sat. Pub grub.

Emerald Palace
26 William St. ☎ 267706.
1630-0200 Mon-Sat, until 2400 Sun. Chicken, pizza, chips.

★ **EVERGLADES HOTEL** ♀
Prehen Rd. ☎ 46722.
Last orders 2145, Sun 2115.
Set meals, à la carte. £££

★ **FIORENTINI'S** ⊛
47 Strand Rd. 0900-2130
Mon-Fri, 0900-1730 Sat & Sun. Earlier closing in winter.
Snacks, ice cream.

Co. LONDONDERRY — Londonderry

Forum ♀
24 Foyle St. ☎ 360066.
1200-1430 & 2100-2300
Mon-Sat. Sandwiches, burgers, salads.

Gallery & Gilhooly's ♀
14 Dungiven Rd. ☎ 43698.
1230-1430 & 1730-2200
Mon-Sat. Steak, salmon.

The Galley
12a Shipquay St. ☎ 370260.
0900-1730 Mon-Sat. Baked potatoes, roasts, lasagne. £.

Glue Pot ♀
34 Shipquay St. ☎ 267463.
1130-1500 Mon-Sat. Soup, sandwiches, toasties, sweets.

Grand Central ♀
27 Strand Rd. ☎ 267826.
1200-2300 Mon-Sat,
1230-1430 Sun. Soup, hamburgers, salad, pies.

Gweedore Bar ♀
59 Waterloo St. ☎ 263513.
1200-1500 Mon-Sat.
A la carte, high tea.

Hennessey's ♀
64 Strand Rd. ☎ 371833.
1200-1430 Mon-Sat. Grills, set lunch.

T & E Howie
23 The Diamond. ☎ 262168.
0900-1730 Mon-Sat, until 1900 Fri. Baked potatoes, quiche, salads.

India House ♀
51 Carlisle Rd. ☎ 260532.
1800-2330 Mon-Thur,
until 2400 Fri & Sat, 2230
Sun. Indian.

Inn at the Cross ♀
171 Glenshane Rd. ☎ (0504) 301480. 1200-1600 &
1730-2200 Mon-Sat,
1230-1430 & 1730-2200 Sun.
Pub grub. A la carte. E£.

Iona House ♀
17 Spencer Rd. ☎ 43529.
1200-1500 Mon-Sat. Pub grub.

Kam House
14 William St. ☎ 372166.
1200-0200 Mon-Sat, 1630-0030 Sun. Chinese, European.

Kentucky Fried Chicken
2 Strand Rd. ☎ 372016.
1100-2400 Mon-Wed, until 0200 Thur, 0230 Fri & Sat, 1600-2300 Sun. Chicken, burgers, coleslaw.

Leprechaun
23 Strand Rd. ☎ 363606.
0930-1730 Mon-Sat. Set lunch. Scones, hamburgers, salads.

Linenhall Bar ♀
Market St. ☎ 371665.
1230-1500 & 1800-2100
Mon-Sat. Pub grub.

Lisnagelvin Leisure Centre
☎ 47695. Open Mon-Sun.
Snacks. Café in leisure centre.

Co. LONDONDERRY

McCourt's Bar 🍷
91 Ardmore Rd. ☎ 49492.
1130-2300 Fri-Sun. Pub grub.

Magnet Bar 🍷
161 Culmore Rd. ☎ 354497.
1130-2300 Mon-Sat,
1900-2200 Sun. Pub grub.

Malibu 🍷
6 Bishop St. ☎ 371784.
0930-1730 Mon-Sat, until
2030 Fri. Set lunch, Ulster fry.

Mandarin Palace 🍷
134 Strand Rd. ☎ 264613.
1630-0100 Mon-Thur, until
0200 Fri & Sat, 0030 Sun.
Chinese & European.

Marlene's ☺
33 Shipquay St. ☎ 370145.
1100-1800 & 2030-0300
Mon-Wed, until 0400 Thur,
0430 Fri & Sat, 2030-0230
Sun. Grills, salads.

Martha's Vineyard 🍷
Brunswick Superbowl.
☎ 371999. 1200-1430 &
1800-2230 Mon-Sun.
Chicken, fish.

★ **METRO** 🍷
3 Bank Place. ☎ 267401.
1200-1430 Mon-Sun.
Soup, beef stew.

Morton & Simpson
Lisnagelvin Shopping Centre.
☎ 45446. 0930-1700 Mon,
Tues & Sat, until 2100 Wed-
Fri. Lunch, salads, sandwiches,
sweets.

New Monico 🍷
4 Customs House St.
☎ 263121. 1330-2300
Mon-Sat, 1230-1430 &
1900-2200 Sun. Stew, soup.

New Tower Coffee Shop
Austin's department store,
The Diamond. ☎ 261817.
0900-1700 Mon-Sat, until
2030 Fri. Soup, Irish stew,
daily specials, salads, pastries.
Panoramic view.

Oak Grove Bar 🍷
86 Bishop St. ☎ 260856.
1230-1430 Mon-Sat. Pub grub.

Oval Bar 🍷
94 Duke St. ☎ 244364.
1130-2300 Mon-Fri. Pub grub.

Paolo's Pizzeria 🍷
5 Rockmills, Strand Rd.
☎ 268484. 1200-1500 &
1700-0200 Mon-Sun. Pizza,
pasta, steaks. £.

Parks 🍷
31 Collon Lane. ☎ 362712.
1200-1430 & 1700-2200
Mon-Sun. A la carte. £££.

Peking Pagoda 🍷
33 Foyle St. ☎ 267271.
1200-0030 Mon-Thur, until
0100 Fri & Sat, 1700-2400
Sun. Chinese & European. ££.

Piemonte Pizzeria
Clarendon St. ☎ 266828.
1130-0100 Mon-Sun. Pizzas.

Co. LONDONDERRY — Londonderry

Pilot's Row Leisure Centre
Rossville St. ☎ 269418.
1200-1430 & 1900-2200
Mon-Sat. Coffee, hamburgers.

Pizza Prima
22 Shipquay St. ☎ 264627.
1200-1400 & 1700-2330
Mon-Sun. Pizza, pasta,
kebabs. £.

P J's Bar ♀
74 Spencer Rd. ☎ 311722.
1230-1430 Mon-Sun.
A la carte, high tea.

Rafters ♀ ⊙
Northland Rd. ☎ 266080.
1200-1500 & 1700-2245
Mon-Sat, 1230-1430 &
1900-2230 Sun. Lasagne,
quiche, daily special.

Rosie's Kitchen
8 Sackville St. ☎ 370066.
0900-0200 Tues, Thur & Sat,
until 1600 Wed, 1700-0200
Sun. Steaks, roasts.

The Sandwich Company
61 Strand Rd. ☎ 266771.
0800-1700 Mon-Fri,
1000-1700 Sat. Sandwiches,
rolls. Live music Sat.

★ SCHOONERS ♀
59 Victoria Rd. ☎ 311500.
1200-1430 & 1700-2200
Mon-Thur, until 2300 Fri &
Sat, 2130 Sun. Chillied
vegetable taco, marinated
seafood on a fish paella, trio of
oriental chicken. A la carte,
carvery. ££.

Shantallow House ♀
64 Racecourse Rd. ☎ 353344.
1130-2300 Mon-Sat,
1230-1430 & 1900-2200
Sun. Salads, sandwiches.

Spencers ♀
42 Spencer Rd. ☎ 42900.
1200-1430 & 1730-2200
Mon-Sun. Grills, à la carte.

The Storyteller ♀
45a Carlisle Rd. ☎ 263512.
1200-1430 Mon-Fri, 1730-
2200 Tues-Sun. Steaks,
vegetarian. A la carte. £££.

Superbites
44a Waterloo St. 1100-0230
Mon-Sat, 1800-0030 Sun.
Chicken, fish, burgers.

Terminus Rest
Foyle St. ☎ 268042.
0800-1700 Mon-Sat, 1130-
1600 Sun in winter, until
1800 in summer. Fish & chips.

Thran Maggie's ♀
Craft Village, Shipquay St.
☎ 264267. 1200-2130
Mon-Sun. Steaks, roasts,
à la carte. £££.

Three Mile House ♀
21 Drumahoe Rd. ☎ 311638.
1200-1430 & 1800-2130
Mon-Sat, 1230-1430 & 1900-
2200 Sun. Barbecued
ribs, peppered steak. ££.

Londonderry-Maghera — **Co. LONDONDERRY**

Townsman ☘
33 Shipquay St. ☎ 260820.
1130-1700 Mon-Sat. Soup,
sandwiches, hamburgers,
salads.

Venue ☘
Northland Rd. ☎ 266080.
1230-1430 & 1700-2200
Mon-Sat, 1230-1430 &
1900-2130 Sun. Steak,
chicken, grills, fish. E£.

Villa's Inn ☘
77 Victoria Rd. ☎ 311589.
1200-1430 Mon-Sat.
Grills, steaks. £.

★ **WATERFOOT HOTEL** ☘
Caw Roundabout,
14 Clooney Rd. ☎ 45500.
1230-2230 Mon-Sat, 1215-
1415 & 1700-2115 Sun. Hot &
cold buffet. E££.

Waterloo Bar & Nite Club ☘
3 Strand Rd. ☎ 266067.
1200-1500 Mon-Sat.
A la carte.

Wheeler's
Springtown Shopping Centre,
Northland Rd. 0930-1730
Mon-Sat, until 2100 Wed-Fri.
Snacks.

Wheeler's
30 Shipquay St. ☎ 363337.
1100-0200 Mon-Wed, until
0230 Thur, 0300 Fri & Sat,
1645-2400 Sun. Fish,
sausages, sandwiches.

White Horse Inn ☘
68 Clooney Rd, Campsie.
☎ 860606. Last orders 2215,
Sun 2100. Grill room. Salmon,
steaks. A la carte. E££.

Woodburn ☘
Blackburn Crescent, Waterside.
☎ 41438. 0930-1745 Mon-Sat,
until 1945 Fri. Self-service
snacks. Set lunch. Grills.
A la carte evening only.

MAGHERA
(STD 0648)

Crawford's Coffee Lounge
Main St. ☎ 43877.
0900-1730 Mon-Sat.
Sandwiches, pies, pastries.

Hideout ☘
Main St. ☎ 42315.
1130-1700 Mon-Sat. Pub
grub.

Maggie's Bar ☘
94 Upper Main St. ☎ 43682.
1200-2200 Mon-Sat.
Snacks, grills.

Rab's
6 Coleraine Rd. ☎ 44180.
0900-1800 Mon-Sat, 1130-
1830 Sun. Chicken, quiche,
rolls, cakes.

Co. LONDONDERRY — Magherafelt

MAGHERAFELT
(STD 0648)

The Bay Leaf
Meadowlane Shopping Centre.
☎ 34299. 0900-1730
Mon-Wed & Sat, 0900-2000
Thur & Fri. Soup, rolls,
sandwiches.

BT's Hot Food
Market Square. ☎ 31422.
1200-2400 Mon-Sat, 1700-
2400 Sun. Ulster fry, southern
fried chicken, fish.

★ **CLOISTERS** ♀
23 Church St. ☎ 32257.
1230-1500 & 1700-2200
Mon-Sun. Smoked eel, fillet of
beef with oysters, lamb.

Coachman ♀
58 Rainey St. ☎ 33527.
1200-1400 Mon-Sat.
Pub grub.

Coffee Pot
7 Meeting St. ☎ 31293.
0900-1730 Mon-Sat. Home-
made soup, cakes, rolls. Set
lunch, roasts, chicken.

Coffee Time
9 Broad St. ☎ 33347.
0900-1730 Mon-Sat.
Afternoon tea, set lunch.

★ **DITTY'S BAKERY** ◉

33 Rainey St. ☎ 33944.
0830-1730 Mon-Sat. Home
baking, sandwiches.

★ **FIOLTA'S BISTRO** ♀ ◉
4 Union Arcade. ☎ 33522.
0900-2130 Mon-Sat,
1200-1430 & 1700-2100
Sun. Garlic mushrooms,
lasagne, steak Bushmills. ££.

Greenvale Leisure Centre
Greenvale. ☎ 33410.
0930-2145 Mon-Fri,
1100-1730 Sat, 1400-1800
Sun. Rolls, pizzas, salads,
hamburgers, pastries.

Imperial Palace ♀
15 Queen St. ☎ 31709.
1200-1400 & 1700-2400
Mon-Thur, until 2430 Fri &
Sat, 1700-2400 Sun. Chinese
& European. £.

Karaoke ♀
7 Market St. ☎ 34136.
1230-1430 Mon-Wed & Fri.
Set lunch.

Korner Kafe
51 Rainey St. 1100-2330
Mon-Sat. Ulster fry, burgers,
chicken.

Last Sheaf ♀
31 Rainey St. ☎ 32223
1200-1430 & 1730-2200
Mon-Sat, 1200-2100 Sun.
Steaks, fish, Sunday lunch.
M££.

McErlains
26 Church St. ☎ 32465.
0800-1730 Mon-Sat.
Sandwiches, home baking.

Magherafelt-Moneymore — **Co. LONDONDERRY**

Mary's Bar & Lounge
10 Market St. ☎ 32139.
1200-1430 Mon-Sat. Pub grub.

Nito's
28 Queen St. ☎ 33859.
1200-1430 Mon-Sat. Pub grub.

Snack Box
76 Rainet St. ☎ 33710.
1200-2300 Mon-Sun. Burgers, fish, lunchtime special.

Taste Buds
18 Rainey St. ☎ 32484.
0900-1730 Mon-Sat. Soup, sandwiches, set lunches.

Town & Country Inn
28 Union Rd. ☎ 32473.
1130-2300 Mon-Sat. Chicken, curries.

MAGILLIGAN

Angler's Rest
Seacoast Rd. ☎ 50265.
1200-2200 Mon-Sat, 1230-1500 & 1900-2200 Sun. Pub grub.

Ballymaclary House
573 Seacoast Rd.
☎ (050 47) 50283.
1000-2100 Mon-Sat. Homemade pie of the day (savoury). Lobster, sole, steak specialities. High tea. A la carte E£££. 18th-century country house. £££.

Mallard Bar
401 Seacoast Rd. ☎ 50288.
1200-1430 Mon-Sat, 1800-2100 Mon-Sun. Pub grub. A la carte. E£.

Point Bar
107 Point Rd. ☎ (050 47) 50440. 1700-2130 Mon-Sat. Pub grub.

MONEYMORE
(STD 064 87)

Bier Keller
18 Stonard St. ☎ 48282.
1230-1430 & 1700-2100 Mon-Sat. Pub grub.

Drapers Arms
2 High St. ☎ 48647.
1130-2230 Mon-Sat. Pub grub.

Ivy
4 Smith St. ☎ 48154.
1245-2045 Mon-Sat, 1630-2045 Sun. Fish, steaks, ribs.

Springhill House
☎ 748210. 1400-1900 Mon-Sun July-Aug, closed Tues. Reduced hours rest of year. Coffee shop in National Trust house.

The best of all worlds for the touring traveller-

THE YORK

2 STATION ROAD
PORTSTEWART
CO. LONDONDERRY,
NORTHERN IRELAND
BT55 7DA
TEL: (0265) 833594

Situated on the world famous Causeway Coast with its excellent golf courses, beaches and many local attractions.

Continental style luxury self-catering apartments with traditional pub serving nationally renowned food.

★ Entertainment weekly ★

R·A·F·T·E·R·S
Award Winning Restaurant

OPEN EVERY NIGHT FROM 5.00 - 10.45 p.m.

Monday, Tuesday, Wednesday, Thursday, Friday and Saturday;
also each lunchtime
from 12.00 noon-3.00p.m.

SUNDAY EVENING
7-9.30 p.m. Lunch 12.30 - 2.30 p.m.

NORTHLAND ROAD, DERRY - TELEPHONE: (0504) 266080

Ballymaclary House

Licensed Restaurant
OPEN DAILY

Morning coffee, afternoon tea, high tea, à la carte private functions & barbeque facilities

573 Seacoast Road, Limavady, Co. Londonderry BT49 0LG
Tel. Bellarena (050 47) 50283

Proprietors:
Jane McAuley & Christine Armstrong

Portstewart — Co. LONDONDERRY

PORTSTEWART
(STD 0265)

Anchor Bar ⚟
87 The Promenade. ☎ 832003.
1230-1430 & 1900-2130
Mon-Sat. Pub grub.

Cassonis
Church St. ☎ 834777/832150.
1700-2300 Mon-Sun. Italian.

Cookery Nook
18 The Promenade. ☎ 834103.
0900-1730 Oct-June,
until 2230 summer. Set lunch.
Soup, Irish stew, apple pie.

Edgewater Hotel ⚟
88 Strand Rd. ☎ 833314.
Last orders 2130, Sun 2000.
A la carte. £££.

Galvey Lodge ⚟
158 Station Rd. ☎ 832218.
1200-1430 & 1700-2130
Mon-Sat. Lunch, grills.
A la carte.

Good Food & Company
44 The Promenade. ☎ 836386.
0900-2200 Mon-Sat July &
Aug, 0900-1730 rest of year.
Closed Sun. Home baking.

Heathron Diner
29 The Promenade.
☎ 834569. 0900-2300
Mon-Sat, 1200-2300 Sun in
summer, reduced hours rest
of year. Steaks, salads.

Lis-na-rhin
6 Victoria Terrace. ☎ 833522.
Last orders 1800. Wild
salmon, turbot, brill.
Booking essential. £.

Montagu Arms ⚟
68 The Promenade.
☎ 834146. 1200-2300
Mon-Sun. Grills. ££.

★ **MORELLI'S/NINO'S**
57 The Promenade. ☎ 832150.
1000-2300 Mon-Sun summer
& Easter, 1000-1800 winter.
Baked potatoes, pasta, pizza,
ice cream.

Mulroy
8 Atlantic Circle. ☎ 832293.
Set meals. A la carte.
Booking essential.

Nelly's ⚟
170 Coleraine Rd. ☎ 834238.
1200-2000 Mon-Sat. Pub
grub. Evening à la carte, oak-
smoked salmon, entrecôte
frenzo, gateau. £££.

Peppercorn
67b The Promenade.
☎ 834691. 1700-2400 Mon-
Thur & Sun, until 0200 Fri &
Sat. Indian & European. ££.

Prom Fast Food
The Promenade. ☎ 832586.
1200-1400 & 1700-0200
Mon-Sun. Pizza, vegetarian
burgers, fish.

Co. LONDONDERRY — Portstewart-Swatragh

Sea Splash Hotel ♑
3 Kinora Terrace. ☎ 832688.
Last orders 2030. A la carte.
E£.

Shenanigans ♑
78 The Promenade.
☎ (026 583) 6000.
1230-1430 Mon-Sun,
1730-2100 Mon-Sat, 1900-
2100 Sun. Chargrilled steaks,
lasagne, curry, tagliatelli.

Sundae Garden
53 The Promenade. ☎ 832150.
0930-2230 Mon-Sun
Easter-Sept, 0930-1800
Mon-Sat, until 2030 Sun
winter. Ice cream, coffee,
cakes, fish & chips.

Windsor Hotel ♑
8 The Promenade. ☎ 832523.
Last orders 2000. Set meals.
Local salmon. £.

York Bar ♑
2 Station Rd. ☎ 833594.
1230-1430 & 1730-2030
Mon-Sat, 1230-1415 Sun.
Seafood, steaks, chicken, pasta.

SWATRAGH
(STD 064 888)

Rafters Bar ♑
2 Kilrea Rd. ☎ 206.
1130-2300 Mon-Sat,
1230-1430 & 1900-2200 Sun.
Pies, curries, hamburgers.

COUNTY TYRONE

AUGHER

Queen Anya Steak House
42 Main St. ☎ (066 25) 48615.
0900-1930 Mon-Sat. Steaks, set lunch.

★ **ROSAMUND'S COFFEE SHOP**

Station House. ☎ (066 25) 48601. 0900-1700 Mon-Sat. Set lunch. Wheaten bread, bacon baps, Clogher Valley cheese. Selection of Irish crafts in restored former railway station.

AUGHNACLOY
(STD 066 252)

Lynn's
158 Moore St. ☎ 546. 1700-2400 Mon-Sat, 1700-2330 Sun. Chinese & European.

Peking Garden ♉
69 Moore St. ☎ 269.
1200-1400 Mon-Sat, 1700-2300 Mon-Sun, closed Tues. Chinese & European.

Silver Star ♉
86 Moore St. ☎ 420.
1130-2300 Mon-Sat, 1230-1430 & 1900-2200 Sun. Pub grub.

BALLYGAWLEY
(STD 066 25)

Kelly's Inn ♉
Garvaghey House,
232 Omagh Rd. ☎ 568218.
1130-2200 Mon-Sat,
1230-1430 & 1900-2200 Sun. Pub grub. A la carte ££.

★ **SUITOR GALLERY**

17 Grange Rd. ☎ 68653.
1000-1730 Mon-Sat & bank hols. Soup, scones, tray bakes.

BERAGH
(STD 066 27)

Corner House ♉
29 Main St. ☎ 58155.
1130-2130 Mon-Sat. Pub grub.

Traveller's Inn ♉
134 Curr Rd. ☎ (066 253) 68249. 1130-2300 Mon-Sat, 1230-1400 & 1900-2200 Sun. Pub grub.

CALEDON
(STD 0861)

Arctic Star ♉
1 Castle Park. ☎ 568688.
1230-1430 Mon-Fri.
Hamburgers, pub grub.

Co. TYRONE — Caledon-Castlederg

Caledon Arms ♀
44 Main St. ☎ 568161.
1800-2300 Mon-Sat,
1900-2200 Sun. Set lunch,
grills. A la carte. E£.

Deer Park Lounge & Bar ♀
18 Main St. ☎ 568255.
1130-2300 Mon-Sat. Steaks,
salads, chicken.

CASTLECAULFIELD

Parkanaur House
57 Parkanaur Rd.
☎ (086 87) 61272. Booking
essential.

Quinn's Corner
Edencrannon. ☎ (086 87)
67529. 1230-2200 Mon-Sat,
1230-1430 & 1900-2200 Sun.
Burgers, salads, pies.

CASTLEDERG
(STD 066 26)

Allstar Café
13 Ferguson Crescent.
☎ 70488. 1600-2400
Mon-Thur, until 0200
Fri & Sat. Grills.

Castle Inn ♀
48 Main St. ☎ 71501.
1200-2100 Mon-Sat. Bar snacks.

Crescent Inn ♀
1 Ferguson Crescent.
☎ 71161. 1230-1430 & 1900-
2200 Mon-Sun. Pub grub.
Live music.

Derg Arms ♀
43 Main St. ☎ 71644.
1200-1500 Mon-Sat,
1900-2200 Sun.
Lunch, afternoon tea.
A la carte. E£.

Derg Valley ♀
3 William St. ☎ 71809.
0930-2300 Mon-Sat,
1800-2200 Sun. Set lunch.
A la carte. E£.

Forge Inn ♀
13 Ferguson Crescent.
☎ 70488. Last orders 2100.
Set lunch, à la carte.

Market Bar ♀
59 Main St. ☎ 71247.
1230-1430 Mon-Sun pub
grub. 1900-2200 Fri-Sun
steaks, fish, salads E£.

Punter's Inn ♀
38 Main St. ☎ 71339.
1130-2300 Mon-Sat,
1230-1430 & 1900-2200
Sun. Pub grub.

Vienna Coffee Shop
75 Main St. ☎ 71379.
1000-1730 Mon-Sat, closed
Wed. Soup, stew, salads,
breads, cakes.

Village Inn ♀
☎ (0648) 71490. Pub grub.

Clogher-Coalisland — Co. TYRONE

CLOGHER
(STD 066 25)

The Coffee Shop
31 Main St. ☎ 48605.
0900-1700 Mon-Sat. Soup,
quiche, sandwiches.

Kelly's Café
5 Main St. ☎ 48183.
1130-2300 Mon-Sat,
1500-2330 Sun. Pies, grills,
chicken.

McSorley's Tavern ♀
39 Main St. ☎ 48673.
1130-2300 Mon-Sat,
1230-1430 & 1900-2200
Sun. Soup, toasties, pies.

Rathmore Bar ♀
127 Main St. ☎ 48240.
1130-2300 Mon-Sat,
1230-1430 & 1900-2200 Sun.
Lunch, toasties.

Trident Inn ♀
97 Main St. ☎ 48924.
1130-2200 Mon-Sat. Pub
grub. A la carte from 1900. £.

COAGH
(STD 064 87)

Water's Edge Boat Inn ♀
201 Battery Rd. ☎ 36367.
1800-2300 Fri-Sun. Pub grub.

Hanover House ♀
24 Hanover Square.
☎ 37530. 1100-1300 Tues-Sat,
1200-1500 & 1700-2200 Sun.
Set lunch, high tea. Duckling
in orange sauce. A la carte £.

COALISLAND
(STD 086 87)

Golden Grill
Main St. ☎ 40533.
1030-2300 Mon-Sat,
1030-1330 Wed. Soup,
chicken, fish, chips.

The Greyhound Bar & Restaurant ♀
Barrack Square. ☎ 48230.
1230-1430 & 1700-2130
Mon-Sun. Grills, burgers,
salad.

Landi's Café
The Square, 3 Dungannon Rd.
☎ 40211. 1030-0030 Mon-Sat,
closed Thur. Grills,
sandwiches, sweets.

Pyramid Centre ♀
11 Mountjoy Rd. 1230-1430 &
1600-2300 Mon-Thur, 1130-
0100 Fri-Sat, 1900-2200 Sun.
Steak, fish, chicken.

The Venue ♀
26b The Square. ☎ 40633.
1200-1500 & 1700-2000
Thur-Sat, 1900-2030 Sun. Set
lunch. A la carte.

Co. TYRONE — Cookstown

COOKSTOWN
(STD 064 87)

Al Capone's
58 James St. ☎ 64356.
1100-2400 Mon-Thur, until
0300 Fri & Sat, 1600-0230
Sun. Baked potatoes, burgers.

Braeside Bar ⚲
221 Orritor Rd. ☎ 62664.
1400-2300 Mon-Thur,
1130-2300 Sat. Pub grub.

Brewery Grill Bar ⚲
58 William St. ☎ 65934.
1100-2400 Mon-Sat,
1600-2400 Sun.
Soup, burgers, stew.

The Café
4 Burn Rd. ☎ 64456.
1100-1800 Mon-Sat. Snacks.

Cartwheel
25 James St. ☎ 63672.
1230-1430 Mon-Sat, 1900-2200 Fri & Sat. Pies, burgers.

Chequers ⚲
12 Oldtown St. ☎ 65122.
1130-1430 & 1700-2200
Mon-Thur, 1130-2200 Fri &
Sat. Chicken kiev, set lunch.
A la carte E££.

Clubland & Black Horse ⚲
21 Molesworth St. ☎ 64946.
1230-1430 Mon-Sat. Carvery.

Coffee Room
40 William St. ☎ 63438.
0900-1730 Mon-Sat. Set
lunch. Sandwiches, salads.
Self service.

Conway Inn ⚲
86 Chapel St. ☎ 65028.
1230-1430 Mon-Sat. Pub grub.

Cookstown Leisure Centre
Fountain Rd. ☎ 63853.
1000-2200 Mon-Fri,
1100-1800 Sat. Pizzas,
hamburgers, scones.

★ **COURTYARD**

56 William St. ☎ 65070.
0900-1800 Mon-Sat,
0900-1500 Wed. Set lunch,
savoury pies, home-made
sweets.

Dempsey's Food Depot ⚲
Central Arcade, James St.
☎ 63035. 0900-1730 Mon,
until 2130 Tues-Thur, 2230 Fri
& Sat. Pizzas, grills, salads. E£.

Dragon Palace ⚲
44 Loy St. ☎ 63311.
1200-1400 & 1700-2400
Mon-Thur, until 0100 Fri,
1600-0100 Sat, 1600-0030
Sun. Cantonese & European. E£.

Dunleath Bar ⚲
58 Church St. ☎ 62644.
1130-2300 Mon-Sat,
1230-1430 & 1900-2200
Sun. Pub grub.

Cookstown — Co. TYRONE

Farmhouse Restaurant
95 Cookstown Rd. ☎ 47125.
0900-1900 Mon-Wed, until
2300 Thur-Sat. Grills, snacks.

Gables ♀
40 Cookstown Rd. ☎ 67888.
1230-2200 Mon-Sat, until
2130 Sun. Set lunches.
A la carte ££.

Gaslight ♀
40 Loy St. ☎ 65640.
1130-2300 Mon-Sat,
1230-1430 & 1900-2200
Sun. Pub grub.

Glenavon House Hotel ♀
52 Drum Rd. ☎ 64949. Last
orders 2130, Sun 2100. A la
carte. Hot & cold carvery. E£.

★ **GREENVALE HOTEL** ♀
57 Drum Rd. ☎ 62243. Last
orders 2130. Set lunch.
A la carte. E££.

Halfway House ♀
81 Pomeroy Rd. ☎ 66372.
1800-2300 Thur-Sun.
Pub grub. A la carte £.

Joe Mac's
32 Molesworth St. ☎ 63371.
1130-2330 Mon, Tues & Thur,
until 0100 Fri, 0230 Sat,
1700-2330 Sun. Grills, pizzas,
Ulster fry.

McGlaughlin's
10 James St. ☎ 63493.
0900-1730 Mon-Sat, closed
Wed. Set lunch, salads.

Mill Wheel Bar ♀
60 Dunamore Rd. ☎ 51280.
1230-1500 Mon-Sun,
1900-2200 Fri & Sat. Set
meals, grills.

Mistletoe
13 Old Town St. ☎ 63476.
0900-1730 Mon-Sat, until
1430 Wed. Café behind
confectionery shop. Set lunch.

Otter Lodge ♀
26 Dungannon Rd.
☎ 65427. 1230-1400 &
1730-2200 Mon-Sun.
Carvery, à la carte. E££.

Penny Farthing
54 William St. ☎ 64922.
1030-1630 Mon-Sun, closed
Wed. Pastries, scones.

Prairie ♀
9 Corvanaghan Rd.
☎ 51226. 1900-2200 Wed-
Sun, 1230-1430 Sun. Grills,
salads. A la carte E£.

Railway Bar ♀
63 Union St. ☎ 63278.
1130-2300 Mon-Sat,
1230-1430 & 1900-2200
Sun. Hamburgers, pies.

Rossiter's
19 William St. ☎ 63388.
0900-1700 Mon-Sat.
Pizzas, lasagne.

Royal Hotel ♀
64 Coagh St. ☎ 62224. Last
orders 2145. Steaks, chicken.
A la carte. ££.

Co. TYRONE — *Cookstown-Dungannon*

Sinley
92 Church St. ☎ 64572.
1700-0100 Mon-Sat,
1600-0100 Sun.
Chinese, European. £.

Sperrin Room (Menary's)
39 William St. ☎ 63364.
0900-1730 Mon-Sun.
Chicken pie, lasagne.

Taj-Mahal
8 Orritor St. ☎ 65922. 1700-2400 Tues-Sun. Closed Mon.
Indian & European. ££.

Thatch Lounge
19 Molesworth St. ☎ 63787.
1700-2100 Mon-Fri,
1230-2230 Sat. Pub grub.

White Pheasant
3a Burn Rd. ☎ 64249.
0900-1700 Mon-Thur & Sat,
until 1830 Fri.
Grills, snacks, chips.

DROMORE
(STD 066 282)

Salt & Pepper
30 Main St. ☎ 236.
1200-2400 Mon-Thur,
1130-0130 Fri & Sat,
1730-0130 Sun.
Chicken & chips, curry.

DRUMQUIN
(STD 066 283)

Eddie O'Kane's
22 Main St. ☎ 233.
1900-2200 Thur-Sun.
Pub grub.

Post Inn
2 Main St. ☎ 329.
1900-2100 Thur-Sat.
Pub grub.

DUNGANNON
(STD 086 87)

The Upper Crust
15 Church St. ☎ 22797.
0915-1700 Mon-Sat.
Pies, pastries, vegetarian.

Cohannon Inn
Tamnamore. ☎ 24488.
0900-2200 Mon-Sun. Grills,
fish, carvery. A la carte. E£.

Country Kitchen
88 Granville Rd. ☎ 24254.
0900-1700 Mon-Fri.
Home baking.

Dee's
5 Thomas St. ☎ 52202.
0900-1730 Mon-Sat.
Sandwiches, salads, scones.

Door Step
Coalisland Rd. 0900-1900
Mon-Wed, 0900-2130
Thur-Sat. Grills, steaks.

Dungannon   **Co. TYRONE**

Dunowen Inn
Market Square. ☎ 23144.
1200-2230 Mon-Sat. Set
lunch, pub grub. A la carte.
E££.

Edwin's Place
20 Coash Rd. ☎ 40430.
1230-1430 Wed-Fri, 1800-
2130 Fri-Sun. Baked potatoes.

Fort
33 Scotch St. ☎ 22620.
1230-1430 Mon-Sat.
Pub grub.

Gables
40 Cookstown Rd. ☎ 61580.
1230-2200 Mon-Sat, until
2130 Sun. A la carte E£.

★ **GRANGE LODGE**
7 Grange Rd. ☎ (086 87)
84212. Fri & Sat evenings,
booking essential. Home
cooking in country house. E£££.

★ **HEDLEY'S COFFEE HOUSE**
The Arcade, Scotch St.
☎ 24605. 0900-1700
Mon-Sat. Home-baked pies,
cakes.

★ **INN ON THE PARK HOTEL**
Moy Rd. ☎ 25151. Last orders
2130, Fri & Sat 2200. Steak,
lobster bisque, rainbow trout,
lemon pancakes. ££.

Killymaddy Tourist Centre
Ballygawley Rd. ☎ 67323.
0830-2100 Mon-Sun in
summer, 0900-1800
Mon-Thur, until 2000 Fri-Sun
in winter. Grills, snacks. Sat
evening, dinner only.

Lough Neagh Lodge
Maghery. ☎ (0762) 851901.
1200-2100 Mon-Sat.
A la carte. ££.

Lorna's Grill
64 Church St. ☎ 53222.
0900-1700 Mon-Sat.
Sandwiches, quiche.

Normandy
40 Main St. ☎ 22397.
0800-2200 Mon-Fri,
1200-1900 Sat. Fish & chips.

Northland Arms
Georges St. ☎ 23693.
1200-2230 Mon-Sat. Hot &
cold carvery. Soup,
sandwiches, basket meals.

Pagni's
7 Irish St. 1000-1900
Mon-Sat, until 1430 Wed.
Fish, chicken.

Rainbow Chinese Restaurant
59 Scotch St. ☎ 26556.
1700-0030 Sun-Thur, until
0100 Fri & Sat. Chinese &
English. A la carte.

Rialto
21 Irish St. ☎ 27317.
0930-2030 Mon-Sat. Italian.

COACH INN

**OMAGH
TELEPHONE: 243330**

Special Lunches Daily
12 noon to 3 p.m.
(Chef's special daily)
Full à la carte menu
3 p.m. to 10 p.m.
**Special table d'hote
dinner menu..........for two
SUNDAY LUNCH
12 noon to 2 p.m.
A la carte..7.00 to 10.00 p.m.
Please note: Meals served
to 10 p.m.**
Sunday lunch booking advisable

*   *Large selection of
wines available*   *

Dungannon District

**Stay in the centre of
Ulster and see it all**

 U S GRANT ANCESTRAL HOMESTEAD

PEATLANDS PARK

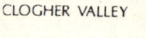 CLOGHER VALLEY

TYRONE CRYSTAL

PARKANAUR FOREST PARK

Try our Package Breaks!

SIGHTSEEING -- PONY TREKKING
GOLFING -- FISHING

Leisure Services Department
Dungannon District Council
Circular Road, Dungannon (086 87) 25311

WOODLANDER RESTAURANT

**Member of
'A Taste of Ulster'
'Healthy Eating Circle'**

Now offering extensive new
à la carte menu, featuring
many new meat, fish, poultry
and vegetarian dishes.
'SOMETHING FOR EVERYONE'
A la carte restaurant open Monday to
Sunday 6 pm to 10 pm.
Bar snacks Monday to Sunday
12.30 to 8 pm
Chef specials Monday to Saturday
12.30 to 2.30 pm.
Not forgetting the popular Sunday
carvery, 12.30 to 2.30 pm.
'An array of fine meat, vegetables
and salads.'
**SO DON'T DELAY BOOK TODAY
OMAGH (0662) 251038**

Floyds

Wine Bar
BALLYMAGORRY,
STRABANE, Co. TYRONE

**Open daily
12 noon - 2.30 pm
5.30pm - 10 pm**

Carvery lunch - £3.50

**Extensive wine bar
menu each evening**

**Function room also
available for that
special occasion**

**Tel:
(0504) 382905**

Dungannon-Gortin — Co. TYRONE

Tally's Bar ♆
Galbally. ☎ (086 87) 58231.
1130-2300 Mon-Sat,
1900-2200 Sun. Pub grub.
A la carte E£.

★ **TOP BAR** ♆

73 Castlecaulfield Rd.
☎ 61349. 1800-2200 Thur &
Fri, 1230-1430 & 1900-2200
Sun. Bistro, à la carte, set
meals.

Tree Tops
15 Northland Place.
☎ 23508. 0900-1730
Mon-Thur, until 2200 Fri &
Sat. Carvery, high tea. £.

Tyrone Crystal Tea Shop ⊙
Killbrackey. ☎ 25335.
0900-1700 Mon-Sat.
Snacks, lasagne, pies.

White Horse Inn ♆
70 Scotch St. ☎ 24130.
1230-1430 Mon-Fri.
Set lunch, salads, grills.

FINTONA
(STD 0662)

Charlie's Grill
53 Main St. ☎ 841266.
1100-2430 Tues-Sat,
1800-2300 Sun-Mon. Grills.

Eccles Arms ♆
128 Main St. ☎ 841220.
1200-2000 Mon-Sat,
1900-2200 Sun.
Hamburgers, pies, grills.

Kitty's Kitchen
☎ 841746. 0900-1800 Mon-
Fri, until 1930 Sat. Home
baking, lunches, lasagne.

FIVEMILETOWN
(STD 036 55)

Chestnut Bar ♆
113 Main St. ☎ 21398.
1130-2300 Mon-Sat.
Pub grub.

Fourways Hotel ♆
41 Main St. ☎ 21260. Last
orders 2300. Mixed grill,
omelettes. E£.

Top Note ♆
100 Main St. ☎ 21830.
1700-2400 Tues-Sat, 1230-
1500 & 1700-2400 Sun.
French & Italian. A la carte ££.

Valley Hotel ♆
60 Main St. ☎ 21505.
Last orders 2200, Sun 2130.
Avocado with prawns, pork
fillet & apple sauce. A la carte.
E££.

GORTIN
(STD 066 26)

Glenelly Kitchen
Sperrin Heritage Centre.
☎ 48142. 1100-1800 Mon-Sat,
1400-1900 Sun. Snacks.

Co. TYRONE — Gortin-Newtownstewart

McCullagh's
16 Main St. ☎ 48157.
1130-2300 Mon-Sat,
1230-1430 & 1900-2200
Sun. Pub grub.

Picador
62 Main St. ☎ 48315.
1130-2300 Mon-Sat,
1230-1430 & 1900-2200
Sun. Pub grub.

MOY
(STD 086 87)

Argory Tea Rooms
The Argory. ☎ 84753.
1400-1800 Sat & Sun April,
May, June & Sept. 1400-1800
Fri-Mon June. 1400-1800
Mon-Sun July & Aug. Garden
tea rooms opened by
arrangement (National Trust).

Ascot
Charlemont St. ☎ 84552.
0900-1730 Mon-Sat. Set
lunch, hamburgers, salads.

Bridge Bar
149 Portadown Rd,
Charlemont. ☎ 84271.
1130-2330 Mon-Sat,
1230-1430 & 1900-2200
Sun. Sausage rolls, pies,
hamburgers.

Grand Bar
24 The Square. ☎ 84840.
1130-2300 Mon-Sat,
1230-1430 & 1900-2200
Sun. Pub grub.

Old Fort Bar
33 Main St, Charlemont.
☎ 84808. 1130-2300 Mon-Sat,
1230-1430 & 1900-2200 Sun.
Grills, salads, stews.

Stables
The Square. ☎ 84629.
1230-1430 & 1800-2130
Mon-Sat, until 2200 Sun. Set
lunch. A la carte. E£.

Traynor's Inn
86 Armagh Rd. ☎ 891753.
1130-2300 Mon-Sat,
1230-1430 & 1900-2200
Sun. Pub grub.

Welcome Inn
Dungannon St. ☎ 84223.
1200-1330 & 1900-2200
Mon-Sat. Pub grub.

MOYGASHEL

Normandy
40 Main St. ☎ (086 87) 22397.
0800-2200 Mon-Fri,
1200-1900 Sat. Fish & chips.

NEWTOWNSTEWART
(STD 066 26)

Castle Bar
1 Castle Brae. ☎ 61039.
1200-1500 & 1800-2100
Mon-Sat. Pub grub.

Coffee Pot
24a Main St. ☎ 61565.
0900-1800 Mon-Sat.
Pies, soup, stew, scones.

Newtownstewart-Omagh **Co. TYRONE**

Country Inn ♀
43 Main St. ☎ 62105.
1230-1430 Mon-Sat. Pub grub.

Corner Bar ♀
2 Carnkenny Rd, Ardstraw.
☎ 61257. 1130-0100 Mon-Sat, 1900-2200 Sun. Pub grub.

Harry Avery Lounge ♀
19 Dublin St. ☎ 61431.
1230-1430 Mon-Sun,
1900-2200 Thur-Sun. Pub grub.

McGuigan's Bar ♀
43 Main St. ☎ 62105.
1230-1430 Mon-Sun,
1900-2100 Wed, Fri & Sat.
Set meals, grills.

Milltown Café
Newtownstewart Rd,
Milltown. ☎ 61609.
0900-2400 Mon-Sat,
1100-2400 Sun. Soup, grills, salads.

Olde Mill ♀
7 Millbrook Rd, Milltown.
☎ 62048. 1030-2130 Mon-Sun. Steaks, chicken chasseur, vegetarian. A la carte. E££.

Wel Cum Inn ♀
36 Main St. ☎ 61276.
1130-2300 Mon-Sat,
1230-1430 & 1900-2200 Sun. Pies, pub grub.

OMAGH
(STD 0662)

Bridge Restaurant
32 Bridge St. ☎ 0830-1800
Mon-Sat, until 1400 Wed.
Salads, soup, sandwiches.

Bridge Tavern ♀
Eskra. ☎ (0662) 841521.
1230-1430 Mon-Sun. Pub grub, basket meals in evening.

Caesar's ♀
26 Bridge St. ☎ 251133.
1200-1400 Mon-Sat,
1700-2400 Mon-Sun.
Pizzas, lasagne, salads.

The Cake Shop
38 Market St. ☎ 251012.
0900-1730 Mon-Sat.
Salads, pastries

Campsie Bake Shop
80 Market St. ☎ 244038.
0830-1730 Mon-Sat.
Lasagne, quiche, Ulster fry.

Carlton Coffee Lounge
31 High St. ☎ 247046.
0900-1730 Mon-Sat. Lasagne, quiche, Ulster fry.

Cellar Bar ♀
Bridge St. ☎ 247577.
1130-1400 Mon-Fri.
Pub grub.

The Clock ♀
Old Market Place.
☎ 247355. 1200-1500
Mon-Sat, 1800-2130 Wed-Sun. Pub grub. River view.

Co. TYRONE   Omagh

Coach Inn
Dromore Tamlaght Rd.
☎ 243330. 1200-1500
Mon-Sat. Set lunch.

Coffee House
26 Bridge St. ☎ 247577.
0930-1730 Mon-Sat. Snacks.

Curry King
8 Campsie Rd. ☎ 246502.
1200-2400 Mon-Sun.
Burgers, pizza.

Dragon Castle
2 High St. ☎ 245208.
1200-1400 & 1700-2345
Mon, Tues, Thur & Sun, until
0100 Fri & Sat. Chinese &
European. £.

Eddie's Crossroads Bar
Greencastle. ☎ (066 26)
48266. 1800-2200 Mon-Sat.
Grills, salads.

El Paso
62 Market St. ☎ 243125.
1130-2300 Mon-Sat.
Pub grub.

Expressway Restaurant
1 Mountjoy Rd. ☎ 246487.
0900-2400 Mon-Thur, until
0300 Fri & Sat. Salads, scones
coffee.

Giovanni's
9 John St. ☎ 252025. 1200-
1400 Mon-Fri, 1700-2400
Mon, Thur & Sun, 1700-0300
Fri & Sat. Italian.

★ **GREENMOUNT LODGE**
58 Greenmount Rd,
Gortaclare. ☎ (0662) 841325.
1900-2130 Fri & Sat. Dinner.
Booking essential. E£.

Halfway House
Tattyreagh. ☎ 42605.
1130-2300 Mon-Sat,
1900-2200 Sun.
Soup, sandwiches.

Omagh Leisure Centre
Old Mountfield Rd.
☎ 246711. 1000-1430
Mon-Sat, 1530-2100
Mon-Fri, 1500-1700 Sat,
1400-1700 Sun. Snacks.

Libbi
52 Market St. ☎ 242969.
0900-1730 Mon, Tues &
Thur-Sat, until 1400 Wed.
Coffee, cakes.

Old McDonald's
6 Bridge St. ☎ 247666.
0800-1900 Mon-Sat.
Pub grub.

McElroy's
30 Castle St. ☎ 244441.
1200-1900 Mon-Sat.
Pub grub.

McGirr's of Gortnagarn
Mountjoy East. ☎ 242462.
1230-1430 & 1900-2100
Mon-Sat. Grills. A la carte Fri
& Sat.

Omagh — Co. TYRONE

★ MELLON COUNTRY INN 🍷 ⊙
134 Beltany Rd. ☎ (066 26) 61224. 1030-2130 Mon-Sat, 1200-2030 Tues. Set lunch. A la carte evenings. E£££.

Mill 🍷
212 Gorticashel Rd. ☎ 248451. 1800-2300 Mon-Sat. Pub grub.

Mr G's 🍷
2 Old Market Yard. 0930-1730 Mon-Sat, until 1400 Wed. Quiche, home baked scones, hoagies.

Nichol & Shiels
41a Market St. ☎ 247379. 0900-1730 Mon-Sat. Home-made pies, tray bakes, coffee.

Number Seven 🍷
7 John St. ☎ 246587. 1230-1430 Mon-Sat. Savoury lunches, sweets.

Omanni 🍴
2 Derry Rd. ☎ 247500. 1700-2400 Tues-Thur, 1600-0100 Fri & Sat, until 2330 Sun. Chinese, Asian & European. £.

Pink Elephant
19 High St. ☎ 249805. 0900-1800 Mon-Sat, 1200-1500 Sun. Snacks, lunches.

Pizzarama
78 Market St. ☎ 244799. 1200-1400 Mon-Fri, 1700-2400 Mon-Sun. Pizzas, salads, garlic bread.

Royal Arms Hotel 🍷
51 High St. ☎ 243262. Last orders 2130, Sun 2030. A la carte. ££.

Sally O'Brien's 🍷
35 John St. ☎ 242521. 2100-2300 Fri & Sat. Grills.

Shoppers Rest
58 High St. ☎ 243545. 0730-1800 Mon-Sat. Toasties, lunches, salads.

Silverbirch Hotel 🍷
5 Gortin Rd. ☎ 242520. Last orders 2100. £.

Taste of India 🍴
8 Campsie Rd. ☎ 248342. 1630-2430 Mon-Sun. Indian. E£.

Village Inn 🍷
Killyclogher. ☎ 243865. 1130-1530 Mon-Sat, 1230-1430 & 1900-2200 Sun. Pub grub.

★ WOODLANDER 🍷 ⊙
28 Gortin Rd. ☎ 251038. 1200-1800 Mon, until 2200 Tues-Sun. Sole, red snapper, beef Robert, home-made desserts. M£. E£££. A la carte.

Co. TYRONE — Plumbridge-Sion Mills

PLUMBRIDGE

Pinkertons Café
25 Main St. ☎ (066 26) 48327.
1100-2200 Mon-Sat,
1400-2100 Sun.
Steak, chicken, curries.

Sperrin Heritage Centre
Cranagh. ☎ (066 26) 48142.
1100-1800 Mon-Fri,
1130-1800 Sat, 1400-1900
Sun. Sandwiches, scones,
pastries. 8 miles east of
Plumbridge, on B47.

POMEROY
(STD 0868)

Corner Bar ♀
81 Main St. ☎ 758709.
1130-2300 Mon-Sat,
1230-1430 & 1900-2200
Sun. Pub grub.

SION MILLS
(STD 066 26)

Marshall's ♀
☎ 58638. 1130-2300
Mon-Sat, 1230-1430 &
1900-2200 Sun. Pub grub.

McGIRR'S of GORTNAGARN
LOUNGE BAR & RESTAURANT

★ Daily lunches ★ evening meals

★ Private functions ★ weddings ★ exhibitions

Meals available from 12 noon till 10.00 p.m.

Entertainment • Dancing
Telephone: Omagh 242462/245841

Otter Lodge

26 Dungannon Road, Cookstown, BT80 8TL Tel(064 87) 65427

Wine Bar • Lunches 1200 - 1400 Mon - Sun £
Evening Meals • 1900 - 2130 Fri - Sat, 1730 - 2130 Sun £
Restaurant • 1900 - 2130 Fri - Sat ££ booking essential
Sun lunch 1200 - 1400 • Sun evening 1730 - 1930 £
Functions • Weddings • Parties etc for groups up to 90

Sixmilecross-Strabane — Co. TYRONE

SIXMILECROSS

Tavern ♇
12 Main St. ☎ (066 27) 58461.
1130-2300 Mon-Sat,
1900-2200 Sun. Pub grub.

Whistler's Inn ♇
26 Main St. ☎ (066 27) 58349.
1100-1900 Mon-Thur, until
2230 Fri & Sat. Set lunch.
Steak, chicken.

STEWARTSTOWN
(STD 086 873)

Drumcairn Inn ♇
32 The Square. ☎ 216.
2100-2300 Mon-Sat.
Pub grub, grills.

Duffy's ♇
32 The Square. ☎ 216.
2000-2400 Thur-Sat. Pub grub.

Hoff's ♇
The Square. ☎ 402.
2000-2400 Thur-Sun.
A la carte E£.

Lakeview Inn ♇
15 The Square. ☎ 8106.
1130-2300 Mon-Sat.
Pies, burgers.

STRABANE
(STD 0504)

Butlers
19 Abercorn Square.
0900-1800 Mon-Thur, until
0200 Fri & Sat. Fish & chips,
pies.

Ballymagorry Arms ♇
421 Victoria Rd, Ballymagorry.
☎ 382905. 1230-1430
Mon-Sat, 1230-1430 &
1900-2200 Sun. Pub grub.

Blue Parrot ♇
19 Castle St. ☎ 382687.
1200-1500 Mon-Sat.
Snacks. A la carte.

Bonne Tasse ⌒
Abercorn Square. 0900-1730
Mon-Sat. Hot & cold snacks,
sandwiches, drinks.

Buttery Tavern ♇
30 Market St. ☎ 884466.
1200-1430 Mon-Sat. Set
meals. Pub grub. A la carte. E£.

Coach Inn ♇
366 Victoria Rd. ☎ (050 484)
362. 1130-2300 Mon-Sat,
1230-1430 & 1900-2200 Sun.
Pub grub.

Country Kitchen
Lower Main St. ☎ 382621.
0900-1730 Mon-Sat.
Breakfast, afternoon tea,
home baking.

Fir Trees Lodge Hotel ♇
Melmount Rd. ☎ 382382.
Last orders 2130.
A la carte. E££.

Flann O'Brien ♇
3 Derry Rd. ☎ 884427.
1230-1430 Mon-Sat.
Set lunch, grills.

Co. TYRONE — Strabane-Trillick

Floyd's ♌
421 Victoria Rd. ☎ 382905.
1230-1430 & 1730-2200
Mon-Sat, until 2130 Sun.
A la carte, carvery. E£.

Home Cuisine
55 Main St. ☎ 382002.
0930-1715 Mon-Sat.
Snacks, grills.

Kelly's Bar ♌
Abercorn Square. ☎ 883551.
1130-2300 Mon-Sat,
1230-1430 & 1900-2230 Sun.
Pub grub.

Kurly Wurly's ♌
9 Bowling Green. ☎ 383353.
1100-2300 Mon-Sat, 1200-
1500 & 1700-2200 Sun. Soup,
sandwiches, pies.

Mill House Inn ♌
37 Patrick St. ☎ 382690.
1200-1400 Mon-Fri,
1800-2300 Mon-Sun.
A la carte. E££.

Piccolo
Abercorn Square. ☎ 382784.
0900-1800 Mon-Sat.
Grills, sandwiches.

Railway Bar ♌
64 Railway Rd. ☎ 882366.
1130-2300 Mon-Sat,
1230-1430 & 1900-2200
Sun. Pub grub.

Teashop
29 Abercorn Square.
0800-1730 Mon-Sat.
Salads, lasagne, chips.

Town Hall Bar ♌
Market Centre, Market St.
☎ 382424. 1200-1500
Mon-Sat. Fish, quiche.

Welcome Inn ♌
38 Patrick St. ☎ 382528.
1130-2300 Mon-Sat,
1230-1430 & 1900-2200 Sun.
Sandwiches, pies.

Wembley
10 Castle Place. ☎ 382307.
0900-1900 Mon-Sat.
Fish & chips.

TRILLICK
(STD 036 555)

Bridge Inn ♌ ⊙
2 Kilskeery Rd. ☎ 201.
1130-2300 Mon-Sat,
1230-1430 & 1900-2200 Sun.
Pub grub.

McAloon's ♌
19 Main St. ☎ 208.
1200-1400 & 1700-2000
Mon-Sat. Pub grub.

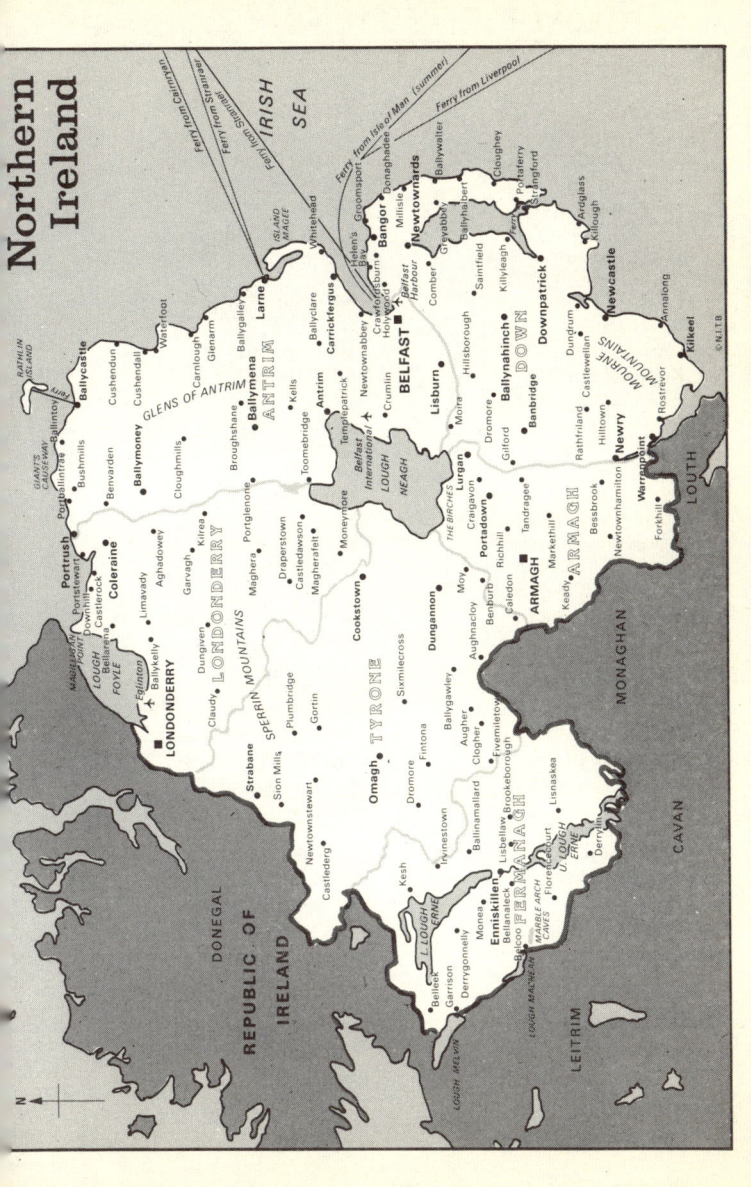

Index to towns and villages

Aghadowey 163
Aghalee 99
Ahoghill 65
Aldergrove 65
Annalong 111
Antrim 65
Ardglass 111
Armagh 99
Augher 183
Aughnacloy 183

Ballinamallard 153
Ballintoy 67
Ballycastle 67
Ballyclare 68
Ballygalley 69
Ballygawley 183
Ballykelly 163
Ballymena 69
Ballymoney 74
Ballynahinch 112
Ballywalter 113
Banbridge 113
Bangor 115
Belcoo 153
Belfast 29
Bellanaleck 153
Belleek 153
Belleeks 101
Beragh 183

Bessbrook 101
Blackwatertown 101
Brookeborough 153
Broughshane 75
Bushmills 75

Caledon 183
Camlough 102
Carnlough 76
Carrickfergus 76
Carrowdore 119
Carryduff 121
Castlecaulfield 184
Castledawson 163
Castlederg 184
Castlereagh (see Belfast)
Castlerock 164
Castlewellan 121
Claudy 164
Clough 122
Clogher 185
Cloughey 122
Cloughmills 78
Coagh 185
Coalisland 185
Coleraine 164
Comber 122
  (for La Mon see Belfast)
Conlig 123
Cookstown 186
Craigavon 102

Index to towns and villages

Cranfield 123
Crawfordsburn 123
Crossgar 123
Crossmaglen 103
Crumlin 78
Cullybackey 79
Cultra 124
Cushendall 79
Cushendun 79

Derry (see Londonderry)
Derrygonnelly 154
Derrylin 154
Dervock 79
Doagh 80
Donaghadee 124
Downpatrick 125
Draperstown 167
Dromara 126
Dromore (Co. Down) 127
Dromore (Co. Tyrone) 188
Drumquin 188
Dunadry 80
Dundonald (see Belfast)
Dundrum 127
Dungannon 188
Dungiven 167
Dunmurry 80

Ederney 154
Eglinton 168
Enniskillen 154

Fintona 191
Fivemiletown 191
Florencecourt 158
Forkhill 103

Garrison 158
Garvagh 168
Giant's Causeway 81
Gilford 127
Glarryford 81
Glenariff 81
Glenarm 83
Glengormley 83
  (see also Newtownabbey)
Gortin 191
Greenisland 84
Greyabbey 129
Greysteel 168
Groomsport 129

Hamiltonsbawn 103
Helen's Bay 129
Hillsborough 130
Hilltown 130
Holywood 131

Irvinestown 158

Katesbridge 133
Keady 104
Kells 84

Index to towns and villages

Kesh 159
Kilkeel 133
Killinchy 134
Killough 134
Killylea 104
Killyleagh 134
Kilrea 168
Kinawley 161
Kircubbin 135
Knockcloghrim 169

Larne 84
Letterbreen 161
Limavady 169
Lisbellaw 161
Lisburn 86
Lisnarick 161
Lisnaskea 161
Londonderry 171
Loughbrickland 135
Loughgall 104
Lurgan 104
  (see also Craigavon)

Maghera 177
Magherafelt 178
Magilligan 179
Mallusk 91
Markethill 106
Middletown 106
Millisle 135
Moira 136

Moneymore 179
Mountnorris 107
Moy 192
Moygashel 192

Newcastle 137
Newry 140
Newtownabbey 91
Newtownards 144
Newtownbutler 162
Newtownhamilton 107
Newtownstewart 192

Omagh 193

Plumbridge 196
Pomeroy 196
Portadown 107
Portaferry 147
Portballintrae 92
Portglenone 93
Portrush 93
Portstewart 181

Randalstown 96
Rathfriland 147
Rathlin Island 96
Richhill 109
Roslea 162
Rostrevor 149

Index to towns and villages

Saintfield 150
Seaforde 150
Sion Mills 196
Sixmilecross 196
Stewartstown 196
Stoneyford 96
Strabane 196
Strangford 150
Swatragh 182

Tandragee 109
Temple 150
Templepatrick 97
Tempo 162
Toomebridge 97
Trillick 198

Waringstown 151
Warrenpoint 151
Waterfoot
 (see Glenariff)
Whiteabbey
 (see Newtownabbey)
Whitecross 110
Whitehead 97

Please note

This book is intended only as a convenient reference guide to eating out in Northern Ireland. Care has been taken to ensure entries are up to date. However, information has been gathered from a wide range of sources and the Northern Ireland Tourist Board does not accept responsibility for errors and omissions. In addition, changes will inevitably occur after the book goes to press, so it is advisable to make your own enquiries.